The 2005 TOUR de FRANCE

Armstrong's Farewell

John Wilcockson and Andrew Hood

VELO press

BOULDER, COLORADO

2005 Tour de France
© 2005 VeloPress®

Printed in the United States of America.

10 9 8 7 6 5 4 3 2 1

Distributed in the United States and Canada by Publishers Group West.

Library of Congress Cataloging-in-Publication Data

Wilcockson, John.
 2005 Tour de France : Armstrong's Farewell / John Wilcockson & Andrew Hood.
     p. cm.
 ISBN 1-931382-68-9 (pbk. : alk. paper)
 1. Tour de France (Bicycle race) (2005) 2. Cyclists.
I. Hood, Andrew 1964- II. Title.
 GV1049.2.T68W547 2005
 796.6'20944—dc22

2005026962

VeloPress®
1830 North 55th Street
Boulder, Colorado 80301–2700 USA
303/440-0601
Fax 303/444-6788
E-mail velopress@insideinc.com

To purchase additional copies of this book or other VeloPress® books, call 800/234-8356 or visit us on the Web at velopress.com.

Book cover and interior design by Erin Johnson
Cover photos by Getty Images

The 2005

TOUR de FRANCE

Armstrong's Farewell

Contents

Acknowledgments

We would like to thank all our colleagues at the Tour de France who contributed their ideas, enthusiasm, and support. In particular, Rupert Guinness of Australia's *Daily Telegraph* contributed insider information from the Aussie contingent and his special brand of repartee; *VeloNews* associate editor Neal Rogers brought much-needed quotes and a rookie Tour reporter's special insights, as did Nate Vinton of *Ski Racing*; and senior technical writer Lennard Zinn gave his expert knowledge.

We would also like to thank for their assistance the team liaisons Bryan Nygaard at CSC, Jacinto Vidarte at Liberty Seguros, Alessandro Tegner at Quick Step, Luuk Eisinger at T-Mobile, Dan Osipow and Jogi Müller at Discovery Channel, along with the many American, Belgian, British, Canadian, Danish, Dutch, French, German, Italian, Spanish, and Swiss journalists with whom we shared race details and rider information.

Thank you to Graham Watson for the wonderful images that help bring the Tour alive, and to the staff at VeloPress and *VeloNews*, especially Renee Jardine, Jade Hays, Ted Costantino, and Kip Mikler, for their diligence and support throughout this project. And finally, a special thanks to our respective wives for sort of understanding our passion for a bicycle race in France, or there wouldn't be another Tour for either of us.

INTRODUCTION
The Last Time?

Well this could be the last time,

This could be the last time,

Maybe the last time,

I don't know.

—from "The Last Time," by Mick Jagger and Keith Richards

When *Austin-American Statesman* sportswriter Suzanne Haliburton called the just-retired Lance Armstrong on September 5, 2005, to write a short story about the Tour de France champion's engagement to pop singer Sheryl Crow, she got quite a shock. Not only did she get details of how Armstrong discussed the engagement with his three children before popping the question to Crow on a mountain biking vacation in Sun Valley, Idaho, but Haliburton also received an earful about a French campaign to discredit his Tour career with doping allegations. Armstrong then said he was considering coming out of retirement and riding another Tour. "I'm thinking about it," Armstrong told her. "I'm thinking it's the best way to piss them off."

The "them" Armstrong was referring to were the French media, particularly the national newspapers, *L'Équipe* and *Le Monde*, titles that are highly respected in France. *L'Équipe*, an all-sports publication with a stature similar to *Sports Illustrated*, is the country's biggest-selling daily thanks to its blue-collar readership, while *Le Monde* is the insider political forum for the intellectual set. They may be at opposite ends of the social spectrum, but both papers began raising questions about Armstrong as soon as he started dominating the Tour de France in 1999.

After the Texan rode away from Europe's best climbers on the now infamous stage to Sestriere, *L'Équipe* published an editorial titled *Cyclisme à deux vitesses* ("Cycling at two speeds"), which echoed a claim by French racer Jean-Cyril Robin that "95 percent of the French riders are clean," while most of the foreigners were doped. The sports daily also ran a long interview with Christophe Bassons, a young French rider who had a clean reputation when it came to performance-enhancing drugs, and who said that no one could win the Tour without using the blood-booster EPO. Armstrong was mad with Bassons for saying what he said, and mad at *L'Équipe* for publishing the indirect allegations against him.

A few days after the Bassons interview, following a hard mountain stage to Piau-Engalay in the Pyrénées, Armstrong was walking away from a press conference when a journalist from *Le Monde* stopped him. The writer thrust a faxed copy of the next day's paper in front of the Texan and asked him if he knew anything about the report it contained, claiming that Armstrong had tested positive for corticosteroids on the first day of that Tour. At the next day's press conference, Armstrong pointed at "Mister Le Monde" and, supported by a bulletin from the Union Cycliste Internationale (UCI), told him the steroid was from a topical ointment used to clear up a saddle sore.

The French "doping" campaign against Armstrong continued through the rest of his career. When a judicial investigation was started in late 2000 into his team's alleged use of a product called Actovegin, a derivative of calf's blood believed to increase the body's uptake of oxygen, Armstrong threatened to boycott the following year's Tour. Even though that investigation was eventually dropped, the situation was so bad by 2002 that fans at the roadside on the climb to Mont Ventoux shouted *"dopé, dopé"* as the American rode past.

Because of his continued "difficult" relationship with the French, Armstrong was asked during the 2005 Tour whether his more laid-back demeanor in his final appearance was part of a plan to conquer the hearts of the fans.

"I get asked that question a lot," he replied, "and I don't know how differently I can answer it. I'm a guy that's completely devoted to their event. I'm a guy who completely and almost always defends this country and its people at a time when there's not a lot of people in America defending this country, this country of France, and their position. I can't say enough good things about it so I don't know what else I can tell you. The people on the roadside are very supportive."

But weren't there, as one questioner put it, "a few guys who seem to know everything and have a lot of nasty things to say?"

"Of course," Armstrong replied, "four or five per day. But that shouldn't cloud out the thousands of other ones who yell supportive things. I'm comfortable here, I love the race, and ultimately, I think we'll have a fine relationship."

That relationship summarily ended a month after Armstrong won his seventh successive Tour de France, when *L'Équipe* released its controversial story claiming it had proof that the American used EPO when he first won the Tour. The paper reported that a French laboratory had retested urine samples kept frozen since the 1999 Tour, and six of seventeen samples alleged to be Armstrong's had tested positive for the banned drug EPO—a test that wasn't introduced to the Tour until 2001.

Four days after Armstrong made his threat to return to racing in 2006, he was somewhat exonerated by the UCI, which issued a long statement that criticized the ethics of *L'Équipe*, the French lab, and the World Anti-Doping Agency. It said in part: "We deplore the fact that the long-established and entrenched confidentiality principle could be violated in such a flagrant way, without any respect for fair play and the rider's privacy. This aspect forms part of our thorough and vigorous investigation into this matter."

Perhaps the eventual results of that investigation would allay any qualms Armstrong retained. In any case, ten days after his tantrum threatening to return to racing, Armstrong confirmed in a conference call that the 2005 Tour de France was indeed his last. "I am not coming back," he stated. "I am happy with the way my career went, and I am happy with the way it ended. There is no way I can go back there. I would be crazy. . . . I know if I go back, there is no way I am going to get a fair shake on the roadside, in doping control, or in the labs. . . . I am sick of dealing with this shit."

This harsh conclusion in mid-September was in sharp contrast to the mellow thoughts Armstrong had during the July race. For instance, when he was asked at Briançon what was different about this Tour compared to the others, he said, "Two things. We have a different title sponsor, with a three-year commitment. My commitment to Discovery Channel was to race the Tour once, and to race it with all I had. I'm trying to do that and live up to that promise.

"Also, this is my final Tour. Every day I get on the bike it's a countdown. I know I only have eleven days to go, ten days to go. It's an interesting thought every day, when I'm on the bike. I'm going to miss it, but at the same time, I'm ready to move on." At Mende, just three days before he finished the race in Paris, Armstrong said, "You enjoy yourself more when you know it's almost over. My career is almost over; it's a nice feeling."

And when it was all over, and Armstrong had completed his unprecedented seventh-in-a-row victory, his future wife Sheryl Crow said, "It's very emotional. So much went into preparing for this race for all the riders, not just Lance. Lance wanted so much to end his career like this."

As for the champion himself, he said, "It's nice to win one with a cushion, and say that you put in a good sporting performance, but it wouldn't be fair to say to next year's winner, 'Well, you're lucky I didn't show up.' Let's just watch next year's race and let the champion be the champion."

That champion, definitively, won't be Lance Armstrong.

2005 TOUR DE FRANCE
Race Map

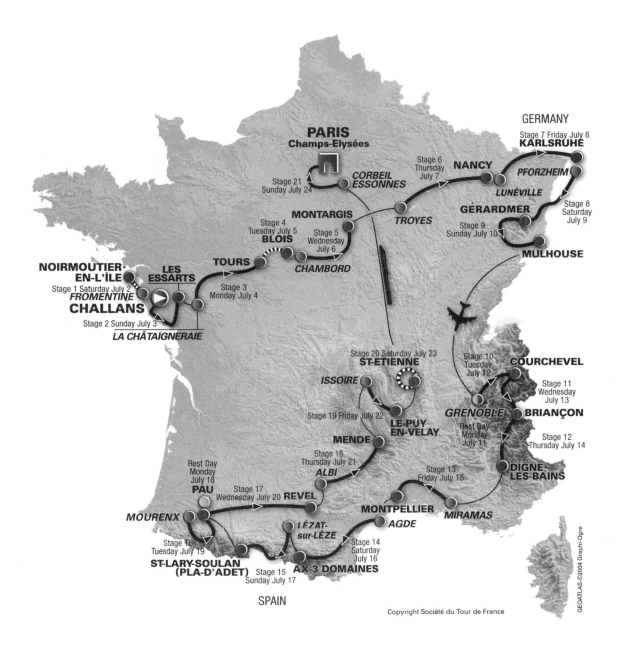

GERMANY

PARIS
Champs-Elysées

Stage 21
Sunday July 24

*CORBEIL
ESSONNES*

Stage 6
Thursday
July 7

NANCY

Stage 7 Friday July 8
KARLSRUHE

PFORZHEIM

LUNÉVILLE

Stage 8
Saturday
July 9

MONTARGIS

Stage 4
Tuesday July 5
BLOIS

Stage 5
Wednesday
July 6

TROYES

GÉRARDMER

Stage 9
Sunday July 10

MULHOUSE

**NOIRMOUTIER-
EN-L'ÎLE**

**LES
ESSARTS**

TOURS

CHAMBORD

Stage 1 Saturday July 2
FROMENTINE
CHALLANS

Stage 3
Monday July 4

Stage 2 Sunday July 3

LA CHÂTAIGNERAIE

Stage 20 Saturday July 23
ST-ETIENNE

Stage 10
Tuesday
July 12

COURCHEVEL

ISSOIRE

Stage 11
Wednesday
July 13

Stage 19 Friday July 22

**LE-PUY
EN-VELAY**

GRENOBLE

BRIANÇON

MENDE

Rest Day
Monday
July 11

Stage 12
Thursday July 14

Stage 18
Thursday July 21
ALBI

Stage 13
Friday July 15

**DIGNE-
LES-BAINS**

Rest Day
Monday
July 18

PAU

Stage 17
Wednesday July 20 **REVEL**

MONTPELLIER

MIRAMAS

MOURENX

*LÉZAT-
sur-LÈZE*

AGDE

Stage 16
Tuesday July 19

Stage 14
Saturday
July 16

**ST-LARY-SOULAN
(PLA-D'ADET)**

Stage 15
Sunday July 17

AX-3 DOMAINES

SPAIN

Copyright Société du Tour de France

GEOATLAS-©2004 Graphi-Ogre

2005 TOUR DE FRANCE
Start List

92nd Tour de France
France, July 2–24, 2005

DISCOVERY CHANNEL
Lance Armstrong (USA)
Jose Azevedo (P)
Manuel Beltran (Sp)
George Hincapie (USA)
Benjamin Noval (Sp)
Pavel Padrnos (Cz)
Yaroslav Popovych (Ukr)
Jose Luis Rubiera (Sp)
Paolo Savoldelli (I)

T-MOBILE TEAM
Jan Ullrich (G)
Giuseppe Guerini (I)
Matthias Kessler (G)
Andreas Klöden (G)
Daniele Nardello (I)
Stephan Schreck (G)
Oscar Sevilla (Sp)
Tobias Steinhauser (G)
Alexander Vinokourov (Kaz)

TEAM CSC
Ivan Basso (I)
Kurt-Asle Arvesen (N)
Bobby Julich (USA)
Giovanni Lombardi (I)
Carlos Sastre (Sp)
Luke Roberts (Aus)
Nicki Sörensen (Dk)
Jens Voigt (G)
Dave Zabriskie (USA)

ILLES BALEARS–CAISSE D'EPARGNE
Francisco Mancebo (Sp)
José Luis Arrieta (Sp)
David Arroyo (Sp)
Daniel Becke (Sp)
Isaac Gálvez (Sp)
Jose Vicente García Acosta (Sp)
Vladimir Karpets (Rus)
Alejandro Valverde (Sp)
Xabier Zandio (Sp)

DAVITAMON-LOTTO
Robbie McEwen (Aus)
Mario Aerts (B)
Christophe Brandt (B)
Cadel Evans (Aus)
Axel Merckx (B)
Leon van Bonand (Nl)
Fred Rodriguez (USA)
Johan Vansummeren (B)
Wim Vansevenant (B)

RABOBANK
Denis Menchov (Rus)
Michael Boogerd (Nl)
Erik Dekker (Nl)
Karsten Kroon (Nl)
Gerben Löwik (Nl)
Joost Posthuma (Nl)
Michael Rasmussen (Dk)
Marc Wauters (B)
Pieter Weening (Nl)

PHONAK HEARING SYSTEMS
Santiago Botero (Col)
Bert Grabsch (G)
Jose Enrique Gutierrez (Sp)
Robert Hunter (RSA)
Nicolas Jalabert (F)
Floyd Landis (USA)
Alexandre Moos (Swi)
Oscar Pereiro (Sp)
Steve Zampieri (Swi)

FASSA BORTOLO
Fabian Cancellara (Swi)
Lorenzo Bernucci (I)
Claudio Corioni (I)
Mauro Facci (I)
Juan Antonio Flecha (Sp)
Dario Frigo (I)
Massimo Giunti (I)
Volodimir Gustov (Ukr)
Kim Kirchen (Lux)

SAUNIER DUVAL–PRODIR
Juan Manuel Garate (Sp)
Rubens Bertogliati (Swi)
David Canada (Sp)
Nicolas Fritsch (F)
Jose Angel Gomez Marchante (Sp)
Chris Horner (USA)
Leonardo Piepoli (I)
Manuel Quinziato (I)
Constantino Zaballa (Sp)

LIBERTY SEGUROS–WÜRTH

Roberto Heras (Sp)
Joseba Beloki (Sp)
Alberto Contador (Sp)
Allan Davis (Aus)
Igor Gonzalez de Galdeano (Sp)
Jörg Jaksche (G)
Luis León Sanchez (Sp)
Marcos Serrano (Sp)
Angel Vicioso (Sp)

CRÉDIT AGRICOLE

Christophe Moreau (F)
Laszlo Bodrogi (Hun)
Pietro Caucchioli (I)
Patrice Halgand (F)
Sébastien Hinault (F)
Thor Hushovd (N)
Sébastien Joly (F)
Andrei Kashechkin (Kaz)
Jaan Kirsipuu (Est)

LIQUIGAS-BIANCHI

Stefano Garzelli (I)
Michael Albasini (Swi)
Magnus Backstedt (S)
Kjell Carlström (Fin)
Dario Cioni (I)
Mauro Gerosa (I)
Marcus Ljungqvist (S)
Luciano Pagliarini (Bra)
Franco Pellizotti (F)

COFIDIS, LE CREDIT PAR TELEPHONE

Stuart O'Grady (Aus)
Stéphane Augé (F)
Frédéric Bessy (F)
Sylvain Chavanel (F)
Thierry Marichal (B)
David Moncoutié (F)
Janek Tombak (Est)
Cédric Vasseur (F)
Matthew White (Aus)

QUICK STEP

Tom Boonen (B)
Wilfried Cretskens (B)
Kevin Hulsmans (B)
Servais Knaven (Nl)
Michael Rogers (Aus)
Patrik Sinkewitz (G)
Bram Tankink (Nl)
Guido Trenti (USA)
Stefano Zanini (I)

BOUYGUES TÉLÉCOM

Didier Rous (F)
Walter Bénéteau (F)
Laurent Brochard (F)
Pierrick Fédrigo (F)
Anthony Geslin (F)
Laurent Lefèvre (F)
Jérôme Pineau (F)
Matthieu Sprick (F)
Thomas Voeckler (F)

LAMPRE-CAFFITA

Eddy Mazzoleni (I)
Gianluca Bortolami (I)
Salvatore Commesso (I)
Gerrit Glomser (A)
David Loosli (Swi)
Evgeni Petrov (Rus)
Daniele Righi (I)
Alessandro Spezialetti (I)
Gorazd Stangelj (Slo)

GEROLSTEINER

Georg Totschnig (A)
Robert Förster (G)
Sebastian Lang (G)
Levi Leipheimer (USA)
Michael Rich (G)
Ronny Scholz (G)
Fabian Wegmann (G)
Peter Wrolich (A)
Beat Zberg (Swi)

FRANÇAISE DES JEUX

Bradley McGee (Aus)
Sandy Casar (F)
Baden Cooke (Aus)
Carlos Da Cruz (F)
Bernhard Eisel (A)
Philippe Gilbert (B)
Thomas Lövkvist (S)
Christophe Mengin (F)
Francis Mourey (F)

DOMINA VACANZE

Sergei Gonchar (Ukr)
Alessandro Bertolini (I)
Alessandro Cortinovis (I)
Angelo Furlan (I)
Andrei Grivko (Ukr)
Maxim Iglinski (Kaz)
Jörg Ludewig (G)
Rafael Nuritdinov (Uzb)
Alessandro Vanotti (I)

EUSKALTEL-EUSKADI

Iban Mayo (Sp)
Iker Camano (Sp)
Unai Etxebarria (Ven)
Iker Flores (Sp)
David Herrero (Sp)
Inaki Isasi (Sp)
Inigo Landaluze (Sp)
Egoi Martinez (Sp)
Haimar Zubeldia (Sp)

AG2R–PREVOYANCE

Jean-Patrick Nazon (F)
Mikel Astarloza (Sp)
Sylvain Calzati (F)
Samuel Dumoulin (F)
Simon Gerrans (Aus)
Stéphane Goubert (F)
Yuriy Krivtsov (Ukr)
Nicolas Portal (F)
Ludovic Turpin (F)

CHAPTER 1 | LE GRAND DÉPART
Back to Basics
in the Vendée

The Tour de France likes to start with a bang. As the world's biggest bike race, it only seems right to make *le Grand Départ* as grand as it can possibly be. The last time the Tour kicked off in the Vendée region of western France it was 1999, and huge crowds came to see the official presentation of the teams. One by one, the teams marched in line onto pontoons floating on a lake for their group photos. A ruined medieval castle provided an appropriately grand backdrop. When night fell, the lake became the centerpiece of a huge sound-and-light show, in which a thousand participants reenacted battles that ravaged the Vendée region over a 700-year time span.

In contrast to that spectacle, the 2005 Tour opened with a low-key presentation of the twenty one *équipes* at the local sports hall in Challans, an agricultural town of 18,000 people. As the starters were introduced, each team coasted out of the building on their bikes and leisurely circled a barricaded, 900-meter circuit where a good-natured crowd politely applauded the riders.

It was an odd send-off for the world's largest annual sports event, but no matter: The real fireworks had already taken place.

In the hours before the presentation, Jan Ullrich, leader of the German T-Mobile squad and defending champion Lance Armstrong's biggest rival, was feeling so good that after a morning training ride with his teammates he decided to take one more look at the first stage's flat time trial course. He was riding at race speed behind a team car driven by his *directeur sportif* Mario Kummer when, 11km into the course, they approached a round-about that connects to a side road leading to the infamous Passage du Gois—infamous because it was the scene of a huge pileup in the 1999 Tour. But on this showery day with no other cyclists in sight, a race-ending tangle was the last thing on Ullrich's mind.

The only traffic Kummer saw as he approached the roundabout was a truck coming from the opposite direction. He expected it to head straight on; instead, it continued around the traffic circle and headed toward the Gois. Kummer had no time to warn Ullrich on his radio before he slammed on the car's brakes. The 1997 Tour champion smashed into the back of the station wagon, breaking the rear window with his helmet, which cracked in two.

The left side of Ullrich's neck was cut by the glass, but it just missed piercing a vein. Even so, he was rushed back to the Hôtel Mercure in the seaside village of St. Jean-de-Monts, where his team doctor patched him up and a small pack of journalists gathered to see if the German's Tour was going to be compromised. Luckily, officials said, Ullrich was not badly injured. The German was in a state of shock, but more lasting perhaps would be the whiplash to his shoulder and back.

It was a lousy start to a race that was shaping up as the most important of Ullrich's career. Since his 1997 victory, Ullrich had not fared so well. Though six-time winner Armstrong repeatedly named Ullrich as his main rival for Tour honors, and Ullrich's four second-place finishes in four starts between 1998 and 2003 had seemingly earned him that distinction, the German's performances were somewhat erratic. The closest he came to dethroning Armstrong was in 2003, but he couldn't take advantage when the champion was weakened by chronic dehydration, and he finished 1:01 behind at the end. His 2004 result was worse. He failed to finish on the podium for the first time, taking fourth place behind Armstrong, T-Mobile teammate Andreas Klöden, and CSC's Ivan Basso.

Now, with T-Mobile touting Ullrich as the leader of a team that was focused purely on the yellow jersey, it was time to show the world what he could do. At 31, Ullrich was at the peak of his powers. T-Mobile's team manager Walter Godefroot inferred as much in a pre-Tour review of his team's strategy. By combining Ullrich's strength with the uphill power of Klöden and the relentless combativeness of Alexander Vinokourov, Godefroot envisioned attacking Armstrong and his Discovery Channel team on three fronts.

"I've been trying for a long time to prove that there is strength in numbers, but I've never been able to get everything to come together," said Godefroot the day before the Tour start. "Ullrich was absent one year, then Vinokourov the next. I'm crossing my fingers. Since the cohabitation of Jan Ullrich and Bjarne Riis [at my Telekom team] in 1996 and 1997, I've known that it's possible to get strong personalities to work together."

Possible, yes, even on the famously fractious T-Mobile squad, where deathly silences often ruled the dinner table. But Godefroot insisted that the motivation of defeating Armstrong had unified the team around Ullrich. No longer was there a need to win stages; star sprinter Erik Zabel had been dropped from T-Mobile's 2005 Tour roster.

There was still an odd undertone of caution in Godefroot's remarks, though. Pre-Tour interviews are usually full of confident bluster, yet Godefroot admitted to some doubts. Assessing Ullrich's form, he said, "I think his morale has never been as positive as this year in the past five years. I believe he can beat Armstrong. But it all depends on how strong our team will be."

Godefroot also spelled out T-Mobile's strategy for unsettling Armstrong. "In all of his six victories, Armstrong never really attacked in the mountains; he won in the time trials. His team was always so strong that he could wait until the end of the last climb and then gain 30 seconds or a minute in a very short amount of time," said the veteran Belgian, who was managing his Tour team for the last time before stepping down. "We have to keep him busy for the entire three weeks. And maybe attack early, maybe already on the next-to-last climb. Vinokourov would be the man who can do such a thing."

It all added up to a hopeful if somewhat lukewarm assessment. With Ullrich as leader, Klöden as backup, and Vinokourov as the wild card, T-Mobile's chances were probably as good as anyone's. But now with Ullrich's crash, the question would be, was he ready? And if not, who, really, could unseat Armstrong?

FEELING GOOD

Ullrich was not the only rider who would start the race in less than perfect shape. Armstrong, too, was still a little banged up from crashing on his time trial bike during a training ride in Nice ten days before the Tour. First he was distracted by a bee sting. Then he hit a bump in the road, which caused his bike to lock up and sent him spinning over the handlebars. "It was a silly crash," Armstrong reported a few days later. "I hit my head, which cracked the helmet in two. It wasn't that serious—no breaks, no stitches . . . just road rash and a little beat up."

But Armstrong added, "I feel very good on the bike and I'd even venture to say I feel better than I've ever felt." That observation was confirmed by his personal coach Chris Carmichael, who said Armstrong would be having one last performance test in the week before the Tour. "I'll never forget looking at the results of a similar test . . . four days before the 1999 Tour de France began," Carmichael said. "He had reached the level where he was capable of winning the Tour . . . and he has consistently returned to that level every year since. I'm confident that this last performance test will again show he's 100-percent ready."

And indeed, with his final prep behind him, Armstrong looked calm and prepared— despite a lingering black eye from his crash—on arriving at his Nantes hotel a few days before the start of the Tour. He didn't seem bothered that he had yet to win a race in 2005. When asked at the team's pre-race news conference why he seemed so relaxed compared with the nervousness he showed before starting the 2004 Tour in Belgium, he replied, "I was nervous last year because I had the impression I was up against, not really a demon . . . but in 101 years none of the greats have been able to win a sixth Tour. Many people said that means it is simply not possible, for some . . . *higher* reason. That's an incredible burden to get rid of. For me, I am not chasing a legacy [this year]. I am just here to have a good time, enjoy my last Tour, and enjoy the good form I *think* I have."

Having fun is something Tour riders generally don't mention until the end of their careers. Frenchman Bernard Hinault, for example, didn't broach the subject until he was ready to start his final Tour de France in 1986. And have fun he did. The five-time Tour winner went on the attack whenever he felt like it. He won both the long time trials, finished first at L'Alpe d'Huez and wore the yellow jersey for five days. But he didn't win that Tour. He had promised to help his young prodigy, Greg LeMond, take his first title. And the American did win, despite the deliberate head games played by Hinault.

When another five-time champion, Miguel Induráin, began his last Tour in 1996, he didn't make any predictions, but he was the red-hot favorite and hoping to ride triumphantly into his hometown of Pamplona, which was included in the Tour route for the first time. In his buildup to the Tour, the Spaniard won four stage races including an easy victory at the Dauphiné Libéré, in which he took the longest time trial and the toughest mountain stage in the Alps. Perhaps he was overconfident, perhaps he suffered more than the others in the torrential rain that fell through the Tour's opening week, perhaps he bonked on the first alpine stage because of not having his usual focus. Whatever the cause, Induráin stumbled where he should have soared. His best result of that Tour, which he finished in 11th place overall, came in the 65km time trial through the Bordeaux wine country the day before the finish. Induráin was second in the stage, 56 seconds slower than a Tour rookie named Jan Ullrich.

GAME PLAN

So what could the race followers expect from Lance Armstrong's 11th and final Tour? Like Induráin, he was starting the Tour as the odds-on favorite to win. Like Hinault, he wanted to have some fun. But for Armstrong, fun only comes when he is winning. He doesn't like being a runner-up, even if he were to finish the Tour behind a Discovery Channel teammate like his designated successor, Yaroslav Popovych of Ukraine.

Given Armstrong's usual attention to detail, he and team director Johan Bruyneel looked ready to adopt their Tour-tested game plan, which they often summed up as "one successful attack and two good time trials."

For the 2005 Tour that would mean a series of well-executed sorties, beginning with the stage 1 time trial—perhaps even winning it—to plant seeds of doubt in his rivals' minds. Armstrong's other opportunities would come in the stage 4 team time trial, where his disciplined Discovery squad would surely do well, and then in the mountains. Armstrong, as usual, was focusing on the first mountaintop finish in the Alps, at Courchevel, in stage 10. If the "one successful attack" didn't work, he would have two more chances to distance his opponents in the two summit finishes in the Pyrénées, in stages 14 and 15. And the final time trial on the Tour's penultimate day, on a long, rolling course at St. Étienne, would suit Armstrong's skills especially well.

After several years of subjugation, the other main contenders were aware of how the defending champion planned his Tours, so they were either going to try to beat him at his own game (perhaps only Ullrich had that capability) or stay within reach of Armstrong in the time trials and try to catch out the Discovery team with unexpected attacks in the mountains (the declared policy of two former third-place finishers, Ullrich's teammate Vinokourov and the CSC team leader Ivan Basso).

Though Armstrong was the favorite to win the Tour for an unprecedented seventh time, history has shown that upsets do occur. Take the 1965 Tour. That was the year the renowned French film director Claude Lelouch made a superb documentary about the Tour, titled *Pour un Maillot Jaune* (*For a Yellow Jersey*). There was no commentary to the film. Lelouch used only the sounds and sights of France. It was not a story of the race, either. The race told its own story, and it produced a totally unexpected winner: an Italian, a last-minute replacement riding his first Tour, named Felice Gimondi.

Forty years later, a surprise winner of the 92nd Tour was unlikely given Armstrong's solid six-year streak and the total confidence he displayed at the Challans news conference. What remains the same about the Tour is the ceremony surrounding its opening. In Lelouch's film total silence precedes the beginning of the first road stage. A ceremonial tricolor ribbon is held like a finishing tape across the road, the local mayor steps in to cut it loose, and the cyclists move away to the vibrant sounds of the Tour, including *La Marseillaise*, the French national anthem. Another Tour was under way.

CHAPTER 2 | STAGE 1
Rookies & Champions

Shortly after 7:15 at the close of the Tour's first day, and the scenes around the finish line were decidedly mixed. Blaring from the podium of the opening stage time trial, the stirring sounds of the Tour anthem rolled into the mild evening air as the first yellow jersey was awarded to stage-winner Dave Zabriskie, a rider making his first appearance at the race.

A quarter mile away, a rider making his final appearance, a smiling Lance Armstrong, was standing in the open doorway of his Discovery Channel team's camper van. He was being peppered with questions by a scrum of journalists, high on body odor and low on patience, who were squeezed into a five-foot-wide gap between the high-sided Discovery and Liquigas-Bianchi team vehicles.

Nearby, a frazzled, speechless Jan Ullrich was sitting in the front seat of the departing T-Mobile team car, his racing skinsuit still unzipped to the chest as he toweled off his ruddy face, drank from a plastic water bottle, and stared impassively ahead. Following his training crash, he found himself in shock for the second time in two days.

And in the center of the now almost-empty parking lot, Australian yellow-jersey hopeful Cadel Evans was calmly spinning the pedals on his bike trainer, talking about his first day at the Tour.

Like the other 188 starters, Evans, racing for the Belgian squad Davitamon-Lotto, began this overcast Saturday at one of the ten hotels being occupied by the twenty-one teams in and around the city of Nantes. Much of the previous days had been spent in pre-race hoopla: press conferences, medical checks, blood tests, and team presentations. "I'm trying not to get caught up in the hype and stuff," said Evans, a former world-class

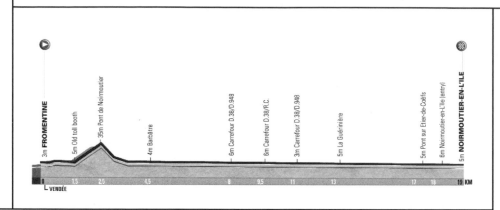

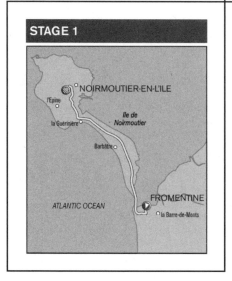

STAGE 1

mountain biker who is a climbing specialist. "I just do my race and do my job and see where it takes me."

Another Tour rookie, Californian Chris Horner on the Spanish team Saunier Duval–Prodir, was equally focused on being ready for his Tour debut. "I'm running into the whole thing kind of blind," he admitted. "We've had three days at the hotel, where you're not getting much [riding]. The weather's been bad, the wind was blowing hard, and you had a lot of ceremony stuff, so there was a lot less riding than I like to do."

But Horner added, with a sense of optimism, "We've got another six, seven days before we get into the mountains, so there's plenty of time to get the legs open. Some guys like Lance can really prepare for a race like this, and then guys like me, we just have to find our wings as we go."

At 33, Chris Horner was in his eleventh season as a professional cyclist, and after winning all the best races in the United States, he had finally reached the show. He readily agreed that the Tour was different from any other race. "Yeah, absolutely," he enthused. "Especially when we drove into the start, and you see all the people cheering and stuff. It's incredible how many people they get out for this."

What was especially amazing was how many spectators were able to cram themselves onto the pan-flat island of Noirmoutier. Although the start in the port town of Fromentine was on the mainland, most of the time trial course was on the island, and to get there, the tens of thousands of fans either walked across the modern bridge the riders would take later or made an early-morning, low-tide crossing of the Passage du Gois, a causeway that can be 12 feet underwater at high tide.

Once they'd found a nice spot to watch the race, families set up their picnic tables and folding chairs. During their long wait (the first rider didn't start until 3:40 p.m.), they had time to visit the food stands and grab hand-fuls of potato pancakes served with seaweed harvested from the salt marshes, a local specialty. And when the vehicles from the Tour's publicity caravan drove through, they could buy the official €15 Tour kit of T-shirt and souvenirs, get a €1 ice cream or collect freebies like the red and

Their close ranks and excited chattering, a hum and buzz that rose and fell and then exploded into cheers as each rider exited the start house . . .

white Champion supermarket peaked caps, giant green PMU cardboard hands, or Haribo jellybeans thrown out by college students hired by the sponsors for the month of festivities.

Because the 585-meter-long Noirmoutier Bridge was closed to spectators, those who hadn't made it across early in the day were now jammed six-deep in the opening 2.5km. Their close ranks and excited chattering, a hum and buzz that rose and fell and then exploded into cheers as each rider exited the start house, added to the tension and trepidation felt by the riders as they accelerated into their time trials.

EARLY STARTERS

Canny *directeurs sportifs*, anticipating changing conditions from the island weather, placed their specialist time trialists near the front of the field. And indeed, by midafternoon a substantial breeze was blowing parallel to the roadway, a nice boost that would be felt for most of the 19km route. So it was with special interest that savvy observers followed four riders in the opening hour (the 189 riders started at one-minute intervals): 11th starter Laszlo Bodrogi of Crédit Agricole, 19th starter Zabriskie of CSC, 41st starter Andreas Klöden of T-Mobile, and 60th starter Vladimir Karpets of Illes Balears.

Bodrogi, a 28-year-old Hungarian, was clearly off to a good ride when with 5km to go he passed his minute man, Michael Albasini of Liquigas-Bianchi, and at the finish was within 100 meters of catching his two-minute man, Stéphane Augé of Cofidis. Bodrogi's time was an excellent 21:50, with an average speed of 52.2kph. But his performance looked puny compared with Zabriskie's.

CSC's 26-year-old American, who won the first long time trial at the Giro d'Italia in mid-May, simply flew out of the start house, zipped through the sharp crowd-lined turns in town, and then powered up to the 114-foot-high crest of the concrete bridge. Once on the island, he gracefully swept through the first of the course's three roundabouts before heading north on the wide, flat highway.

Settled into his ride, Zabriskie's long, lean legs were now churning a steady 95–100rpm, despite the fact that they were pushing a leg-popping 54x11 gear. When he hit the halfway split in a time of 10:15, he was averaging more than 55kph and showing no signs of slowing down. At 10km, Zabriskie raced past his minute man, Spaniard Xabier Zandio of Illes Balears, in such a rush that Zandio barely had time to spot Zabriskie's number disappearing in the distance. Then, in an incredible display of power, Zabriskie caught his two-minute man, Belgian Mario Aerts of Davitamon-Lotto, 4km from the finish.

> **"I just wanted to open up the legs, and I felt good. There wasn't any pressure to make a good ride."**

When he sped across the finish line in 20:51, Zabriskie had broken Greg LeMond's Tour time trial speed record of 54.545kph by 0.131kph, a record that had stood for sixteen years. It was, to say the least, a time that would be tough to match.

That was confirmed when 2004 Tour runner-up Klöden came through two minutes slower (22:52), followed by defending under-26 champion Karpets more than a minute back (21:56). Klöden's ride was a big disappointment, both for his T-Mobile squad and for race followers expecting the 30-year-old German to again be a threat overall. Perhaps the conditions had already changed because when a weary Horner, who started an hour after Klöden, came home with an identical time (22:52), he said, "It was incredibly hard. There's a cross-headwind out there. The only place to get a rest was at a couple of roundabouts."

But another American in a similar time slot, sprinter Fred Rodriguez of Davitamon-Lotto, who actually caught Rabobank climber Michael Rasmussen for a minute in his 23:00 performance, said, "I just wanted to open up the legs, and I felt good. There wasn't any pressure to make a good ride."

There *was* pressure on the men who started in the 103rd and 104th starting slots, CSC's Jens Voigt and T-Mobile's Vinokourov. Voigt's team expected a strong performance from the German veteran to give them a boost in the team competition. The total time of the top three riders on each squad determines the classification, and the leading team would start last in the stage 4 team time trial, a big advantage.

When Voigt reached the 9.4km split in 10:37 (second only to Zabriskie at that point), it looked as though he was on a great schedule. He faded in the second half though, crossing the line 1:04 slower than his American teammate. Voigt was in the red zone for the final few kilometers, as evidenced at the finish by his scarlet face, zip pulled down to the waist, and the long time he needed to regain his breath.

By now, a pale sun had broken through the haze of the 70-degree afternoon, but the humidity remained high. The toughness of the conditions was confirmed by Vinokourov, who was just one second faster than Voigt at halfway. Vino started with high hopes. This wasn't a course that suited the squat Kazakh champion's strengths, but he raced to 100 percent of his capabilities. Though he continued to lose time to Zabriskie—40 seconds back at 15km and 53 seconds at the line—Vinokourov had moved into second place with 85 riders still to come.

Informed of his good time right after finishing, sweat glistening in his light-blond hair and trickling down his flushed face while drool hung from his chin, Vinokourov said, "I was going flat out, flat out. My time is good, it's okay, so I am happy. Happy. As for the course, it's very flat and fast. For me, it would be better to have it a bit more rolling. But I did my best. The time trial is always difficult on the first day."

It was 6 p.m. before the crowd's attention was refocused on the warm-up area in Fromentine. Armstrong was still 48 minutes away from his start time, but he was spinning the pedals on his stationary trainer at an impressively high cadence alongside teammate George Hincapie, who was also expected to do a stellar ride. Archrival Ullrich, still wearing a bandage on his head wound, was downplaying his accident of the previous day, telling his team officials that he was "100 percent." But his injuries would almost certainly make it difficult for him to hold a stretched-out arm position on the flat 19km course. As for third favorite Basso, he was quietly warming up on his road bike, knowing that the board-flat course would make it hard for him to match power riders like Ullrich and Armstrong.

All of them, though, were waiting to see how four other American challengers fared in the next half hour. CSC's Bobby Julich started conservatively but finished strongly to record 21:58, four seconds behind teammate Voigt. Gerolsteiner's Levi Leipheimer made an even slower start, level with Klöden at halfway, but he picked up the pace and was actually fourth fastest over the final 4km. His 22:04 equaled the time of his teammate Michael Rich, a former world time trial champion. Team Phonak's Floyd Landis also had a fast finish to record 21:53. Hincapie was slower than Landis and Leipheimer on the second half, but his more even ride netted him an excellent 21:48. This eventually was the day's fourth fastest time, and boosted Armstrong's confidence that a winning performance was possible at this tail end of the day.

Evans, who started three minutes ahead of Ullrich, four in front of Armstrong, confirmed that the wind "dropped off for the evening riders," although he admitted, "I was concentrating on where I was going, not on the wind. The wind didn't bother me too much, which probably means I had pretty good legs." Evans went on to record a solid time of 22:32, which proved 50 seconds faster than the next starter, Francisco Mancebo of Illes Balears, and 15 seconds slower than Basso. But those three rides gained zero attention because of the much-ballyhooed duel starting right behind them.

BATTLE OF THE HEAVYWEIGHTS

Ullrich versus Armstrong '05 was being hyped as a replay of their '03 Tour battle on the penultimate day in the time trial from Pornic to Nantes. Heightening the competition was the proximity of the two venues; Pornic is only a 16km boat ride from Noirmoutier. In 2003, Ullrich needed to overcome a 66-second deficit in 49km to win the Tour, but he crashed heavily on a slick roundabout, sending a spray of sparks into the air, and conceding 11 seconds to Armstrong. Now, on a course 30km shorter, they were both fighting for an advantage that would give the winner a huge psychological boost.

Despite his crash twenty-four hours earlier, Ullrich believed he had the makings of good ride when he puffed out his cheeks and rumbled down the start ramp in Fromentine. He had comfortably won a 36km time trial at the Tour of Switzerland in mid-June and his legs were feeling good. The flat course would play to his strength, where his powerful, slow cadence would not be interrupted by hills. But his biggest challenge was not in front of him. It lay 60 seconds behind.

Armstrong, by far the Tour's most consistent time trialist in recent years, had decorated his TT bike in fresh war paint. Painted on the fork was a lazy "L" (for Lance), which looked like a stylized "7" from the cockpit, while the iconography on the rear disc wheel designed by former New York graffiti artist Lenny McGurr (aka Futura 2000) included several small 7s. The six-time Tour champion was ready for battle. Perhaps that flirtation with fate caused Armstrong's right foot to shoot out of the pedal as he pounded down the start ramp. The slip cost him no more than a second, though, and he was soon spinning a massive 55x11 gear at close to 100rpm.

Accelerating rapidly out of the start village, he shifted down for the short climb to the top of the bridge, where he caught his first glimpse of a pink jersey: Ullrich hammering along the highway ahead. The target was irresistible. Armstrong accelerated again. At the halfway point, the Texan was within 21 seconds of catching Ullrich with a time just 3 seconds off Zabriskie's. Steadily at first, then faster and faster, Armstrong relentlessly closed in on Ullrich until he burst past his disbelieving rival with 3.2km remaining.

In Lance Armstrong's rush to catch Ullrich, he had pulled dead even with Zabriskie's incredible time. But he couldn't quite bring it home. The flags were hanging limp as he roared across the finish line just two seconds short of his former teammate's winning time of 20:51.

He hadn't won the time trial, and he didn't achieve his goal of taking the yellow jersey, but Armstrong couldn't have been happier with his performance. No one expected the Tour's superstar to defeat his main rival by a minute on a course that better suited the German.

Ullrich, shattered after crossing the line six seconds behind Armstrong to take an uncharacteristic 12th place, rode silently to his team car as Armstrong, his sweat-streaked face unwiped, happily bantered with the swarming mob of reporters around his camper van. A French television interviewer shouted over the din, "That was really a great moment in this Tour when you overtook Jan Ullrich." Armstrong didn't disagree. A fan cried, "Lance, Lance, make them work for it" as Armstrong said, "I gave it the maximum to try to get the yellow jersey." He didn't get the jersey that evening, but by eclipsing the times of his chief opponents he had made it clear that three very long weeks lay ahead.

As Armstrong drove away in the van with its curtains drawn, the diligent Evans was still riding his stationary trainer in the parking lot. "I'm feeling all right," said the rookie, "not too bad for a time trial that didn't suit me."

Over at the winner's podium, that other rookie, Zabriskie, was feeling even better. "The feeling is amazing, unbelievable," he said after slipping on the first yellow jersey of his career, and after waiting in the CSC team bus for almost three hours since his phenomenal ride. "I really don't know quite what to say. It was very stressful and nervous to [wait and] watch that on TV. But I am happy it worked in my favor. It may be difficult to sleep tonight."

By the time Zabriskie was driven away in a team car, the locals were preparing a celebratory firework display. Past midnight, children who'd just witnessed the pyrotechnics after a long day at the Tour fell asleep on their parents' shoulders as they traipsed back with crabs and mussels scavenged from the sea to their cars parked a lifetime ago. And 70km away in the Hôtel Océania at the Nantes airport, after *his* very big day, Dave Zabriskie went to sleep using one of yellow-jersey sponsor Crédit Lyonnais' toy lions as an extra pillow.

STAGE 1: FROMENTINE-NOIRMOUTIER TT

1. Dave Zabriskie (USA), CSC, 19km in 20:51 (54.676kph); 2. Lance Armstrong (USA), Discovery Channel, 20:53; 3. Alexander Vinokourov (Kaz), T-Mobile, 21:44; **4. George Hincapie (USA), Discovery Channel, 21:48; 5.** Laszlo Bodrogi (Hun), Crédit Agricole, 21:50; **6. Floyd Landis (USA), Phonak, 21:53; 7.** Fabian Cancellara (Swi), Fassa Bortolo, s.t.; **8.** Jens Voigt (G), CSC, 21:55; **9.** Vladimir Karpets (Rus), Illes Balears, 21:56; **10.** Igor Gonzalez de Galdeano (Sp), Liberty Seguros, s.t.

CHAPTER 3

Zabriskie's Long and Lonely Road to the Yellow Jersey

Many of the key moments in Dave Zabriskie's rocky cycling career have happened when he was alone. Whether it was a four-hour solo break to win a breakthrough stage of the 2004 Vuelta a España, or the long, lonely days struggling to overcome a broken leg and arm a year earlier, Zabriskie has often been forced to look inward for the strength to overcome his professional and personal roadblocks. He found himself in that familiar position yet again several hours right after the two most significant victories of his life: the opening time trial of this 92nd Tour de France and the stage 8 time trial of the Giro d'Italia, seven weeks earlier.

Anyone who came across a 6-foot, 150-pound American lying on a park bench in Florence, Italy, on May 15 might have thought he was a college backpacker searching for the meaning of life. In fact, it was iconoclastic U.S. bike racer Zabriskie, waiting to see if anyone would beat his time in the Giro's 45km time trial starting in Lamporecchio.

"I went off early [19th of 186 riders] and had to wait close to three hours," Zabriskie said. "So I found a bench and laid down and looked at the trees, and I took some pictures of some interesting-looking people."

What else could he do? After roaring over the course in 58:31, Zabriskie had to wait for another 167 riders to complete the stage. With the CSC team bus still at the start in Lamporecchio, Zabriskie had nothing else to do but while away the time in the park. Finally, the waiting became so excruciating that he went to the team car and watched the big guns come through on a mini television set. The closest was his CSC team leader Ivan

Basso, 17 seconds slower. "I watched the last few guys," said Zabriskie. "When [eventual Giro winner Paolo] Savoldelli didn't beat it, I knew I had won."

The victory put the Utah native in elite company as the sixth American to win a Giro stage. Greg LeMond, Ron Kiefel, and Andy Hampsten won stages in the 1980s, Tyler Hamilton took a stage in 2002, and Fred Rodriguez bagged one in 2003.

"It was a pretty good one," said Zabriskie, who a few weeks earlier came second to Floyd Landis (and ahead of Lance Armstrong) in the time trial stage of the Tour de Georgia. "After my time trial in Georgia, I knew I could have a good ride. I was pretty confident, and [CSC team manager Bjarne] Riis told me I'd have a good chance."

Key to Zabriskie's Giro stage victory was his intimate knowledge of the course, which started with a rolling 9km through the vineyards of Tuscany before climbing 1,200 vertical feet in 9km to the crest of Monte Albano. From there, a fast 9km descent to Tornante was followed by a flat 17km run alongside the Arno River into Florence. Zabriskie figures he rode the climb at least twenty times during the team's grueling training camps in January and February, when CSC resided at a nearby Medici family castle. "I knew the climb and the descent really well, and when I got to the straight, it was just full gas. I could have used an extra gear I was going so fast," said Zabriskie, who rode a 55x11 gearing.

It was clear Zabriskie was flying. He even passed his six-minute man, Unai Etxebarria (Euskaltel-Euskadi), in the final kilometers. Zabriskie said he averaged 55kph over the final flat section. "My head was really clear," he continued. "When I came through, I thought 'Someone's going to have to go fast to beat me.'"

Unlike Basso, who has worked intensely on improving his time trial performance, Zabriskie's natural aerodynamic position leaves little room for improvement. "Dave has the most natural time trial position I've ever seen," Riis said. "It would be a waste of time to do wind-tunnel testing with him."

It also helps that Zabriskie feels right at home in Riis's big red machine, CSC, a team that gives every rider a chance to flourish. "He's a really serious guy who really believes in his team," Zabriskie said of Riis. "That belief carries over to all the riders: We believe we're strong, and we go out there to prove it."

Riis helped transform Zabriskie from a young rider with huge potential into America's third-ever Tour de France yellow jersey. At CSC, Zabriskie no longer feels he has to fight his battles alone. He has finally found the support he always longed for.

THE PAIN GAME

Zabriskie's road to the yellow jersey was filled with speed bumps. Growing up in Salt Lake City, he turned to bicycles after breaking his arm at junior high school. Raised by a single mother and three sisters, Zabriskie often found sanctuary on his bike and soon fell in love with plying the steep canyon roads near his Utah home.

"I wasn't Mormon and it was difficult to make friends. Growing up that way wasn't the best experience, but it made me who I am," Zabriskie told the *Boston Globe*. "That helped me to be able to deal with being alone so much in Europe."

When Zabriskie was 17, his mother drove him to Colorado for one of the Lance Armstrong Junior Olympic Race Series events, which qualified him for a stint at the U.S. Olympic Training Center in Colorado Springs. That expert training helped him develop the superb time trialing ability that later carried him to the elite level of cycling.

As a senior amateur racer, his natural ability to ride time trials soon became obvious. He won the 1998 national under-23 (U23) time trial championship, and followed this in 1999 with a time trial stage win at Italy's challenging Giro delle Regioni and took a stage of Oregon's Tour of Willamette with the Nutra-Fig team. By 2000, riding for 7Up–Colorado Cyclist, Zabriskie showed other qualities, too. He came in second at the early-season Redlands Classic stage race (equal on time with winner Chris Horner), took his second national U23 time trial title, won the U23 division of the prestigious Grand Prix des Nations in France, and then placed fourth at the world U23 time trial championship.

Zabriskie's career looked like it was really taking off when in 2001, at age 22, he signed a four-year contract with the U.S.

Zabriskie's career looked like it was really taking off when in 2001, at age 22, he signed a four-year contract with the U.S. Postal Service team to ride alongside his hero, Armstrong.

Postal Service team to ride alongside his hero, Armstrong. But Zabriskie, with his introverted personality and natural shyness, got lost in the hustle and bustle surrounding Postal's established stars. Things came to a head during a team presentation at Solvang, California, one January as each rider was introduced to a packed room of journalists, sponsors, and family. When Zabriskie's turn to talk came around, he clammed up. By the time he could finally muster some words, the microphone had problems, and the room was filled with awkward silences. Zabriskie stood red-faced as they moved on to the next rider.

On the road, though, he made steadier progress. He won the prologue time trial at California's Sea Otter Classic and finished 120th in his first start at a three-week grand tour, the 2002 Vuelta a España. Then, while training in May 2003 for the prestigious week of races culminating in the USPRO Championship at Philadelphia, everything came to a halt.

Zabriskie was barreling down one of the canyons in Utah's Wasatch Range when an SUV pulled out in front of him. He smashed headlong into the vehicle, breaking his left femur and arm, and the post-crash surgery left him with three screws permanently in his left knee. "I remember when I went to see him, his leg had atrophied like this," said Dan Osipow, a Postal team official, who mimicked an emaciated leg with his thumb and index finger. After a long convalescence, a grim Zabriskie returned to racing at the Redlands Classic in March 2004. He crashed again, this time falling on chip-seal pavement on a long descent, leaving horrible scrapes and gashes on the right side of his body. He also suffered a concussion and was evacuated by helicopter.

"Dave is an example of perseverance and determination," said Osipow, now with the Discovery Channel team. "He was down not once, but twice. For him to come back from his injuries and to be in the yellow jersey is incredible."

"I've had some bad luck with crashes," Zabriskie said with understatement at his Tour de France press conference in Noirmoutier. "Maybe that's why you haven't heard too much about me."

Incredibly, Zabriskie pushed through the pain to come back again, for what he vowed would be his last attempt to conquer the sport he loved. If he had any more difficulties, he said, he would retire.

Slowly, Zabriskie's legs came around. He won the U.S. national time trial title in June 2004 and returned to Europe for the second half of the season. He promptly went on a huge breakaway at the Championship of Zürich World Cup classic in August, attacking with Spanish rider Carlos Barredo to build an 18-minute lead that ended only 22km from the finish.

Zabriskie carried that form into his second Vuelta start, helping U.S. Postal Service win the first-day team time trial to put Floyd Landis into the leader's jersey. In stage 11, from San Vicente del Raspeig to Caravaca de la Cruz, Zabriskie attacked early in the 165km stage across the barren flats of Murcia. Zabriskie was once again alone in what turned out to be the equivalent of a four-hour time trial. He crossed the line with the win, a tidy 1:11 ahead of the peloton.

Next, Zabriskie went to the world time trial championships in Bardolino, Italy, hoping to surprise the favorites. "All I needed was to get some muscle back in the left leg. It's like I've been pedaling with one leg. Now that I have almost two legs, it's a lot better," he said after finishing fifth, 1:36 behind winner Michael Rogers of Australia. "I haven't been able to do that since my crash [in 2003]."

Despite the late-season successes, Zabriskie rolled across the world's finish line near Lake Garda not sure if he'd ever race a bike again. Little did he realize that Riis already had him in his sights. Bobby Julich recommended Zabriskie and Christian Vande Velde after Riis expressed an interest in signing up more Americans on his CSC team.

REBUILDING

Within the close-knit world of professional cycling, Zabriskie's quirky sense of humor is legendary. Known for his ironic witticisms and his lounge-act singer routine before races, he immediately surprised his new, sometimes very serious, Danish teammates. "Dave is different, but behind that joking face is a very serious rider," Riis said. "People may think he's kind of goofy, but we're impressed with him."

Zabriskie's turn at the infamous CSC team-building training camp held each December almost proved too much. He jokes about it now, but at the time there were doubts about whether he would have the resilience to endure the team's rigorous pro-gram. "I looked death in the eye," he recalled with a touch of sarcasm. "It helped make me the man that I am today and I can't wait to go back [to camp]."

Zabriskie arrived in Denmark jet-lagged, tired, and unsure about his future and his new team. He soon found himself marching through cold, wet Danish forests dressed in army fatigues. Under the guidance of BS Christensen, a retired NATO Special Forces com-mando and team assistant to Riis, riders underwent a series of challenges that included climbing walls, swimming across the sea in darkness, and sleeping overnight in the woods without extra clothing or gear.

It was all too much for Zabriskie, who left the camp and checked in at a local hospital suffering from exhaustion. He was the first rider to have walked away from one of Riis's survival camps in four years. "When he came to us, he was locked, a very closed person,"

Christensen said. "We had to open him up. He was a tough one because he was so closed. He needed to feel safe and comfortable like he was with a family, then he could open up."

When Zabriskie returned to the team's first training camp in Tuscany in mid-January, he let his legs do the talking. Known for his time trialing strength, it was Zabriskie's climbing skills that earned him a ticket on CSC's 2005 Giro d'Italia squad. Team captain Basso was going for the victory and Riis brought a team stacked with talent.

Though Zabriskie brilliantly won that stage 8 time trial into Florence, Riis was more impressed with how his young recruit rode in the mountains to support Basso. Zabriskie was then short-listed for CSC's Tour de France team and told that he shouldn't travel back to the United States to defend his national time trial title. The orders were clear: Rest and get ready for the Tour.

The 26-year-old American's Tour started like a dream when he played giant killer in the opening individual time trial. A worldwide audience was stunned by his performance in setting a new Tour record for the fastest-ever nonprologue time trial and beating ex-boss Armstrong by two seconds. "I didn't think it would happen," said Zabriskie, who now had taken a stage victory in three consecutive grand tours.

Cycling hacks were soon guffawing at Zabriskie's sardonic wit. When asked how it felt to be in the yellow jersey on the Fourth of July, he opined that he'd like to be back home, "drinking that drink that everyone likes to drink." Perhaps Zabriskie was thinking about one of his famous one-question interviews with riders in the peloton that he publishes on his Web site. It could have been the one conducted during the 2005 Giro with Australian Trent Wilson of the Colombia–Selle Italia team:

DZ: Trent, if you could make a rubber-band bracelet, what would it stand for?

TW: Something to do with beer.

TW (two hours later): Actually, the band would be black and it would say "Don't Fight It." For example, if there is a *gruppetto* forming and you are in it, don't try to jump to the group in front. Don't fight it.

DZ: Thanks for the interview, Trent.

CHAPTER 4 | STAGES 2–3
Warring Sprinters

Moments after zooming across the finish line of the opening road stage in the little town of Les Essarts, the gregarious Belgian racer Tom Boonen made a sharp U-turn and headed for the winner's podium. He began weaving his way between the suddenly ragged ranks of cameramen and reporters when he came face-to-face with his Italian American teammate Guido Trenti. The two big men paused momentarily before engaging in a zealous embrace, with wide grins on their tan faces. A third Quick Step–Innergetic teammate, Michael Rogers of Australia, added his congratulations with an uncharacteristically affectionate hug.

They were celebrating like young kids because all three knew how important this opening sprint victory was for their team and its sponsors. Not many stages at this Tour were going to end in mass sprints, and by taking the very first one Boonen was establishing a psychological advantage over his main competitors for the green jersey, which is awarded to the rider scoring the most points in stage finishes (weighted to favor the sprinters with 35 points for winning a flat stage but only 20 for a mountain stage) and intermediate sprints (where 6, 4, and 2 points go to the first three riders across the line).

This Tour was notable for the absence of three of cycling's greatest sprinting stars. Not toeing the line were Italian super-sprinter Alessandro Petacchi (whose season was focused on the Giro d'Italia and Vuelta a España), six-time green jersey Erik Zabel of Germany (not selected by his T-Mobile team), and Spain's world champion Oscar Freire (still recovering from saddle-sore surgery).

Instead, Boonen's main opponents would be three Australians, the fastest of whom was Davitamon-Lotto's Robbie McEwen, 33, who won the points jersey in 2002 and 2004, and

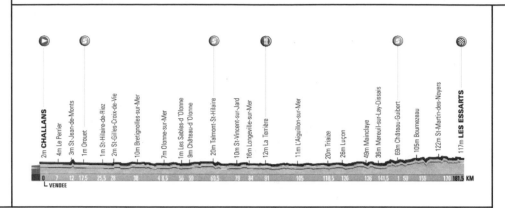

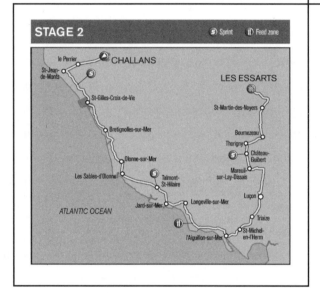

seems to get better with time. He's known as much for his aggressive tenacity in the final kilometers of a race as he is for his ability to seemingly come out of nowhere for the win.

Not quite as good in a mass sprint, but with day-in, day-out consistency, was the Cofidis team's Stuart O'Grady, 31, who wore the green jersey in 2001 all the way to the Champs-Élysées only to lose it in the final inter-mediate sprint to Zabel. The third Aussie, Française des Jeux's Baden Cooke, 26, won the points jersey in 2003, but he battled an illness in 2004 and the closest he had come to a grand tour stage win in two years occurred at the 2005 Giro, where he crashed into the bar-riers after being cut off by Italy's Olympic road champion Paolo Bettini.

Another clear candidate for the green jersey was Norwegian Thor Hushovd, 27, who took over as Crédit Agricole's main sprinter when O'Grady left the team at the end of 2003. At the 2004 Tour, Hushovd won the uphill stage 8 sprint into Quimper and twice finished second to McEwen in mass sprints. As for Boonen, 24, he had won two stages in his debut Tour, the first at Angers (after a mass pileup left only a dozen riders in con-tention) and the second on the Champs-Élysées (where he majestically outsped all of the main sprinters).

DOWN TO BUSINESS

In sharp contrast to the relatively cool and windy conditions of Saturday's time trial opener, riders woke up Sunday for the Tour's first road stage to a hot, muggy French summer day. Temperatures were soaring into the 90s as they gathered for the stage 2 start back in Challans.

In the 36 hours since the team presentation there, Boonen had started taking antibiotics to numb the pain from a toothache that almost prevented him from starting the Tour, Armstrong had confirmed his status as the man to beat, and the Danish team, CSC, had celebrated its first-ever Tour de France yellow jersey with a champagne toast Saturday night. Now, everyone was anxious to get down to business: Boonen by getting his troops to ensure a sprint finish through controlling attacks, Armstrong by drilling his eight Discovery teammates into a cohesive unit for the remainder of the Tour, and CSC by protecting Zabriskie's jersey on the notoriously nervous opening road stage.

"It's great to have the jersey, but at the end of the day, we're here to work for Ivan Basso," said Zabriskie, trying to downplay the media spotlight that always shines on the man in yellow. "This doesn't change anything. I never even dreamed I

"It's great to have the jersey, but at the end of the day, we're here to work for Ivan Basso."

would have the yellow jersey. I don't know how long I will keep it, but sooner or later, the yellow jersey is probably going to go away from Dave Zabriskie."

Even so, the talk of the peloton in Challans surrounded Zabriskie's shocking time trial win and Armstrong's drubbing of his main opponents. Vinokourov and Landis were the only contenders to finish within one minute of the Texan, though Phonak's Landis wasn't too concerned by his deficit going into stage 2. "Ordinarily, I am inconsistent in the opening prologue or time trial, and yesterday was a little bit longer than usual," Landis said, "but I'm happy with my performance."

Landis also indicated he wasn't surprised by Zabriskie's performance. The two Americans share an apartment at their European base in Gerona, Spain, and in the weeks leading up to the Tour Landis said he repeatedly told Zabriskie, "Dude, you've gotta aim at winning that Tour prologue."

CSC team boss Bjarne Riis was not surprised by his young charge's success either, but he cautioned that the native Utah rider still had a lot to learn—and some weight to shed— before growing into the role of an overall contender. "Dave needs to lose 3 to 4 kilos [about

8 pounds] to climb better in the mountains," Riis said. "If he can do that, I'm sure he can be a threat for the Tour someday."

Winning the time trial opener was a first step in that process. The next was wearing the yellow jersey and having his teammates protect him in this first road stage of 181.5km. The stage featured three intermediate sprints and the Tour's first rated climb, the Cat. 4 Côte du Lac de la Vouraie with 16.5km to go. After crossing flat marshland to the sand dunes of the Atlantic coast, the course pushed southeast past the yachting communities of St. Hilaire-de-Riez and Les Sables d'Olonne before turning inland with 75km remaining. From there, the peloton would roll through a bucolic landscape of patchwork fields, often on narrow, twisting backroads, dipping in and out of low valleys, to a tricky finish in Les Essarts.

RAPID OPENING

"It's going to be chaos out there," warned 2003 Paris-Roubaix winner Magnus Bäckstedt of Liquigas-Bianchi. "There's no big sprinter team to take control of the race, so guys are going to be attacking all over the place." The Swede, who said he would be racing the stage for his Brazilian sprinter teammate Luciano Pagliarini, was precisely right.

Frenchman Sylvain Calzati of ag2r made the first attack of the 2005 Tour after just 9km. He was joined by thirteen others after the left turn at St. Jean-de-Monts, where the riders first benefited from a brisk northwesterly wind. The change of pace contributed to a pileup at 23km, with five riders making the day's medical report for minor injuries.

Soon after the Tour's first intermediate sprint at Orouet, taken by Phonak's South African sprinter Robbie Hunter, Calzati attacked again, this time taking with him the Hungarian strongman Laszlo Bodrogi, the French 2004 Tour yellow jersey hero Thomas Voeckler of Bouygues Télécom, and Spanish aggressor David Cañada of Saunier Duval–Prodir. The quartet quickly gained two minutes, which moved Bodrogi, who placed fifth in the time trial, into the Tour's virtual lead.

The gap was up to 4:15 through the day's feed zone at half-distance, but CSC didn't seem overly concerned. "We didn't let the break get too far away," said CSC manager Riis, "and we got some help from the others." Even so, for many kilometers, his entire nine-man team was lined out at the head of the peloton, with Zabriskie on the seventh wheel, just behind Voigt and just ahead of Julich. "With the yellow jersey, the first day's a little easier," noted Julich, "but it's always nervous."

After leaving the coast, the roads narrowed and the number of crashes multiplied. "It was a stressful first day," confirmed Cofidis' Matt White, the Australian who had finally got to the Tour after six years of trying with three different teams. "There was plenty of crashes and bingles, but it's all a bit of a blur. I just tried to stay out of trouble." Many others weren't so lucky. Veteran sprinter Jaan Kirsipuu of Crédit Agricole and Iker Camano of Euskaltel-Euskadi were involved in a spill at 80km. Janeck Tombak of Cofidis got the worst of another crash when the peloton whipped through a tight corner, while two more hit the pavement at 138km.

With less than an hour of racing left, the Française des Jeux, Crédit Agricole, Quick Step, and Davitamon-Lotto teams took over the chase from the relieved CSC men. They trimmed the lead to 1:30 with 35km to go, but each of the day's four attackers still harbored hopes of gaining the first Tour stage win of his career. Voeckler, who valiantly defended the yellow jersey for ten days in 2004, was particularly motivated. One of his Bouygues team's main cosponsors is the Vendée region, whose roads they were racing on. It was on one of these departmental roads that Voeckler shot past the attacking Cañada to take the day's only King of the Mountains (KoM) sprint to give his sponsor some nice podium time in the polka-dot jersey.

"We hoped to arrive together at the finish to try to win the stage, but it's okay to get the climber's jersey," said the always-smiling Voeckler. "[Seven-time KoM winner] Richard Virenque was a great climber. I'm not at that level, so I can't dream about having it in Paris, but for right now, it's okay."

During the roller-coaster run-in to Les Essarts, the peloton inevitably closed in on the leaders. Bodrogi was the first to be gobbled up by the fast-charging pack. Voeckler dangled a little longer. Then Calzati and Cañada shook hands as the field surged past them with 6km to go.

RAGGED SPRINT

With five changes of direction in the final kilometer, including the last left turn only 280 meters from the finish line, all the sprinters wanted to be positioned near the front for the finale. Typically, this means a lot of maneuvering and hard riding by the sprinters' teammates, such as Boonen's Aussie colleague Rogers. "I helped Tom get up there with 5 kilometers to go. There's not much I can do in the lead-out. I'm a bit skinny to be up at the front," said Rogers, the world time trial champion, who was still ruing a disappointing 45th place on opening day.

While teams with sprinters work to keep the field together, the other squads do their best to disrupt things. That was the case with local team Bouygues Télécom. With Voeckler's effort thwarted, it was the turn of his veteran teammate Walter Bénéteau to bolt out of the peloton with 4.5km to go. But he had no more success than Saunier Duval's Constantino Zaballa, who tried his hand with 2.5km to go. He held out for about a kilometer before the speeding peloton guaranteed a collective charge to the line. "There's nothing quite like a mass sprint finish at the Tour de France," enthused Hushovd, who was moving through the peloton behind teammates Kirsipuu and Sébastien Hinault.

These two workers and the other lead-out men were pulling their sprinters to the front on a turn just inside a kilometer to go, when the peloton's smallest rider, 5' 2" Sammy Dumoulin of ag2r, clipped a barrier and saw his bike go careening across the street. No one else fell, but only the first twenty-five riders made it though the corner unimpeded.

With fewer riders to worry about, the final sprint should have been straightforward. Think again. Rounding the last turn, McEwen was positioned perfectly. "I was on Boonen's wheel," said the power-packed Aussie. "As soon as we straightened up, I went with 250 meters to go, and that was too early." What McEwen hadn't realized is that half of the final stretch was downhill before kicking up to the line in the last 100 meters. "When I went . . . my gears didn't work straightaway. I was on my 12 with nothing to push on for a while."

As McEwen attempted to get up to top speed, both Cooke and Boonen went for his back wheel. Cooke's version of what happened next took awhile to put together. He didn't heed a request to talk to reporters after the finish. But at his team bus, after he came out of the shower, Cooke was overheard saying to a friend as he gestured with his arms, smacking his hands together, "Boonen pushed me into the fence." Right then, the bus driver said sorry and punched a button that closed the door with a hiss.

The next day, Cooke reported that with 200 meters to go Boonen came into him at a 45-degree angle for about 5 to 10 meters, and almost sent him into the barriers. "I had to stop pedaling, and it's hard to get a 54x12 going again," noted Cooke, who perhaps was also held back by a memory of his similar confrontation with another Quick Step rider, Bettini, at the Giro that sent him to the tarmac. In that case, Bettini was relegated from first place; but here, at the Tour, his teammate Boonen came through unscathed.

With just McEwen to worry about, the Belgian made a thundering burst on the final kick-up to the line into a headwind that saw him finish a length clear of the Aussie, who was passed in the final meters by a fast-finishing Hushovd. "It's very nice to get [a win] early," said Boonen. "I was very motivated today because I wanted to get some points for the green jersey. The first win is always important."

As Boonen received the day's honors, McEwen pedaled disconsolately away to his Davitamon-Lotto team bus, telling a reporter running alongside him, "I'm really disappointed with my own sprint. I should have waited a little bit more and let Boonen start [the sprint]. Too late now. I'll have another go tomorrow."

> **"I'm really disappointed with my own sprint. I should have waited a little bit more and let Boonen start [the sprint]. Too late now. I'll have another go tomorrow."**

TOURS DE FORCE

That night, after the teams had returned to the same hotels they'd been stuck in for almost a week, forked lightning lit the night sky over the Vendée. The crashing thunder woke some of the riders, and torrential rain beat down on the wheat, barley, corn, and sunflower fields that lined the following day's route through the rolling hills of Anjou to the Loire Valley. The storm broke the heavy humidity and stifling heat, and led to temperatures in the 70s and light winds for stage 3's curving trip through the chateau country to Tours.

With the all-important team time trial coming up twenty-four hours later, Armstrong's Discovery team was hoping for another (for them) quiet day. Commenting on the first road stage, team member Hincapie said, "It was a pretty uneventful day. Pretty easy to sit on the wheels." And at the end of the stage, the Discovery men were the first to get to their team bus, which was parked at the head of the line (and the nearest to the freeway), ready to make a quick getaway. Discovery's logistical expertise was particularly important in this Tour, which had long transfers to team hotels almost every evening. Every minute saved gave the *soigneurs* more time for massage sessions and allowed mechanics more time to work on the bikes. The time savings also equated to an earlier mealtime, and, most importantly, extra rest and relaxation for the riders.

Although the speeds were again high in stage 3—averaging 46kph compared with stage 2's 47kph—Armstrong's men had another day of following wheels. And though Basso's CSC

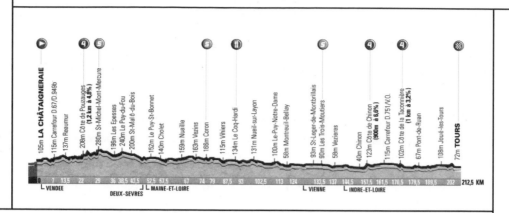

team still had Zabriskie's overall lead to maintain, the squad managed to ride conservatively. "If you have the yellow jersey I think you have to defend it," said team boss Riis. "We can do that . . . without using all the riders on the team . . . because we want to save something for the more important days to come."

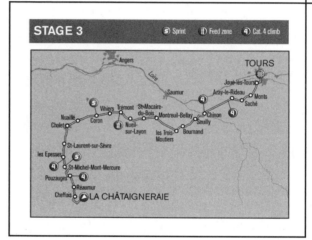

That wasn't the case for teams that had started the Tour with a goal of winning stages. On this 212.5km day, the squads that threw riders on the attack were Rabobank, whose Dutch veteran Erik Dekker began the major escape by sprinting clear of the pack 25km into the stage; Saunier Duval, whose Swiss strongman Rubens Bertogliati soon caught Dekker; and ag2r, whose willing Frenchman Nicolas Portal provided the third pair of legs in the lead group.

After the trio gained a maximum lead of 5:30 at the feed zone halfway through the stage, just before leaving a wide *route nationale* for a long spell on narrower back roads, the chase was stepped up by McEwen's Belgian teammate Johan Van Summeren and Boonen's Rogers. By the time the race curled around the round-towered, eleventh-century castle at Chinon with 52km to go, the gap was down to 1:45. And after spending almost four hours at the front the trio was in the pack's sights with four minutes left in the stage.

This scenario was déjà vu for Dekker. At October 2004's 252.5km Paris-Tours classic, he raced all day in a breakaway group before jumping clear on the never-ending Avenue de

Grammont. Dekker held off the pack all the way to the line to win the race by less than a second. This time his final solo attack coming onto the same boulevard fell short by 2.7km.

After most of the day's chasing had been done by the Quick Step and Davitamon-Lotto teams, it was Crédit Agricole that attempted to set up a winning train for Hushovd on the dead-straight ride into the heart of Tours. But the French squad didn't seem to take into account the gusting wind blowing from their left between the city's modern apartment blocks. Its support man Hinault "died" with 500 meters left, forcing Kirsipuu to start his lead-out too soon. In turn, Hushovd was forced to start his sprint more than 300 meters from the line.

Behind the big Norwegian, McEwen looked ready to pounce, but Boonen was on the Aussie's wheel and waited until the 200-meter mark before standing on his pedals and flying past on the Aussie champion's left. McEwen immediately responded and was headed into Boonen's draft when he found himself locked between Gerolsteiner's Austrian Peter Wrolich on his left and O'Grady to the right.

"Boonen came past. Stuey was trying to come on Boonen's wheel and I was just trying to stay upright,"said McEwen, who claimed that O'Grady leaned on him and then stuck out his elbow. "My arm was trapped by his elbow. That twisted my back and pulled my head toward him." But all that the judges saw was McEwen's head turning and apparently "butting" O'Grady. They relegated him from third to 185th place, and docked him the 26 sprinting points that would make a huge difference to the outcome of the green jersey competition in the weeks to come.

For now, Boonen was king, and McEwen's challenge would have to go on hold until after the stage 4 team time trial.

STAGE 2: CHALLANS–LES ESSARTS

1. Tom Boonen (B), Quick Step–Innergetic, 181.5km in 3:51:31 (47.038kph); **2.** Thor Hushovd (N), Crédit Agricole; **3.** Robbie McEwen (Aus), Davitamon-Lotto; **4.** Stuart O'Grady (Aus), Cofidis; **5.** Luciano Pagliarini (Bra), Liquigas-Bianchi, all s.t.

STAGE 3: LA CHÂTAIGNERAIE–TOURS

1. Boonen, 212.5km in 4:36:08 (46.170kph); **2.** Peter Wrolich (A), Gerolsteiner; **3.** O'Grady; **4.** Bernhard Eisel (A), Française des Jeux; **5.** Allan Davis (Aus), Liberty Seguros, all s.t.

GENERAL CLASSIFICATION

1. Dave Zabriskie (USA), CSC, 8:48:31

2. Lance Armstrong (USA), Discovery Channel, 00:02

3. Laszlo Bodrogi (Hun), Crédit Agricole, 00:47

4. Alexander Vinokourov (Kaz), T-Mobile, 00:53

5. George Hincapie (USA), Discovery Channel, 00:57

CHAPTER 5
Mighty Tom
Goes for Green

Tom Boonen is as ambitious as he is tall. At 6' 3" and the ripe age of 24, the big Belgian sprinter wants it all. Right now.

Posing shirtless and being interviewed in the European edition of *Playboy*, dating a former Miss Belgium, and driving fast cars, Boonen loves life in the fast lane.

He's done a good job at accumulating trophies in his prolific young career. Winning the Tour of Flanders and Paris-Roubaix classics back-to-back in April 2005 earned him free drinks in any Belgian pub for the rest of his life. He had already earned the fans' respect by taking two stages of the Tour de France on his debut in 2004. He gained further accolades for bagging two stages of Paris-Nice and the Tour of Belgium on his way to the 2005 Tour.

Boonen stayed out of the pubs after his incredible spring run and showed up at the Tour intent on coming out of the blocks with a vengeance. When the wins come easy, there's no reason to slow down.

"My goal is to win stages, then we'll worry about the green jersey," Boonen said a day before the Tour started. "There's no need worrying about the green jersey if you can't win stages."

The world was seeing a newly confident, more experienced Boonen. Until this Tour, he had been the prodigy, the young prince in waiting, an unproven rider who could some-day take the place of the former classics king Johan Museeuw.

It all began with Boonen's breakthrough ride at Paris-Roubaix in 2002, where the 21-year-old finished third after his U.S. Postal Service team leader, a fatigued George

Hincapie, faltered and fell into a ditch while they were chasing the winning breakaway rider, Museeuw. Since then, Boonen has steadily grown into one of the sport's strongest, and smartest, riders.

The pressure was huge when he moved from Postal to a Belgian team, but Boonen handled it with aplomb beyond his years. The strong support of his Quick Step team only bolstered his confidence.

"I told him, 'Don't panic, don't get crazy by the press, do what you have to do in the winter, and someday you will win,'" said Quick Step manager Patrick Lefévère. "He has the motor, the look, everything. He has the future in front of him; some guys have the future behind them already."

Boonen's gain was the Postal team's—and its successor, the Discovery Channel's—loss. Boonen made his professional debut with U.S. Postal in 2002 and quickly earned the team's first Paris-Roubaix podium at age 21.

"I knew from the beginning that he has big potential," said Discovery *directeur sportif* Dirk Demol, a former Roubaix winner and fellow Belgian. "It's a pity that we lost him, because I know on our team he was happy, and it's a shame that he went away."

Boonen arrived at the start of the 2005 Tour all smiles. Little did the world know there was pain lurking behind his toothy grin.

CLASSICS OR SPRINTS?

Every time that Boonen wins a field sprint, he's asked whether he's a better classics rider or sprinter. "I've already been asked that question about a hundred times," Boonen said. "I think I can be both. In the classics I was super. I'm not going great now, but I'm still good enough to compete here with the other best sprinters in the world."

For the Tour, Boonen undoubtedly had the look and the team to suit a sprinter. While Michael Rogers was the team's leader for the overall, Boonen was the man the team was built around. Lefévère left behind such climbers as Juan Miguel Mercado, a winner of a Tour stage in 2004.

Italian veteran Stefano Zanini, Boonen's favorite catapult from the previous two seasons, was back on the roster along with new addition Guido Trenti, the Italian-born rider who rides as a phantom American thanks to his mother's Boston roots.

"It's always better to have two than one," Boonen said, referring to his favorite lead-out tandem. "It's very important to have a good lead-out man. I stay back in around 15th place with Guido. In the closing stages, Stefano [takes] me to the front, and then Guido [takes] over in the last kilometer."

Quick Step is not quite as power-packed as the Fassa Bortolo squad of Italian sprinter Alessandro Petacchi, but Petacchi didn't start this Tour and so there was no dominating lead-out train to drive home the sprints every day. Boonen's one-two punch would work just fine.

Big Tom's first chance to win came in the 181.5km stage 2 from Challans to Les Essarts. The stage unfolded predictably: an early break was brought back with 5km to go where there ensued a fast lead-in to the finish. Liquigas-Bianchi tried to steal Boonen's thunder, but he sprang clear to grab the victory ahead of Thor Hushovd and defending green jersey champion Robbie McEwen. Boonen's arms shot straight up in his trademark double victory salute.

On the Saturday of the opening time trial, Boonen woke up with intense pain in one of his molars. An emergency visit from a dentist and some prescribed antibiotics helped get him through the pain.

When the wins come like clockwork, anything else is a disappointment. "It was very important to have won today, of course," he said. "If not, everyone would have asked me why I hadn't."

Boonen hit replay the very next day. Perhaps the setting foretold a Boonen victory as stage 3 finished along the barreling straightaway of the Avenue de Grammont, the finishing stretch of the sprinter's classic, Paris-Tours. And in holding off Austrian Peter Wrolich and the Aussie tag-team of Stuart O'Grady and McEwen for the win, Boonen's green jersey hopes took a boost while McEwen's were tanked after he was relegated to last place in the peloton for dangerous sprinting.

"Last year, I had to wait until the Champs-Élysées to win my second stage," Boonen beamed. "Now I've done as well after only three days. It's really good for the green jersey."

That toothy grin almost spelled his doom, however.

On the Saturday of the opening time trial, Boonen woke up with intense pain in one of his molars. An emergency visit from a dentist and some prescribed antibiotics helped get him through the pain.

"It was very bad," he said. "It wouldn't have been possible to ride as I had such a headache, but we found a dentist and he sorted it out. I just hope I don't have any further complications."

A toothache wasn't going to wipe away the smile in Boonen's very rosy world. He reportedly signed a contract with Quick Step through 2008, giving him the security to chase down his dreams. And after his Paris-Roubaix press conference, Boonen boldly named two objectives for the remainder of the 2005 season: the green sprinter's jersey at the Tour de France and a victory at the world road championship. It seemed that he was already on the way to achieving the first of those goals.

CHAPTER 6 | STAGE 4
Fast Duels Fate:
CSC Versus Discovery

Bjarne Riis and Lance Armstrong know a thing or two about team time trialing. Both men have been on winning team time trial (TTT) squads at the Tour de France. Riis won as a *domestique* with French team Super U in 1989, and then six years later as a leader with Italian team Gewiss–Ballan. That 1995 TTT victory, on a rolling 67.2km course between the Normandy towns of Mayenne and Alençon, saw Riis's men set a record Tour speed of 54.93kph that still stood ten years later.

In his very first tour, Armstrong finished third with Motorola in the 1993 TTT. He didn't have a winning experience until U.S. Postal Service aced the Joinville to St. Dizier stage in 2003, whereupon he repeated the experience a year later with his Postal squad at Arras.

Meanwhile, Riis managed teams that often came close to winning the Tour TTT. In 2002, his CSC squad was leading at every checkpoint until a key rider flatted 20km from the finish in Château-Thierry. Some riders waited, others didn't, and the resulting confusion caused them to eventually place third. Two years later, in the rainy Cambrai-Arras TTT, CSC suffered two flats and a three-man crash, and still managed to finish fifth. So Riis knew that his squad had the ability to come out on top, and he fully believed that the stage 4 team time trial at this 2005 Tour would be his team's crowning moment. He had his best crew ever, and he drilled them at pre-season training camps in January and February to perfect their technique in this unique, collective discipline.

The squad's time trialing strength was confirmed in stage 1 when Zabriskie (1st), Voigt (8th), and Julich (11th) gave CSC the team win over Discovery Channel's Armstrong

(2nd), Hincapie (4th), and José Luis Rubiera (16th) by four seconds. That small time difference translated into CSC getting the favored final starting position in the TTT, five minutes behind Discovery, where they would have the advantage of knowing the time splits of their competitors.

Bjarne Riis was convinced that his CSC team was going to win the stage. "I will be upset if we lose," Riis said on the eve of what is always one of the most important tests at the Tour. With a win in the TTT, CSC would not only retain Zabriskie's yellow jersey but also help Basso regain some of the 84 seconds he conceded to Armstrong in the individual time trial.

Riis was right to be confident. In Julich, Voigt, Nicki Sörensen, Giovanni Lombardi, and Kurt-Asle Arvesen, the team had discipline, experience, and strength. The speed of newcomers Luke Roberts (Olympic team pursuit gold medalist) and Zabriskie was undeniable, while team leaders Basso and Carlos Sastre have always done well in this group effort.

Although Armstrong's team had won the two previous years, there were some questions about its new riders Yaroslav Popovych and Paolo Savoldelli, who didn't have the TTT knowledge of the injured Viatcheslav Ekimov and the departed Floyd Landis. Ekimov in particular brought the keen sense of discipline and rhythm that are so important in this event. Armstrong agreed that the team missed Ekimov. "He's the best guy on the team in this event," said the Texan. "Not only is he the strongest but he's the steadiest. He's a picture of team time trial perfection and he loves this event."

On the other hand, Armstrong would again be the chief motivator, and team stalwart Hincapie, who had shared in all six of his boss's overall wins, was ready to take on Ekimov's "reliability" role. Furthermore, Hincapie was on the best form of his life as he revealed later when he talked about his confidence for the upcoming test. "I wanted to ride my 56 [chainring]," he said, referring to a monstrously high gear that only the strongest riders can push. To his regret, Hincapie added, "They wanted us all to ride the same gears, so we rode 55s."

FAST, FAST, FAST

With a strong tailwind from the west, teams were flying through the flats that made up two-thirds of the 67.5km course at a pace of one kilometer per minute. The final section contained four rollers and one significant climb, however, which caught out many of the

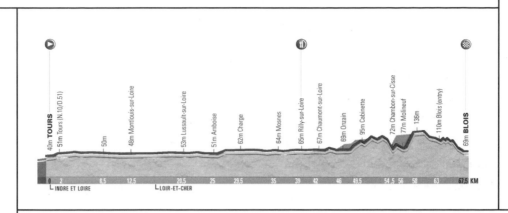

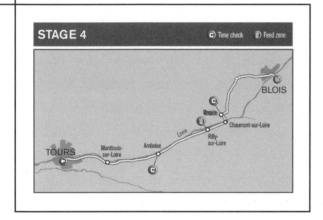

formations. And as Armstrong pointed out, there weren't going to be big time gains on the flat section: "You can't do 45 kilometers in one direction with such a tailwind with such a straight road and such perfect pavement, and expect to be 30, 40 seconds ahead of . . . your chief rival. We knew the race would come down to the last 20 kilometers where you turn left, have some crosswind, and have some rolling hills, so we tried to focus on that and not lose too much time in the beginning."

Armstrong was right. After the opening 25km out of Tours along a gradually curving levee on the left bank of the Loire, Riis's CSC team led by 15 seconds over Discovery and T-Mobile. Then, after turning left on a high modern bridge crossing the wide river at Chaumont-sur-Loire and reaching the 46km point, where the flat roads ended, T-Mobile came through in 47:15. A quarter hour later Discovery's split was 47:14. Armstrong's men saw they were leading by a second, but they still had the disadvantage of racing in front of CSC. "You know that you have to wait five more minutes when you go through and see the clock," said Armstrong. "[It's] stressful to say the least." And when the results at that intermediate check came through, Armstrong's men learned they were still six seconds slower than CSC. It was going to be close.

The surprise so far was the performance of Liberty Seguros, the team of Spanish climber Roberto Heras and German all-rounder Jörg Jaksche. They went through the

25km check in second place, only six seconds down on CSC, and they were still in fourth place, 20 seconds down, on entering the hills.

While Liberty was the surprise, Phonak was the disappointment. In 2004, the Swiss squad came in second to Postal at the Tour's team time trial, despite suffering a half-dozen flat tires and ending with the minimum five riders (a team's finish time is taken when its fifth rider crosses the line). A year later, Phonak would again finish with only five men, but this time the riders left behind didn't have flats; they could not hold the pace on the hills.

Phonak's new team leaders, Landis and Colombian Santiago Botero, rode strongly throughout, as did the team's only two Spanish riders Oscar Pereiro and José Enrique Gutierrez, but Phonak missed the other three Spaniards it had in 2004, particularly Santos Gonzalez. Despite all that, Phonak managed to come in fifth on the day, albeit 1:30 down on the eventual winners.

As Armstrong predicted, the final 20km were proving decisive. T-Mobile lost three riders on this section, while CSC's Giovanni Lombardi fell back. Only the Discovery nine remained intact. Besides having the advantage of starting last, CSC had cleverly placed an observer in one of the cars following the Discovery team to relay the exact time the American team passed certain landmarks. This helped Riis's men pace their effort even better, and according to their unofficial time splits they maintained their six-second lead entering the final, mostly downhill 5km.

LIGHTNING BOLT

By the time Basso's team heard the encouraging news, Discovery had crossed the Blois finish line in 1:10:39, which bounced Ullrich's T-Mobile team from the top spot by 35 seconds. CSC was still ahead of Discovery's pace inside the final 2km when its eight remaining riders sped through a series of tight downhill curves past a sixteenth-century chateau. Then, 200 meters after the road flattened out, and halfway along the Rue Porte-Côté (a street in Blois named after an ancient gateway that pierces the city ramparts), race leader Zabriskie's front wheel suddenly turned, dumping him on his left side at perhaps 65kph. He narrowly missed colliding with the metal barriers, and a gendarme standing just inside them was forced to jump out of the way when Zabriskie's red bike went skidding by. The three riders following the yellow jersey—Roberts, Basso, and Julich—acrobatically managed to avoid their fallen colleague and his mangled, careening bicycle. "The others waited to see what would happen," Riis later said, "and I yelled at them to keep going to the finish as fast as they can, not to wait."

The few seconds of hesitation before the other three caught up almost certainly cost CSC the stage. By the time they dashed across the line 1.5km later, all nine Discovery Channel riders had piled into their team bus to watch CSC completing its effort on a small TV. Seeing that victory was theirs by two seconds, the bus exploded in celebration. The Postal/Discovery squad had triumphed in the Tour TTT for its third successive year.

Zabriskie would have been credited with the same time as his colleagues (and kept the overall lead) had his crash happened in the final kilometer. As it was, he rolled across the line 1:28 behind the others, his dreams as bloodied and torn as his yellow jersey. The polite French fans were shocked to see that the maillot jaune had crashed and, as he passed, they cheered, "Bravo!" Zabriskie disappeared into the team camper without speaking to journalists. X-rays later revealed no broken bones, but to some degree the tumble had broken his spirit.

"The crash is unexplainable to me. A freak accident," Zabriskie said the next morning. "One second we're going, and I'm about to get out [of the saddle], and the next I'm sliding along the road."

Maybe it was fate, as posited by teammate Julich, who was racing two places behind Zabriskie. Perhaps a shot fired through that pierced rampart? "I saw a lightning bolt come down and strike one guy that definitely didn't deserve it," Julich said. "For me the only explanation was he lost his chain somehow when we started to accelerate. It was [as if it] just jumped off the big chainring. I've never seen anything like that. It was like someone had a voodoo doll, just pulled it out, and struck him down with it. It really ripped our guts out."

Commenting on the team's morale after having victory inexplicably turned to defeat, Julich added, "We lost [the stage] by two seconds, and we definitely lost more than two seconds in that [incident]. We were a few seconds away from drinking champagne and smoking cigars. Instead, it was like a funeral."

"Immediately after the race, it *was* a big down," Zabriskie agreed. "But it came back up again quickly. We had a team meeting on the bus; everyone supported me 100 percent. We'll stick together."

For Zabriskie, the hugs and backslaps he got for losing the jersey were almost as important as the plaudits and headlines he earned for winning it. "No one is blaming

Dave for what happened," said CSC team boss Riis. "The team will rally around him and help him."

While CSC could only make the best of a bad situation, Discovery was jubilant. Hincapie, who was now lying second overall behind teammate Armstrong, said, "I did my best team time trial ever. We were really psyched to win by such a close margin. We're both superstrong teams. It was exciting."

It was certainly exciting for Armstrong to win the final team time trial of his career, especially since this is his favorite event, but he still showed his sympathy for longtime teammate Zabriskie. "It's unfortunate what happened to Dave," Armstrong said. "The team time trial is so hard at the end that everybody is on the limit, everybody is a little bit cross-eyed, and then you come into the city and there are a lot of turns and you get the whipping wind. It's easy to make a mistake like that. I can certainly see how it happened but clearly it's bad luck for him. They were flying. They were riding strong. It took everything we had to try and catch up to them."

Just how far modern cycling technology and training have come was clear from the results of this rather extraordinary team time trial. Not only did Armstrong's winning Discovery Channel squad shatter the Tour TTT speed record with 57.324kph, but 14 of the other 20 teams also went faster than the 54.930kph set ten years ago by Italy's Gewiss–Ballan squad. And but for a cruel twist of fate, that Gewiss–Ballan team leader, Riis, would still have had a piece of the record.

STAGE 4: TOURS-BLOIS TTT

1. Discovery Channel (USA), 67.5km in 1:10:39 (57.324 kph); **2.** CSC (Dk), 1:10:41; **3.** T-Mobile (G), 1:11:14; **4.** Liberty Seguros (Sp), 1:11:32; **5.** Phonak (Swi), 1:12:10.

GENERAL CLASSIFICATION

1. Lance Armstrong (USA), Discovery Channel

2. George Hincapie (USA), Discovery Channel, 00:55

3. Jens Voigt (G), CSC, 01:04

4. Bobby Julich (USA), CSC, 01:07

5. José Luis Rubiera (Sp), Discovery Channel, 01:14

CHAPTER 7
Landis Welcomes a
New Role

A handful of journalists was gathered by the door of the Phonak team's distinctive green and white bus in La Châtaigneraie before the start of the Tour's third stage. The man they were anxious to see was Floyd Landis, the hardworking ex-mountain biker whose remarkable journey from his rural roots in eastern Pennsylvania to become a leader of one of the world's strongest professional cycling teams is one of the best stories in the peloton. But that's not what the journalists were curious to learn about. The story everyone wanted to hear about was his acrimonious split with Tour champion Lance Armstrong.

It was no secret in Tour de France circles that Landis and Armstrong had had a falling out after Landis decided to leave U.S. Postal Service (soon to become Discovery Channel) and join Phonak as one of its team leaders. For Armstrong, riders who dared to take their own chances outside the team were regarded as making the ultimate act of disloyalty.

The prospect of the two Americans' quiet rivalry spilling out into the Tour's media-heavy world had tongues wagging, but Landis told the rabble at La Châtaigneraie that he was only here to race. "I'm not motivated by animosity," Landis said. "It's a bicycle race and a competition and I'm motivated by the excitement and the atmosphere, not in any way by anger."

Landis has had one of the most unlikely roads to the elite world of cycling. Raised in the pastoral countryside near Lancaster, Pennsylvania, by Mennonite parents, Landis was never afraid to go his own way. And leaving for the Swiss team Phonak after three seasons at Armstrong's side was just the latest step in his highly unconventional road to the Tour.

At 29, Landis decided he'd reached a point in his career when he was ready to pursue his own path. "The most critical reason for my decision to leave Postal was for my own opportunities," Landis confirmed. "If I was here [at the Tour] for Discovery, I would be working for Lance and that would be it. So I decided it was now or never."

Problems between Armstrong and Landis may have come as a surprise to close observers of the previous few Tours de France. After all, Landis was Armstrong's chosen one, the new American sidekick in the Texan's historic stampede through the Tour's record books. In three years under Armstrong's watchful eye at Postal, Landis grew, matured, and blossomed into a topflight professional. He was a faithful stalwart at the Tour de France, helping the boss capture Tour wins 4 and 5, and the record number 6.

"If I was here [at the Tour] for Discovery, I would be working for Lance and that would be it. So I decided it was now or never."

Landis had become the new Kevin Livingston or Tyler Hamilton—the men who had been Armstrong's strongest support riders in the mountain stages of his first few Tour wins. But as it had with Livingston and Hamilton, the relationship between the boss and the apprentice soured as Landis insisted on a larger role on the team following his breakthrough performance at the 2004 Tour.

That fall, Landis became frustrated as he watched the team sign such future leaders as Yaroslav Popovych and Paolo Savoldelli while his own contract remained unsigned. So when Phonak came with a lucrative two-year offer, Landis grabbed it without looking back. "It was time for a change . . . we'll leave it at that," Landis said.

ACRIMONY

The road from the finish line hugs at the 2004 Tour finish in Le Grand Bornand—where Armstrong encouraged Landis to attack "like you stole something, Floyd" in a bid for stage victory—to the rancor in the spring of 2005 revealed the character of both men. Much was made about the obvious tensions between the two men in April's Tour de Georgia. Landis squared off against his old boss, and won the Mount Alto time trial 1:46 ahead of the sputtering Armstrong.

Two days later, in the decisive climbing stage up Brasstown Bald mountain, Discovery Channel sent Tom Danielson on the attack with Levi Leipheimer (Gerolsteiner) in tow.

Armstrong stayed glued on Landis's wheel, an obvious racing tactic when a teammate is up the road, but Big Tex couldn't help but turn the screws.

Coming into the finish, after Danielson had won the stage and taken the overall lead from Landis, Armstrong bolted ahead across the line, pointed back to the withering Landis and then up at the finish-line clock, giving a final one-arm flourish that could only be interpreted as "up yours." The histrionics caused a stir among the American fans, but Armstrong demurred, saying he was sprinting ahead to take the finish-line time bonus (there wasn't one). Landis fumed at the humiliation.

More tension bubbled beneath the surface at the Dauphiné Libéré race in June, but by the time the Tour rolled around, the pair seemed ready to bury the knives. "We've had our conversations," Landis said. "I think it's unfortunate because I spent three years of my career there. Every last second of every race I was in with him, I was not working for myself ever. And he still feels like I owe him something."

Landis said he respects Armstrong; he just wishes his former boss would return the love. "In the end, I would like him for a friend," Landis said. "I wish he had the same respect for me, but so be it."

Respect was his in spades at Phonak, where Landis was designated as one of the bosses for the team's Tour de France attack. Colombian Santiago Botero and Spanish attacker Oscar Pereiro would also ride with eyes on a top-five finish. In fact, the team was quietly hopeful for a podium spot despite coming off plenty of convulsions in the off-season.

The problems began when former team leader Hamilton tested positive for banned blood doping in September 2004 and was handed a two-year racing ban—something that Hamilton strongly denied and was appealing with the Court of Arbitration for Sport (CAS). Right after that, Spanish teammate Santiago Perez, after finishing second at the 2004 Vuelta a España, failed the same test and was also banned for two years.

The doping allegations caused Phonak to lose its place on cycling's new UCI ProTour roster, and prompted team owner Andy Rihs to fire the management staff and bring in former Tour de France official John Lelangue to right the ship. Phonak's own challenge to CAS earned the squad a ticket back into the ProTour and subsequently to the Tour de France. By the team's January training camp in Majorca, the path was clear: Lelangue gave one speech about the team's troubles and never mentioned them again. Everything was focused on the 2005 Tour.

DISCIPLINE AND DEDICATION

For Landis, the team's upheaval and reinstatement meant that he would become a team leader for the first time in his career. In his first season outside of the Postal/Discovery program, Landis hooked up with Colorado-based sports physiologist Dr. Allen Lim. The pair spent all of May and June together in Europe, as Landis rode key Tour climbs and raced the Dauphiné Libéré while Lim analyzed his daily power data.

"Every day has been hands-on," said Lim, who added that he learned more from Landis than the other way around. "I've learned just how much will and discipline and dedication it takes to execute. It's one thing to talk about an ideal plan and how much you have to train, but to see someone actually commit and do that, it teaches you a lot about what individuals are capable of doing and capable of committing to."

Going into the Tour, Landis said, "I'd like to think I belong among the favorites, but it honestly won't take long to figure out." He proved he'd done his homework with a strong performance in the opening time trial, finishing sixth, 1:02 behind winner Dave Zabriskie. Phonak was hoping for greater success in the team time trial, but it finished a somewhat disappointing fifth, 1:31 behind Armstrong's Discovery Channel team. However, under the Tour's new team time trial scoring system, devised to promote closer competition, Landis was penalized only 50 seconds on overall time.

Intense as ever on the bike, Landis was looking like a new man since leaving the pressure-cooker at Discovery Channel. No longer at the beck and call of Armstrong, Landis felt free to race for himself and simply be himself. "It couldn't be better," he said. "I'm the happiest guy around."

Landis pointed out that he was enjoying himself more at this Tour than he had while riding for the race winner for three years at U.S. Postal. "Nobody wants to believe me when I tell them this, but there's more pressure racing for Lance than being the team leader for yourself," Landis said. "Mentally it's easier, because we don't feel the stress of everybody expecting us to win the race. It's easier because I'm not around Lance and there's not nearly the amount of pressure and stress. Everybody expects Lance to win, and he expects to win, and if you're not as good as you can be then it's not acceptable. The team is entirely focused on Lance's winning the Tour. That's what he deserves, that's how it should be, but anybody with any goals for themselves needs to go."

Landis was hoping to gain from his experience as a team leader and return as a challenger in 2006. But he wasn't expecting to fill anyone's perceived void as the next big American hope for Tour victory.

"I don't pretend to be in any way like Lance," Landis said. "I don't want to be the next Lance Armstrong. I don't want to be the next anybody. In no way do I want what Lance has in life, other than to be the best bicycle racer I can be. The pressure, the fame . . . all of it seems excessive, I would say. In the next few years, I'll continue to race and spend as much time as I can becoming the best bicycle racer I can without risking my family or anything else that makes me happy in life."

CHAPTER 8 | STAGES 5–7
Final Turns

The Tour was still abuzz with Dave Zabriskie's fate and the dramatically close finish of the team time trial when the race entourage gathered the next morning on the park-like grounds of the extravagently handsome chateau at Chambord. And a little more drama was awaiting before stage 5 got under way. On descending from the big silver Discovery Channel team bus, George Hincapie revealed that "Lance isn't going to wear the jersey today."

Armstrong confirmed that news when he left his newly earned yellow jersey in the team car and rode up to the start in his regular Discovery uniform. "I watched television [last night] and I had a sick feeling," Armstrong said. "CSC were very close and without this crash they would have had a good chance of winning the stage. It would have been a matter of tenths or hundredths of seconds. And there is a tradition in the Tour not to wear a yellow jersey when you take it from a mishap. The last I can remember is when Greg LeMond didn't wear it when Rolf Sørensen crashed [in 1991]."

That analogy wasn't exact because when Sørensen, a Dane, crashed and broke his collarbone in stage 4 of the 1991 Tour, he finished the stage and kept the yellow jersey. So LeMond wasn't bound to wear yellow the next stage, even though Sørensen didn't start. But Armstrong was correct about one of the unspoken traditions of the Tour. In 1973, for example, race leader Luis Ocaña crashed out of the race on the first stage in the Pyrénées and Eddy Merckx refused to wear the yellow jersey the following day, even though he had assumed the leadership.

Unfortunately, Armstrong's gesture to recognize the awful luck of countryman Zabriskie wasn't appreciated by Tour officials. Eventually, a deal was struck whereby the race leader wore his Discovery colors on the 5km neutralized section; the peloton then halted

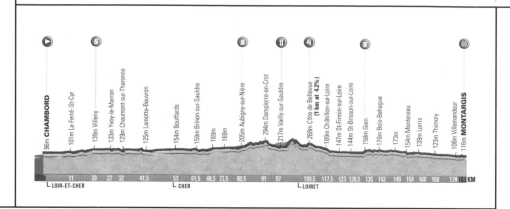

long enough to allow Armstrong to don the jersey. "I just wanted to make a statement," he said. "I understand that the organizers have obligations, and that the fans wait for hours to see the yellow jersey go by. We don't always think of those things."

What most of the fans saw between rain showers during the 183km stage to Montargis

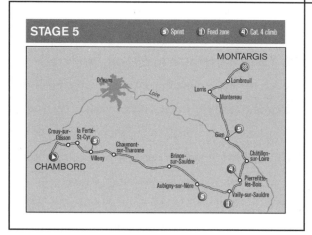

on rolling terrain across the central Loire Valley was a blur. The yellow jersey followed his teammates, who were riding a hellaciously fast tempo (52km, or a bit over 32 miles, in the first hour), to keep a four-man break in check. The break was started by Spanish rider Juan Antonio Flecha of Fassa Bortolo, who gained five minutes on the pack before being joined (eventually) by LaszloBodrogi (who again was the virtual race leader for a while), Italian Salvatore Commesso of Lampre-Caffita and Finland's Kjell Carlström of Liquigas-Bianchi. They were 3:30 clear at the feed zone when a dropped musette bag tangled in the wheel of CSC's Basso, who fell, but escaped with minor injuries.

After holding a 1:40 lead along a tough crosswind section, the four-man break was inevitably swallowed up by the sprinters' teams midway through the wind-assisted final 20km. A mass sprint was again in the cards, although a tricky run-in to Montargis (which produced a pileup with 5km to go) and a 90-degree turn into the narrow finishing straight complicated matters. When a stage of Paris-Nice finished here in 2004, Quick Step rider

Pedro Horillo of Spain attacked out of the tight turn. He managed to hang tough on the uphill rise to the line for a narrow stage win.

Horillo's leader, Boonen, didn't contest that sprint because he had flatted in the final kilometers. But the Belgian obviously knew (and liked) the finish geography, and for this fifth stage of the Tour his team helped him make the final corner just behind the Française des Jeux trio of McGee, Cooke, and Eisel. That narrow turn, from the Avenue Gaillardin into the Rue Jean Jaurès, just past a Chinese restaurant and a kebab shop, acted like a filter—especially when Hushovd (who was involved in the Paris-Nice sprint) dove too fast into the corner, pulled his foot from the pedal, and gapped several riders. Entering the final 500 meters, there were fewer than ten riders with a chance of winning.

> **That narrow turn, from the Avenue Gaillardin into the Rue Jean Jaurès, just past a Chinese restaurant and a kebab shop, acted like a filter— especially when Hushovd (who was involved in the Paris-Nice sprint) dove too fast into the corner, pulled his foot from the pedal, and gapped several riders.**

Cooke and Eisel began the uphill sprint on the right, but they were soon passed by a recovered Hushovd on the left. Boonen, in the green jersey, then dashed though the middle expecting to win in the same manner he took stage 2 in Les Essarts. But he hadn't reckoned on the fighting spirit of McEwen who was getting his first chance for redemption since his disqualification from the sprint at Tours.

Boonen thought he was again executing his sprint perfectly, but this time McEwen zeroed in on the big Belgian's wheel and waited until the last 150 meters before unleashing his fast-twitch muscles with an unbeatable acceleration. The Aussie was going away as he crossed the line, and proudly leaned back in the saddle pointing both forefingers at his chest not once but four times, as if to say "I am the fastest," a message he was sending not only to Boonen but also to the judges whom, he claimed, unfairly declassed him at Tours after his famous "head butting" tussle with O'Grady.

"Our guys really deserve this stage win to pay them back for all their work," said McEwen, who insisted on hugging all his teammates one by one as a race official impatiently waited to escort him to the podium, the same podium where Armstrong would shortly receive a new yellow jersey for his second day in the Tour's overall lead.

MIXED FORTUNES

While the last turn in Montargis opened the door to an exciting sprint finish, the final corner on the next day's stage into Nancy would see a dramatically different outcome, particularly for Française des Jeux's veteran rider Christophe Mengin, T-Mobile's yellow-jersey hope Alexander Vinokourov, and Fassa Bortolo's Italian journeyman pro Lorenzo Bernucci.

Mengin, 36, had won only six races in a career spanning 12 years, with the highlight still being his stage win at the 1987 Tour de France, where he took the semi-mountainous stage 16 at Fribourg, Switzerland, in a twenty-two-man sprint. With retirement in sight, the thoughtful Mengin was hoping that he still had a chance for victory in what was probably his final Tour.

He targeted this 199km sixth stage, the most challenging yet, because he knew that the last of four Cat. 4 climbs was the steepest and came just 13km from the finish. The Frenchman, who lives in the area, also intimately knew the run-in to Nancy, having trained on the roads countless times.

The stage started in sunshine in the cycling-savvy city of Troyes, but the riders were soon pounding through conditions that were very uncharacteristic of July: temperatures in the 50s, torrential rain showers, and for the fourth day a stiff wind blowing from the west. Despite a very fast start (51.5km in the opening hour) over the open, rolling hills of the Champagne region, Mengin instigated the day's main breakaway at 30km. He was soon joined by Italian Mauro Gerosa of Liquigas-Bianchi, Dutchman Karsten Kroon of Rabobank, Estonian Jaan Kirsipuu of Crédit Agricole, and Frenchman Stéphane Augé of Cofidis.

These five were still together almost three hours later, leading by 1:05, when they began the 3km Côte de Maron climb with 16km to go. When Mengin put on the pressure halfway up the winding hill, the other four soon fell back to be absorbed by a peloton being strung out by a strong surge from Basso's CSC team. In heavy rain, Mengin used the long, winding descent into Nancy to his advantage, racing through the slick turns faster than the pack and eking out an initial 40-second lead, which dwindled to 25 seconds at 10km, and 12 seconds at 5km to go. "I didn't have great legs today," Mengin admitted later, "but I had the morale to try something. You have to give 100 percent when you've got the chance."

His lead was still 150 meters when the peloton's pace momentarily eased with 2km remaining. This lull was a cue for the ever-aggressive Vinokourov to make a surprise attack.

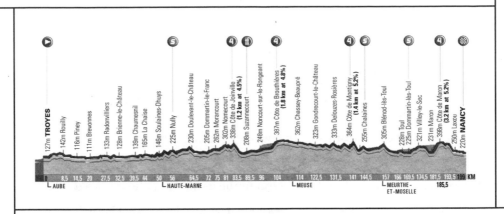

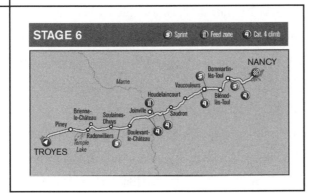

As the Kazakh rounded the second-to-last turn, Bernucci took up the chase. The Italian, who was hired by Fassa Bortolo to lead out star sprinter Petacchi after three winless seasons at Landbouwkrediet–Colnago, was closing in on Vinokourov, who in turn was closing in on Mengin, and all three were headed into the final right-angle corner just inside the final kilometer.

Mengin knew that the turn from the Rue d'Auxonne into the Rue de Metz could be taken at speed. But when he was at its apex and looking ahead toward the finish line, his tires suddenly lost traction on what turned out to be spilled diesel fuel. Mengin's bike skidded out and he smashed into the barriers, his dreams suddenly ended.

Vinokourov just missed hitting the fallen Frenchman, but as he juggled his bike to stay upright he momentarily unclipped from his right pedal, giving Bernucci the chance to rush past. If the Italian *gregàrio* had turned his head, he would have seen rider after rider sliding on their backs on the slick pavement, blocking the road.

Much was made of Fassa Bortolo's Cancellara, one of the blocked riders, screaming to Bernucci into his team radio transmitter to "go full gas!" But the Italian's earpiece wasn't working, and as it turned out he didn't need the encouragement. He knew instinctively to keep riding flat out until he crossed the line. The elated Bernucci kept his small advantage to take his first career win, while, with his second-place time bonus, Vinokourov gained 19 seconds to slot into third place overall, 1:02 behind Armstrong. The Texan downplayed

Vinokourov's performance, but in his calculating mind the race leader must have been concerned about an opponent prepared to take big risks for even the most modest of gains.

And so another stage was over, one neatly summed up by first-timer Chris Horner as he pedaled slowly in the rain toward his team bus in the heart of ancient Nancy. "Now *that* was a stage," said the Californian. "That was a great stage; that was really fun. That one took a little something out of everybody, I'm sure."

It certainly took something out of the unfortunate Mengin, who managed to get back on his bike and cross the line two minutes behind Bernucci before talking to French TV. "I feel more like a boxer after a fight than a cyclist," he said. "I've got a bit of a black eye where I think a brake lever or gear shifter hit it. And I've got a sore hip on my left side." He also discovered later that he had fractured a bone in his face; he would have to pull out of the Tour the following evening.

The stage also took its toll on Zabriskie, who arrived seven minutes down in an eight-man group. Still recovering from his unfortunate crash in the team time trial, Zabriskie was putting on a brave face when he said, "I was just hanging on until I saw the 25 kilometers to go banner. I'm still very stiff, but hope to come back and help Ivan [Basso] later in the race."

By the time Zabriskie crossed the line, Bernucci was being lauded by the press. The stage had sure been fun for the 25-year-old Italian, who gratefully accepted his unexpected success, saying, "This win doesn't change who I am, a humble servant." Perhaps, like Mengin, Bernucci will be back in a decade trying for a repeat.

LAST CHANCE SPRINT

After they tangled in the pileup on the streets of Nancy, Boonen and McEwen rode together to the finish line, chatting in Flemish and probably joking about how they would normally be racing at 70, not 17kph, down the final straightaway. Both knew that it would be another twenty-four hours before they could continue their high-speed sprinting duel, in Karlsruhe, Germany, and that this would be their last chance to win another stage before hitting the mountains.

Points leader Boonen had a rough time getting to Karlsruhe. For the second day, he was involved in a pileup, this one coming only 23km after the pack left the stage 7 start outside a Versailles-style chateau in Lunéville on a cool, showery morning. Describing this latest crash, Boonen said, "I thought my back was broken. Two guys crashed on top of me.

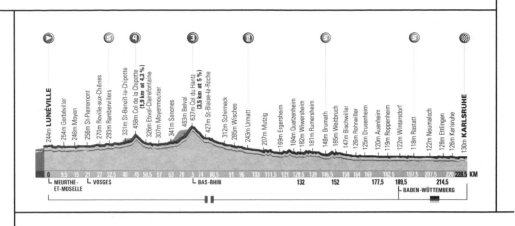

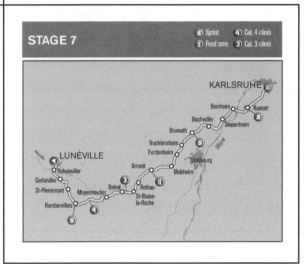

My bike was totally destroyed. I am in a lot of pain in my back and hip."

With ripped shorts and a stiff back, Boonen had a hard 7km chase back to the peloton that was racing through heavy rain at 48kph. He recovered enough to make big efforts to defend his green jersey against Hushovd at two intermediate sprints in the final 100km. But the finish would prove a different story.

McEwen was having a much easier day. He even contributed to the day's longest breakaway. When the young German rider Fabian Wegmann of Gerolsteiner jumped clear to take the KoM prize on the first of two easy climbs in the Vosges foothills, the Col de la Chipotte after 26km, McEwen chased and caught him on the descent. "I said to him, 'Okay, if a group of seven or eight guys comes in the next 10 kilometers, we will go. If they don't, I'm going back and you have a nice day,'" McEwen reported.

After 11km together, no one had joined them. They were one minute ahead of the pack, and, according to McEwen, "in a place I didn't want to be." Then, instead of just sitting up and waiting for the peloton, a playful McEwen revealed, "I actually hid behind a bush until the peloton came past and then I jumped on the back, so a lot of guys didn't know I was back with them."

Everyone knew where Wegmann was. After taking more King of the Mountains points, he secured the overall lead in the climber's competition, and then took a maximum lead of 8:30 in a break that lasted 158km. The last part of his escape took place after the Tour crossed over into Germany, where many of the estimated 700,000 spectators lining the highways and streets leading in to Karlsruhe held up posters of the popular blond Wegmann. "You couldn't seen the road at times," said McEwen, "there were so many people."

McEwen's plans to win were threatened when his two lead-out men, Dutch champion Leon Van Bon and three-time USPRO champ Fred Rodriguez, had crashes coming into Karlsruhe. Rodriguez hit the deck on a slick railroad crossing with 20km to go when "Some guys in front of me slid out and I just ran right into them. I landed on my Achilles, on my ankle. I lost a bit of nerve there . . . so I wasted some energy trying to get back up to the front."

He was back at the head of things within 10km when, McEwen said, "I told my boys, 'Just relax and wait.'" That's not the instruction you would expect an ace sprinter to give his men as they headed at 60kph toward the finish. But knowing the course would turn back into the wind with 4km to go, the Australian champion counseled patience.

For most of the final 3km, on a wide, straight boulevard, the Française des Jeux riders Carlos Da Cruz and McGee set the pace for their sprinters Cooke and Eisel. Then Crédit Agricole's Hinault and Kirsipuu pulled through for teammate Hushovd, while three Liquigas-Bianchi riders seemed to be preparing the sprint for their Argentine fast man Luciano Pagliarini.

The result was a mass charge to the line that stage winner McEwen called "a difficult, unorganized sprint." But at least McEwen's Davitamon-Lotto team had a plan. Sort of. McEwen was still following his two lead-out riders into the final kilometer when, as described by Rodriguez, Van Bon "hit a spectator [who was leaning out taking a photo] with the side of his head, face, and body, right when we were going up the right side [of the peloton] in the last 800, 900 meters."

Rodriguez then made his strongest pull to take McEwen to the head of the peloton in the last half kilometer. "Rob and I just hugged the right side of the barriers," said the American. "It was one of those sprints where everybody wanted to be at the front. Everybody thought they were a sprinter for the day, more guys than you usually have, so we played it late . . . because you saw the guys were trying to pull the sprint from a long way out. We just rode right through them."

The stiff-backed Boonen didn't have the snap to freelance his way through what McEwen called "just a ball of riders at the front." Instead, Liquigas let loose not Pagliarini but big, beefy Bäckstedt, who seemed headed for the stage win.

With about 150 meters to go, Liberty's young Aussie Allan Davis headed for the Swede's wheel, but his left-to-right switch forced Illes Balears' Isaac Gálvez to fall into Domina Vacanze's Angelo Furlan and later caused the judges to relegate him from the sprint. Miraculously, no one else went down.

"I was still in seventh or eighth and still couldn't see a way though," reported McEwen, who probably hadn't seen that the wide road jogged to the right in the last stretch, opening up a lane on that side. "I took a bit of a gamble in going on the right, and came between Cooke and the barriers."

McEwen probably had the most shelter on that side because once past Cooke (who finished fifth), he had a straight shot to the line against Bäckstedt. "The last 50 meters were hard," admitted McEwen, who threw his bike at the line to take the decision by a wheel, with Eisel pushing home in third, a couple of bike-lengths back.

"It was really satisfying to win again," said McEwen. "People say, 'You're 33 now, and you should start slowing down.' But that's not what I think."

STAGE 5: CHAMBORD-MONTARGIS

1. Robbie McEwen (Aus), Davitamon-Lotto, 183km in 3:46:00 (48.584kph); **2.** Tom Boonen (B), Quick Step–Innergetic; **3.** Thor Hushovd (N), Crédit Agricole; **4.** Stuart O'Grady (Aus), Cofidis; **5.** Angelo Furlan, Domina Vacanze, all s.t.

STAGE 6: TROYES-NANCY

1. Lorenzo Bernucci (I), Fassa Bortolo, 199km in 4:12:52 (47.218kph); **2.** Alexander Vinokourov (Kaz), T-Mobile, s.t.; **3.** Robert Förster (G), Gerolsteiner, at 0:07; **4.** Furlan; **5.** Hushovd, all s.t.

STAGE 7: NANCY-KARLSRUHE

1. McEwen, 228.5km in 5:03:45 (45.136kph); **2.** Magnus Bäckstedt (S), Liquigas-Bianchi; **3.** Bernhard Eisel (A), Française des Jeux; **4.** Gerrit Glomser (A), Lampre-Caffita; **5.** Baden Cooke (Aus), Française des Jeux, all s.t.

GENERAL CLASSIFICATION

1. Lance Armstrong (USA), Discovery Channel

2. George Hincapie (USA), Discovery Channel, 00:55

3. Alexander Vinokourov (Kaz), T-Mobile, 01:02

4. Jens Voigt (G), CSC, 01:04

5. Bobby Julich (USA), CSC, 01:07

CHAPTER 9
Aussie Dynamo:
McEwen Shows No Signs of Slowing Down

"Good afternoon. Thank you for waiting."

It was hardly the formal opening words you would expect from the mouth of a Tour de France stage winner at his post-race press conference. But that's how Robbie McEwen started his Q&A session more than a half hour after he had scorched across the finish line in the German city of Karlsruhe to take his seventh Tour-career stage win. The veteran Aussie with the youthful disposition was late because he had been happily chatting about the stage at the finish line.

If you hadn't seen the sprint finish that day, you could have figured that McEwen had won because of the beaming smile that remained on his boyish face long after he had crossed the line. Right after the finish, from the mêlée of reporters mobbing him down on the street outside the Karlsruhe Expo Center, came a question asking McEwen if he was happy. Not seeing that the questioner was a Spanish reporter who spoke far from perfect English, McEwen said, "What do you think? You'll have to come up with a better question than that."

Some people say that the 33-year-old Australian is cocky, and it's true that his mouth and his actions have sometimes gotten him in trouble. At the 2004 Tour, after he was brought down in a high-speed pileup at the kilometer-to-go sign on the stage finishing in Angers, McEwen stood up, picked his way between other fallen riders, and then let loose a stream of invectives—"It was all your fault! You've done it again!" [the polite version]—at the man he believed caused the crash, Austrian sprinter René Haselbacher. At the time, Haselbacher was lying on the street, screaming in pain, and being attended to by the Tour's medical team.

At this Tour, the day after he felt he was wrongly relegated to last place for "dangerous sprinting" in stage 3's field sprint finish at Tours, the outspoken McEwen said, "It is a pretty harsh decision. I want to make it very clear, I am not trying to blame anyone. I definitely didn't make the first move and it didn't affect the classification of the stage, it didn't affect any other riders. I was more than disappointed, not at the actions of any rider, but more in the decision of the race jury.

"I have watched the video enough times, the pictures enough times. There are other people who definitely know what they are talking about who agree with me. One of them is Sean Kelly. He's not a nobody. He has won the green jersey five times. Eddy Merckx has won the Tour five times and he agrees with me as well. Nobody should have been disqualified."

> **"There are other people who definitely know what they are talking about who agree with me. One of them is Sean Kelly. He's not a nobody. He has won the green jersey five times. Eddy Merckx has won the Tour five times and he agrees with me as well. Nobody should have been disqualified."**

SLOW RISE

McEwen has fast lips and fast legs, but his rise to the top of the world sprinting ranks wasn't as sudden. It was a steady progression that began in 1996, when he turned professional with Rabobank after a successful amateur career with the Australian national team.

He said during the 2002 Tour, when he first raced for Lotto, a Belgian team, "I have a lot more experience now. It has been a buildup. Finally, things are just going right. I haven't had any big problems. I've reached a level this season that I feel is my level, a level where I really belong."

His seesaw battle with Erik Zabel for the green jersey was one of the highlights of that Tour. It typified how McEwen had stepped up to meet the pressure of being one of the best sprinters in the world, and inevitably one of the most targeted.

"It is kind of stressful," he said of the points competition, in which he finished fourth in 1999 ("without going for any intermediate sprints") and second in 2000, when he said he only went for a couple of sprints near the end "because I realized there was more prize money for second place," before winning it in 2002 and 2004.

Cash has always been a big incentive for McEwen, who first started winning prizes in cycling as a BMX rider back in his native Brisbane. That discipline also helped him develop the dynamic sprint and uncanny bike-handling skills that have been the hallmarks of his career as a world-class road sprinter. He's not as big or powerful as stereotypical sprint specialists Tom Boonen, Alessandro Petacchi, or the recently retired Mario Cipollini. McEwen has to rely on his brain, rather than brawn.

Take the annual battle for the Tour's green jersey, the sprinters' most prestigious award. McEwen believes that battling for this honor is as much a game of the mind as of speed. "You have to be concentrating all day and know where the sprints are—if they are downhill, uphill, or flat. Even if it is for 8th or 12th place, you have to sprint."

Putting his brain to work along with his legs helped him take that next giant step forward. While some credit his becoming a father for greater maturity—McEwen's Belgian wife Angelique, an optometrist, gave birth to their son Ewen on the eve of the 2002 Giro—McEwen says fatherhood didn't have much effect on his cycling career.

"People say it makes you settle down and that you feel more responsibility," he said. "You feel more responsibility in life generally; but as far as affecting your riding, I don't think so. It is great having a little boy. But to do well on the bike you have to be concentrating on what you are doing on the bike."

What made the difference between his being just another sprinter and one who earned two green jerseys and a silver medal (the best ever by an Australian) at the 2002 road world's was when he stepped up his weight lifting and the number of training sessions he did in the hills outside Geraardsbergen, where the McEwens live in Flanders. While he once only hit the gym in the off-season, he now fits in two four-week weight-training blocks during the racing season as well.

The first block is normally in April after the early part of McEwen's season, which usually sees him winning stages of the Tour Down Under in Australia. During that block McEwen has a ten-day spell where he stays off his bike altogether. He takes another break after contesting, and usually winning, the initial stages of the Giro d'Italia in May, a race he often abandons in the second week. During this second break, he rides his bike, but not hard. The second block of weight training comes in August as preparation for the road world championships at the end of September.

HEAVY STUFF

Weight training "has made a difference," McEwen said. "In the racing season you get a lot of muscle breakdown, and you have to get that back up. It is especially important for a sprinter. You have to have that explosive power. And there is only one place to get it—the gym. [The weight-training block] has to be three to four weeks. . . . If you start a gym program from nothing it takes three weeks to get any result. When you are already trained in racing, after two weeks you start to get some benefit, then after three weeks you get really strong. I can feel it myself after a couple of weeks. I get stronger and start pushing bigger weights. You need that strength to go day after day."

McEwen said he focuses on leg presses. In a workout, he will push six sets of 26 repetitions with the weights set at 200 kilograms (440 pounds). "I have to be careful with my knees," he said. "It is not excessively heavy. I know I can push 320 kilos (700 pounds), which I have done before, but I do repetitions for strength and endurance."

Little wonder that McEwen is no longer the cheeky, pint-sized sprinter who when he first arrived at the Tour was better known for doing wheelies at the end of mountain stages than fighting for stage victories. Now, McEwen is as fast as he once was daring, and he is far more powerful at the top end. And after taking three stages off Petacchi at the 2005 Giro and beating Boonen at the Tour, he is close to being crowned the king of the sprinters, especially following Cipollini's retirement.

Asked if he commands authority in the peloton, McEwen, who has now beaten all of his rivals in key sprints, gives an unequivocal thumbs-up. "Yeah, I do," he said. "Whereas before I was hoping I could get a gap, now I deserve to start up the front. It is my right to start at the front."

It wasn't so long ago that McEwen found that just getting to the front could be a leg-breaking effort. He still remembers his first two Tours, in 1997 and 1998, when his Rabobank team refused to lead him out and forced him to fight the lead-out trains towing Zabel and Cipollini by himself.

"In my first year on the Tour I was basically doing it on my own," McEwen said. "I was trying to move myself up in the wind, then starting to sprint, and being completely stuffed in the last kilometers. I would be trying to set myself up and would be starting to sprint from eighth position and finishing fourth."

The little Aussie still garnered a handful of fourth and fifth places in 1997, and graduated to seconds and thirds the year after. They were a testimony to his natural speed and courage.

Now, with Davitamon-Lotto, he has experienced lead-out men like Dutchman Leon Van Bon and American Fred Rodriguez. The 2005 Tour was McEwen's first real experience of having Rodriguez as the final teammate setting him up for the sprint. And, after two stages getting used to each other's dynamics, they truly clicked at Montargis and Karlsruhe.

"Working for Robbie is very gratifying," said Rodriguez. "As long as I do my job and keep him safe and we can win, it's always good times. Winning is the most important thing for me, so if it's me or if it's my teammate, it's just as big."

FINDING LOTTO

The first confirmation of McEwen's great potential at the sport's highest level came at the 1999 Tour, when he won the final stage into Paris on the Champs-Élysées. That break-through victory just happened to come a day after he bravely made public his intention to leave the Rabobank team at the end of that season.

Finding a new team to support him was not easy. At Farm Frites, which McEwen joined in 2000, he fell into conflict with *directeur sportif* Patrick Lefévère. Then, in 2001, Lefévère did not select him for the Domo–Farm Frites' Tour team.

McEwen, who reportedly earned a reputation among directors as hard to deal with, returned to Australia at the end of that season without a contract for 2002. That changed when Lotto expressed interest in him, and the two parties eventually worked out an acceptable agreement. At first, it was modest in salary, but rich in performance-based incentive bonuses. And there was another angle to the deal. Lotto guaranteed that McEwen would be given every bit of help to win races. Finally, he would have teammates to lead him out for sprints.

"I have a good team around me that can position me," he said in the first of his four seasons racing with Lotto. "Now I am starting in second or third, and winning. That's been the story." And, like McEwen himself, it's a story that just keeps getting stronger.

CHAPTER 10 | STAGE 8
Into the Hills of the
Black Forest and Vosges

Exactly one week after he pulled on the yellow jersey to open his Tour de France career in mythical style, Dave Zabriskie was in deep trouble. Zabriskie was at the back of the race, and he'd been riding alone for almost 100km. By now, partway up stage 10's final climb, the 17km Col de la Schlucht, he was almost 50 minutes behind the leaders. "Just getting to the top of the climb was the most difficult part," he said the next day. "The crowds helped me a lot. They kept cheering me on even though I was one of the last guys." Zabriskie was so fatigued, he didn't realize he was the *very* last guy. He also didn't know that he was in great danger of being eliminated from the Tour. The lead pack had already crossed the finish line in Gérardmer, and he had to get there within the day's official time cut of 54:43, calculated as 18 percent of the winner's time of 5:03:54. But with "everything still hurting," Zabriskie wouldn't give in to the temptation of quitting.

The Tour's fastest-ever opening week (an average of 47.368kph, or just over 29 miles per hour, for the first 1,081km!) had been unkind to injured riders like Zabriskie. The constant high speeds, nerve-wracking crashes, and frequent rain showers gave him no chance to fully recover from his traumatic stage 4 pavement encounter. That was particularly true on this day's journey, which began in Pforzheim, Germany, with four challenging Cat. 3 climbs in the first 50km.

Each of the climbs was mobbed by tens of thousands of fans packed in tight beneath the pine trees of the Black Forest. On the first of these hills, the 6km, 6 percent climb to the town of Dobel, police estimated the number of spectators at more than 100,000. Presciently, some fans had temporarily changed Dobel's town sign to "L'Alpe d'Obel," in

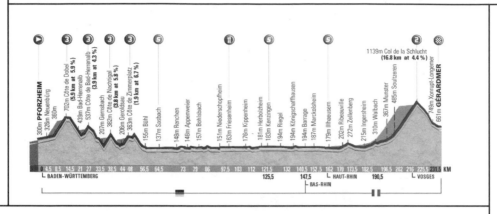

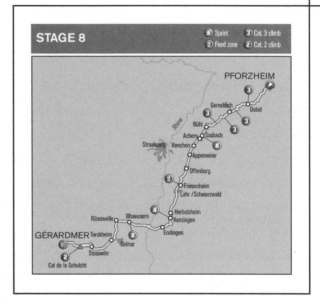

honor of that other crowd-packed, better-known climb in the Alps. To Zabriskie and some of the heavy-legged sprinters, this opening climb probably *did* feel like L'Alpe d'Huez when they fell back from the fast-moving peloton. And with more than five hours still to ride, they knew they were beginning a long battle for survival.

The pace at the front end of the peloton was unbelievably fast for a stage of 231.5km that featured so many climbs. The high pace had been triggered by an attack at kilometer zero by German Jörg Ludewig of Domina Vacanze and Swiss Rubens Bertogliati of Saunier Duval. The two men raced as hard as they could up a deep, tree-covered valley leading to the snaking Dobel climb, where they were quickly passed by a much more threatening move. It came from CSC's Jens Voigt of Germany, Rabobank's Michael Rasmussen of Denmark, Crédit Agricole's Andrey Kashechkin of Kazakhstan, Française des Jeux's Sandy Casar of France, and Discovery Channel's George Hincapie, who started the stage in second place overall, only 55 seconds behind teammate Armstrong.

This could have been the catalyst for a winning break, which would have put Hincapie or Voigt into the yellow jersey, but Ullrich's T-Mobile squad didn't want a potentially dangerous rival like Hincapie to have a free ride to the yellow jersey. The German team soon took up the chase, putting six riders on the front of the peloton. "Johan wanted me to be in the breakaway," Hincapie said, referring to instructions he got from Discovery team director Bruyneel. "I was told to work [in the break] because T-Mobile was pulling. We were going really hard."

For more than 50km, up and down the challenging hills of the Black Forest, T-Mobile put on a brilliant display of teamwork for their home supporters, pulling the peloton single-file at almost 50kph. Despite the efforts of the five leaders, they were pegged to a maximum lead of 1:40 before the gap steadily closed.

Rasmussen, in his first quest for King of the Mountain points, spent the early part of the break on his own to take first place at all four hilltops, and he duly took over the polka-dot jersey at day's end. With his morning's work done, the lean Dane was the first of the five to drop off the break and wait for the peloton. The others sat up after Hincapie took a six-second time bonus at the day's first intermediate sprint at 64.5km in Sasbach, a village boasting a nice range of red and white Rhine Valley wines.

The combination of sharp climbs and rampant speed engendered by the battle between Discovery and T-Mobile put some forty riders (including green jersey Tom Boonen and polka-dot leader Fabian Wegmann) almost four minutes back. They would have a laborious 100km chase to rejoin the peloton, but only after being aided by a short lull in the racing. Some of the stragglers never caught back. Zabriskie, an off-color Iker Flores of Euskaltel, and the sprinters Jaan Kirsipuu, Luciano Pagliarini, and Jean-Patrick Nazon of ag2r would all continue their rearguard struggle in an effort to beat the time limit.

The midstage lull allowed seven riders, led by CSC's Nicki Sörensen, to break clear as the race left Germany and headed back across the Rhine River into France. With Sörensen were two Frenchmen, Cédric Vasseur of Cofidis and Nicolas Jalabert of Phonak, German Ronny Scholz of Gerolsteiner, two-time Italian national champion Salvatore Commesso of Lampre, the Spaniard Juan Antonio Flecha of Fassa Bortolo and, the last to join up, Rabobank's Dutch hope Pieter Weening. They built a 6:30 lead by Illhaeusern, a town of square, half-timbered houses, 70km from the finish.

With the start of the Schlucht climb less than 40km away, the teams hoping for a stage win knew they had to increase their pace. So, through the rolling vineyards of Alsace, the workers of Liquigas-Bianchi (for their leader Stefano Garzelli) and Bouygues

Télécom (for Laurent Brochard) started the ball rolling. Then Spanish riders on the Illes Balears team (plotting a stage win for Alejandro Valverde) took up the chase, and they cut the lead to 2:47 by the time the route turned west into the Vosges, heading up the Col de la Schlucht.

This is where second-year pro Weening, 24, showed great tactical sense in making a bid for stage victory. "I knew that was the right moment to attack, because if I waited for the group to get closer, I was sure we would be caught," he said. His solo attack, with more than 30km separating him from the finish, was not as crazy as it seemed. A few months earlier, Weening and his Rabobank teammate Rasmussen had scouted this stage, along with the following day's trek through the Vosges, so he knew he would be able to get out of sight of the other six very quickly on the snaking but not overly steep climb.

Once the pack began the long, big-ring ascent, the Balears trio of Vladimir Karpets, Francisco Mancebo and Valverde turned on the screws, and quickly shredded the peloton. Surprisingly, most of Armstrong's Discovery teammates were left behind, and that opened the way for T-Mobile to play their long-desired strategy: go on the attack.

> "I've never seen a team just implode like that. I don't even think Lance understood what was going on there."

Halfway up the Cat. 2 climb, two strong accelerations by the ambitious Vinokourov were chased down by Discovery's Paolo Savoldelli. But that was the Italian rider's limit, and when Vinokourov lifted his solid torso out of the saddle and sprinted for a third time, Armstrong himself had to chase him down. The first riders to follow this latest acceleration were Ullrich, Basso, Mancebo, Rasmussen, and Crédit Agricole's Christophe Moreau, while Savoldelli and all the other Discovery team workers fell back. Shockingly, for the first time since climbing the Col d'Aubisque in the 2000 Tour, Armstrong had none of his teammates in a leading group that had grown to thirty-three riders. So when a counterattack came from T-Mobile's third leader, Andreas Klöden, whose form had truly benefited from the first week of racing, Armstrong had to let the energetic German go.

"I've never seen a team just implode like that," CSC's Bobby Julich said of Discovery's apparent troubles. "I don't even think Lance understood what was going on there." Perhaps the implosion was caused by the overconfidence Discovery had shown by not bothering to scout this stage and putting reliance in an unclear policy Armstrong outlined a few days earlier: "The up-and-down days aren't going to be ultimately the hardest days, but they will be tricky so we'll try to stay at the front and wait for the big mountains."

In the last 3km of the Schlucht climb, where the grade steepened from 4 to 6 percent, a smoothly pedaling Klöden chased and caught the energetic Weening right at the crowd-mobbed summit. The pair crossed ten seconds ahead of Rasmussen and thirty-one others, and then made a pact to work as hard as they could to keep the chasers at bay on the long, fast, winding descent.

Française des Jeux's Brad McGee, without teammates, tried to spark a chase, hoping that he could take the resultant sprint just as he had on a similar stage of June's Tour of Switzerland. But no one seemed interested. Instead, most riders turned to the Illes Balears trio, hoping Valverde *really* wanted the stage win. But Mancebo's men didn't want to fully commit, either, knowing that wasting energy on an uncertain stage win might be costly in terms of their overall aspirations.

As a result, the two leaders' gap, which held at seven seconds for most of the descent, expanded to 27 seconds by the finish. Klöden kept riding hard to maximize his overall time gains, hoping that his speed would be too high for Weening to raise a sprint challenge. But the Dutchman had just enough energy to draw level with Klöden at the line with a brave, vigorous effort. "If the sprint had been two meters longer I wouldn't have made it," said the tall, willowy Weening. "My legs were completely spent."

Neither man raised an arm in celebration. Like everyone else they had to await the verdict of the finish-line judge. It eventually came: decision to Weening by 9.6 millimeters, about one-third of an inch! That translates to two ten-thousandths of a second. There's probably never been a closer finish in Tour history.

Klöden's loss, not unlike his defeat by Armstrong at the final mountain stage of the 2004 Tour, was the only negative in the T-Mobile team's excellent day, and it was a small one. "Our tactics were to attack," said a chirpy Ullrich. "Vino tried first, then it was Andreas's turn. My job was to stay with Lance. That was a lot of fun."

Armstrong wasn't smiling at the finish. He was still in the yellow jersey, but his pride had taken a knock. "I wasn't great," he said. "I was isolated and I was suffering." And where were his teammates? "That's a great question," he replied. "I don't know. Perhaps we've been a little too active, maybe the guys are tired. I can't comment until we sit down with them."

His only teammates to finish within a minute of the 32-strong chase group were Hincapie, Popovych, and José Azevedo. Also gapped by the unexpectedly difficult final climb was an under-the-weather Georg Totschnig, Leipheimer's Austrian coleader at Gerolsteiner. Probably the unluckiest rider of the day was Rasmussen. He was now the proud owner of the polka-dot jersey, true, but he flatted on the final descent, conceded almost two minutes, and fell to 68th in the overall standings, 7:05 behind Armstrong.

There was still a very long wait before Zabriskie appeared at the end of the long, flat, finishing straight. He was still being followed by the broom wagon, which always trails the last rider on the road and sweeps up those who quit the race. He had fought relentlessly to avoid becoming a passenger today. When Zabriskie crossed the line in 180th and last place, his time deficit flashed up as 51:12. He had made the time cut by 3:31. The weary CSC man coasted to a stop at the end of the barricaded finish area. The one remaining journalist said to him, "Good job, Dave. That's probably the hardest effort you've made in your life."

In a shaky, barely audible voice, slurring his words like a drunk, the totally drained, sad-eyed Zabriskie managed to put together fourteen words in reply: "Oh, man, I just don't feel good. My body is just not working right."

In a way, his long, lonely, painful ride said as much about his strength of character as the brilliance of his time trial win over Armstrong the previous Saturday. His plucky performance also added poignancy to something he said a few days earlier: "I have a high tolerance for pain, so I should be okay. I've had really good luck and really bad luck, and that's life. This race shows you life."

STAGE 8: PFORZHEIM-GÉRARDMER

1. Pieter Weening (Nl), Rabobank, 231.5km in 5:03:54 (45.706kph); **2.** Andreas Klöden (G), T-Mobile, s.t.; **3.** Alejandro Valverde (Sp), Illes Balears, at 0:27; **4.** Kim Kirchen (Lux), Fassa Bortolo; **5.** Jens Voigt (G), CSC; **6.** Jan Ullrich (G), T-Mobile; **7.** Cadel Evans (Aus), Davitamon-Lotto; **8.** Christophe Moreau (F), Crédit Agricole; **9. Chris Horner (USA), Saunier Duval–Prodir; 10.** Alexander Vinokourov, T-Mobile, all s.t.

GENERAL CLASSIFICATION

1. Lance Armstrong (USA), Discovery Channel, 1,322.5km in 28:06:17 (47.056kph)

2. Jens Voigt (G), CSC, at 01:00

3. Alexander Vinokourov (Kaz), T-Mobile, at 01:02

4. Bobby Julich (USA), CSC, at 01:07

5. Ivan Basso (I), CSC, at 01:26

CHAPTER 11
Discovery's **High Hopes**
for Popo

At the finish every day, the stage winner and leaders of the various competitions head off to a fenced-off area just behind the podium, where they are bombarded with questions by a line of television and radio reporters. At this Tour, ever since the stage 4 team time trial in Blois, race leader Lance Armstrong and the other jersey holders gladly gave their answers.

All riders but one, that is. The holdout was the man in the white jersey, the best of the riders aged 25 or under, Armstrong's Ukraine teammate Yaroslav Popovych. Popovych would glance around nervously as if he was at the high school dance without a date, rather than a potential Tour de France champion.

When someone would finally ask him a question, Popovych would say as little as possible in his still evolving English, uttering something like "The Tour is harder than any race I know." So, after losing time to his rivals on the stage into Gérardmer, he was probably quite relieved that he dropped to second place in the white jersey stakes, just one second behind the 2004 Tour's best young rider, Vladimir Karpets of Russia.

Popovych may have been fairly anonymous in the first week of his first Tour, but it was a situation he couldn't hope to maintain as the race developed. That's because the 25-year-old Ukrainian is the rider who Discovery team boss Johan Bruyneel believes can replace Lance Armstrong as the team's Tour leader in future years.

"He has the physical qualities to be a [great] stage racer," said Bruyneel. "He has the right mentality and he's a hard worker. He's a real racer, he likes to compete."

Whether Popovych can mature into a major Tour contender has yet to be confirmed, but his impressive debut gave Bruyneel reason to be confident. The Belgian sport director believes that Popovych is on a similar trajectory as Ivan Basso, the Italian who won the best young rider competition in 2002, notched a top ten finish in 2003, and finished on the podium in 2004.

MERCKX OF THE AMATEURS

Popovych was born on January 4, 1980, in Kalinov, western Ukraine, and grew up in Drohobych, an industrial city and mining center in the foothills of the Carpathian Mountains. "It's difficult being a young cyclist in Ukraine," Popovych said. So, when he was 19, he followed the advice of a friend and went to Italy to race. He quickly opened people's eyes with a third-place finish in the Giro della Valle d'Aosta, a highly regarded amateur stage race that takes place in the Alps north of Turin. That result earned Popovych a spot on the top Italian amateur squad, Zoccorinese–Vellutex, where he attracted the attention of famed bike manufacturer Ernesto Colnago.

Popovych earned the nickname "Merckx of the amateurs" in Italy's cutthroat *espoirs* circuit, where he racked up a total of 36 wins in 2000 and 2001. The impressive two-season run was capped by victories in the *espoirs* Paris-Roubaix and the 2001 world under-23 road championship in Lisbon, Portugal.

To give "Popo" a jump-start in the pro ranks, Colnago personally financed part of the Landbouwkrediet team, for whom Popovych raced for three years starting in 2002. The youngster delivered on his promise, taking 12th in his Giro debut. The next year he finished third at the Giro, and in 2004 he had three days in the leader's pink jersey before fading to fifth overall in Milan.

Popovych set up his Italian base in the village of Poggio a Caiano, near Prato in Tuscany. While on a November 2002 racing visit to the French-speaking island of New Caledonia in the Pacific, he made friends with a local track racer, Cindy Baroni, the daughter of a former Italian ambassador. Romance blossomed, and the couple was planning to marry a few weeks after this Tour de France, with a formal church wedding planned in December 2005 for his family at their hometown of Drohobych.

GUY FOR THE FUTURE

Discovery Channel won the bidding war for Popovych's services after the 2004 season, and he's under contract with the American team through 2007. "I'm very happy with Discovery.

Everything is great," Popovych said. "The team has big hopes for me. I hope I can fulfill them."

At 5' 8" and 141 pounds, Popovych has a smaller build than Armstrong, but he resembles the Texan in his riding style. They have the same hunch over the handlebars, the same assassin's look in the eyes. "He's different than Lance, but there are some little things you can see," Bruyneel said. "He has the heart, he's always motivated."

Popovych nearly didn't make it to Discovery after he voted in the "orange revolution" elections that rocked his home country in the winter of 2004. Political turmoil in the Ukraine forced him to return home after Paris-Nice in March to sort out the paperwork. But he managed to make it back in time for Spain's mountainous, seven-day Tour of Catalonia in May, hardly knowing how his form would be. He unexpectedly grabbed the leader's jersey after finishing second in the decisive mountain stage in Andorra before holding off the Spanish mountain goats in a climbing time trial the next day to Arcalis.

> **"He's different than Lance, but there are some little things you can see," Bruyneel said. "He has the heart, he's always motivated."**

Popovych is the kind of rider Bruyneel believes he can transform into a new team leader. There will be a huge hole left with Armstrong's departure, but most of the other riders will remain in place. To Bruyneel, Popovych is the ideal candidate to drop into the team's successful Tour template.

"Popovych is one of the guys who can do it in the future," Bruyneel said. "There won't be a second Lance. It's my challenge now to work with another guy to bring him to another level."

A key step in Popovych's progression was getting used to racing on French roads. He completed both Paris-Nice and the Dauphiné Libéré, where he soaked up some of Armstrong's advice. "I like to see how Lance prepares the race, prepares his training. He's the top professional," Popovych said. "It's like cycling school every day."

Bruyneel said Popovych will slowly progress into the leadership role and make a serious run at the 2007 Tour. "Right now we don't put any pressure on him; he looks around, he listens, he learns," Bruyneel said. "He needs to improve a lot in the time trial. He needs more experience. He still needs to learn a lot on the road."

At the Tour, Popovych was impressive in his first week as prince-in-waiting. He finished in the top twenty in the opening time trial, and was a strong presence in the team time trial, after which he took over the white jersey. His strong, consistent riding put him into the top fifteen overall going into the Alps. When asked if he thought he could win the Tour, Popovych laughed. "Maybe someday," he said.

It was back in June, in the final stage of the Dauphiné, when Popovych offered a tantalizing preview of what the cycling world can expect. The roller-coaster stage ended with seven laps of a finishing circuit that included the short, steep Cat. 3 Côte de Domancy climb that was part of the epic 1980 world road championship won by Bernard Hinault. Popovych and teammate George Hincapie jumped away early on the stage and held off the peloton all the way to the line, where Popo eased up and let Hincapie take the win.

After being awed by his new teammate at the Dauphiné, Hincapie said, "He knows that next year I'll be working for him at the Tour de France. This is the first race I've done with him. I was quite impressed with him. I got to see it up close. I think he's a big rider for the future."

CHAPTER 12 | STAGE 9
Unexpected
Developments

The 180 racers arriving for this Sunday stage in Gérardmer, a small mountain town set on a beautiful pine-tree-surrounded lake, seemed more anxious than normal. Several teams had warmed up by riding from their hotels because the day's climbing would begin with a far-from-easy uncategorized hill as soon as the flag was dropped. This was the Tour's first real mountain stage, although the climbs in the Appalachian-like Vosges are not as steep or as high as the alpine monsters they would be facing later in the week. But everyone knew that a 171km stage featuring four Cat. 3 climbs, the Cat. 2 Grand Ballon, and the Tour's first Cat. 1 challenge, the Ballon d'Alsace, would be physically demanding.

It was also a stage that might answer some of the questions that were making the rounds among race followers: After their Col de la Schlucht meltdown, could Discovery regroup and properly defend Armstrong's yellow jersey on a day of six climbs? Would Ullrich's T-Mobile men again go on the attack and put Armstrong on the defensive? Could Ivan Basso's CSC team take advantage of the rivalry between T-Mobile and Discovery, and put another of its riders in the yellow jersey? Would new mountains leader Michael Rasmussen be able to maintain his momentum after the efforts he made the previous day? And how would the day go for riders like Dave Zabriskie, who struggled to make the time cut in stage 8?

The Tour never lies. So when Armstrong's teammates all reported absent during the previous afternoon's critical attacks, the six-time defending champion had to be concerned. "It was a shitty day," Armstrong told French television later that evening. "Perhaps the team and the boys on the team were *too* confident . . . after we did well at the prologue, and won the team time trial. Like everyone else that shows up at the Tour, we want to win, but there are no guarantees."

What was guaranteed were attacks, especially as this stage would be followed by a rest day, after a post-stage, one-hour flight from Mulhouse to Grenoble. Whether those attacks would come from T-Mobile, CSC, or Rasmussen's Rabobank team, the story would soon unfold.

The stage looming ahead would be especially tough for Zabriskie, who told a small group of reporters at his team car, "I hope I'm better today. It's been a real long roller coaster for me. We'll see . . . ." He then went for a warm-up ride, to see how he felt. Having stayed the night partway along the stage 9 route, he knew that the first couple of climbs would be a challenge.

After Zabriskie left for his warm-up, the reporters crossed the street to speak to Floyd Landis, his roommate in Spain. What was it like to ride alone to make the time limit as Zabriskie did the day before? "It's not fun," said Landis. "He'll be all right though. It'll make him tougher."

It may have made him tougher mentally, but Zabriskie soon found out that his body still "wasn't working right."

He did make it over the first 2km hill, but on the short descent the pack was split by a crash that forced Liberty's Igor Gonzalez de Galdeano to quit the race. The fast pace continued in front as a dozen riders tried to break clear at the start of the the next hill, the Cat. 3 Col de Grosse Pierre, and Zabriskie was gapped. Less than 5km into the stage, the young American pulled to the side of the road and stopped. He knew he wouldn't be able to make it through the day. In moments, a motorcycle-mounted UCI *commissaire* rolled up behind him and ripped off his two race numbers. Number 29 was out of the race. Zabriskie's first Tour was officially over.

JOINT EFFORTS

From the dozen-strong attack, one man surged ahead on the 3km, 6.4-percent Grosse Pierre climb. It was Rasmussen, who took the KoM prize ahead of Italian Dario Cioni of Liquigas-Bianchi, and then continued to push the pace on the much steeper, longer descent into the small valley town of La Bresse. "I went out to get points for the mountains jersey to put some distance between myself and the other contenders for the jersey," said the rail-thin Dane.

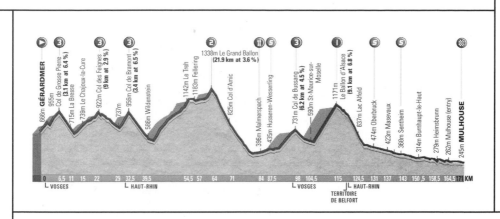

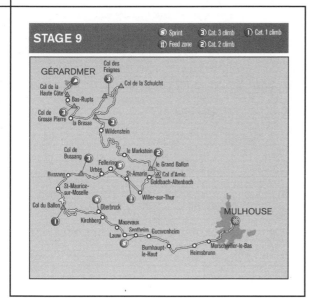

That was the start of what proved to be this Tour's most important breakaway so far. Before it developed though, there was another crash in the strung-out peloton. This one involved Ullrich, and just as Rasmussen's attack would have a long-term effect on the race, so would Ullrich's crash.

It happened on the steep downhill into La Bresse, on the only sharp turn on a smooth, two-lane road that angled across a grassy hillside. "It was caused by a gust of wind that made the peloton suddenly shift," said Ullrich, whose wheels caught a shallow ditch. "I did three or four somersaults." The 1997 Tour champion hurt his left side, but he quickly rejoined when the pack slowed and four teammates waited in the valley to pace him back.

The peloton's pace remained slow on the long, easy climb of the Col des Feignes, on which Cioni joined forces with Rasmussen. They reached the summit with 150km still to race, two minutes ahead of a six-man chase group headed by Christophe Moreau and Jens Voigt, and three minutes in front of the Discovery-led main pack.

Rasmussen was not a name on Discovery Channel's list of dangerous men, especially as he began the day more than seven minutes behind Armstrong on the overall standings. But Rasmussen had prepared well for this stage. "I knew what was coming and that was an advantage," he said, revealing that he had scouted the course with his Rabobank team-mate Weening after Belgium's Flèche Wallonne classic in April. As a result, he knew that the roller-coaster course through the wooded valleys and grass-covered peaks of the Vosges was ideal for a solo move—not unlike the one he made on the Gap-Grenoble stage at the 2004 Dauphiné Libéré that netted him a five-minute stage win over his early break-away companion, Basso.

This time, he again had an Italian, Cioni, for company. The two riders knew each other well, having both raced on the world mountain-bike circuit in the late 1990s before switching to road racing. By the start of the fourth ascent, the Grand Ballon, they had a lead of 2:37 on the chasers and 5:50 on the pack. This was a perfect situation for Rasmussen, who was taking maximum KoM points on every climb while receiving the support of a willing breakaway companion. Cioni's help was invaluable on the fast, big-ring, 23km climb to the 4,390-foot summit of the Grand Ballon. Having a partner was even more important on the mountain's wind-exposed descent and on the subsequent wide, straight highway up the Thur Valley.

Cioni's help kept the six-man chase group at bay by 2:20 along this whole stretch, while the peloton, still following Discovery's steady tempo, continued to lose time—7:50 atop the Grand Ballon, and 9:35 approaching the summit of the day's fifth climb, the Col de Bussang. It was here, halfway up the smooth, straight 6km climb, that Cioni couldn't follow Rasmussen's acceleration. The Dane found himself alone with 76km still to race.

By the tree-lined summit, Rasmussen was a minute clear of Cioni, and three minutes ahead of the Voigt-Moreau group that also included Swiss Alexandre Moos of Phonak, and the Spaniards Angel Vicioso of Liberty Seguros, Xabier Zandio of Illes Balears, and Iñigo Landaluze of Euskaltel-Euskadi.

Voigt and Moreau were the two with the most incentive in this group. Ever since the team time trial, Voigt had been trailing Armstrong on overall time by only one minute, and because the tall German isn't a great climber in mountains like the Alps and Pyrénées, he wasn't considered a real threat by Armstrong's men. Before the start of this stage, CSC boss Riis told Voigt, who likes nothing better than to make long breakaways, that he was free to go for it. As for Moreau, a Frenchman who raced on the Festina team busted for drugs in 1998, he was eager to gain time in a bid to finish top ten at the Tour and pick up points for the climbers' competition.

Not surprisingly, veterans Voigt and Moreau would drop their four companions on the upcoming Ballon d'Alsace. This 9km, 7-percent climb was given a Cat. 1 designation by the organizers, partly because this was the 100th anniversary of the Tour's initial crossing of the Ballon d'Alsace, the event's first-ever serious mountain climb.

A LONG SOLO RUN

In 1905, Frenchman René Pottier rode everyone off his wheel up the Ballon on a 299km stage between Nancy and Besançon. No one expected a rider to make a solo break this year, except perhaps for Rasmussen. Despite having been out front for almost three hours, he rode the legendary climb with great determination, still gaining time on the chasers. Cheered on by a massive, multinational crowd, including a fair number of flag-waving Danes, he crested the 3,842-foot peak 4:20 ahead of Moreau and Voigt, who were a minute in front of the other chasers, and still 9:35 before the pack.

Cheered on by a massive, multinational crowd, including a fair number of flag-waving Danes, he crested the 3,842-foot peak 4:20 ahead of Moreau and Voigt . . .

Wanting to show their regained strength and solidarity, six Discovery Channel riders pulled the peloton up the Ballon d'Alsace, riding hard enough to shed seventy-five riders. But because of the injured Ullrich, there were no attacks from T-Mobile.

Rasmussen still had 55km to ride, including 43km in the valley, before reaching the finish in Mulhouse. But he remained strong—"As the day progressed I just felt better and better," he said—despite a gusting headwind challenging him on the run down through the Alsatian vineyards to the pastures of the Rhine Valley.

Voigt and Moreau are considered two of the strongest *rouleurs* in pro cycling, and yet the lone Rasmussen still held strong. He was 4:10 clear of the chasers, and eight minutes on the pack, at the day's third intermediate sprint with 20km remaining. Shortly after that Voigt flatted, his one slight scare in a quest for the yellow jersey. But Moreau waited for him and they continued in their joint effort. Even so, at the finish, the ecstatic Rasmussen kept more than three minutes of his lead on the two chasers and six minutes on the pack. "I didn't expect us to catch up to him," said Voigt, "but then I did expect to get closer than we did."

Not only had Rasmussen won the stage, he'd also moved into contention on General Classification. The new overall standings showed Voigt in the lead, followed by Moreau at 1:50, Armstrong third at 2:18, and Rasmussen in fourth, a further 25 seconds back.

"I've been a professional cyclist for 23 years," said Rasmussen, referring to the time since he first raced bikes at age eight. "Ever since I started, I was dreaming about winning a stage like today in the polka-dot jersey."

And had he not unluckily conceded those two minutes on the final descent the day before, Rasmussen would have been in a much better position to bid for the yellow, especially with the Alps coming up after the rest day.

While the Rabobank rider rejoiced, Armstrong's main rival, Ullrich, was pleased just to have survived his second serious crash of the Tour. He told reporters in Mulhouse, "My right side is hurting but I can breathe normally. I hope I have a good night and get back in shape. If not I will go to the hospital for a closer examination." The rest day had come at an auspicious moment for Ullrich. But it came twenty-four hours too late for Zabrisksie.

STAGE 9: GÉRARDMER-MULHOUSE

1. Michael Rasmussen (Dk), Rabobank, 171km in 4:08:20 (41.315kph); **2.** Christophe Moreau (F), Crédit Agricole, at 3:04; **3.** Jens Voigt (G), CSC, s.t.; **4.** Stuart O'Grady (Aus), Cofidis, at 6:04; **5.** Philippe Gilbert (B), Française des Jeux, s.t.

GENERAL CLASSIFICATION

1. Jens Voigt (G), CSC, 32:18:23

2. Christophe Moreau (F), Crédit Agricole, 01:50

3. Lance Armstrong (USA), Discovery Channel, 02:18

4. Michael Rasmussen (Dk), Rabobank, 02:43

5. Alexander Vinokourov (Kaz), T-Mobile, 03:20

CHAPTER 13
Chicken Takes to
the Mountains

Michael Rasmussen is fanatical about weight. He doesn't wear the ubiquitous LiveStrong yellow wristband when he's racing because it weighs too much. Even in a sport known for its strong egos and detail-driven obsessive personalities, the 31-year-old Dane stands apart when it comes to eccentricities and curiosities.

Born June 1, 1974, near Copenhagen, the capital of Denmark, Rasmussen nearly gave up racing bicycles for badminton, a sport that's very popular among his countrymen. He's also an accomplished ballroom dancer. Of course neither waltzes nor shuttlecocks rank high on the interest level of most pro bike racers.

More conventional is Rasmussen's fondness for fast cars. In 2005, he was the happy owner of an Audi RS 6, a four-wheeled wolf in sheep's clothing that boasts a powerful 480-horsepower engine humming beneath its hood.

Rasmussen grew up around bikes, but not the kind that are raced. His father owned a bike shop, selling the utilitarian city bicycles that ply the bike lanes of most northern European cities.

Like any young boy in Europe, it was natural that little Michael wanted a racing bike as one of his first gifts. His grandparents bought him a brand-new blue bicycle, but his first ride wasn't terribly successful. He crashed after only a few meters and escaped with cuts and scrapes from his neck to his stomach.

By age 8 he was already racing in the local cycling club, the Holbaek Cykle Ring. Revealing a self-discipline that would be more evident in years to come, he refused to skip a race, even for his church confirmation. After a 9 a.m. start to the bike race, he still made it to the church in time for the ceremony.

Rasmussen's attention to detail is legendary. He's forever fidgeting with his bike, making changes and demanding his mechanics to get everything just perfect. He scans the Web constantly looking for lighter components. The CSC team mechanics admitted that when they heard Rasmussen was leaving their team after the 2002 season to join Rabobank, they bought a bottle of nice red wine and took it over to the wrenches on the Dutch team. "Thanks for taking him," they said.

In a sport where professionals live like monks to keep trim, Rasmussen might rank as the pope of all things food-related. He methodically weighs and prepares his own food, carefully calibrated to the day's activities. For lunch he has 150 grams of pasta if he's been on a long training ride, and 120 grams if it's been shorter. Immediately after a race, Rasmussen will attack a bowl of his favorite mix of nuts, fruit, and yogurt.

And going into this Tour de France, Rasmussen's almost skeletal body was even more emaciated. The 5' 9" climber had shaved a further 3 pounds from his regular racing weight to bring it down to a mere 126.5 pounds.

FROM DENMARK TO ITALY

How a skinny kid from a pan-flat country became a specialist bike climber is often the subject of curiosity. Denmark has hardly anything that resembles a mountain, though there are some abrupt, short hills with ramps as steep as 20 percent. The highest point in the entire country is Yding Skovhøj, which is just 566 feet above sea level.

"I guess it's something you're born with," Rasmussen said. "I could spend from now until Christmas training for sprints and I'd never get any better at sprinting. The only thing I'm good at is climbing mountains. I believe if you have a specialty, you have to work at it and exploit it to the full."

Rasmussen got his first glimpse of Europe's truly high mountains in 1988. He was 14 years old, and went with his hometown cycling club to Bolzano, Italy. He immediately fell in love with the Dolomites and the Italian way of life. He later moved to Italy, and has been living near Varese for a decade.

Rasmussen's frail size didn't jibe well with the bigger, bulkier road racers that Denmark was producing, and by 1989 he decided to switch to the burgeoning mountain bike scene. He enjoyed quick success and, as a junior, won a bronze medal at the 1992 world championships. Denmark already had its mountain biking hero in Henrik Djernis, who won an unprecedented three consecutive world titles from 1992 to 1994, and overshadowed Rasmussen's efforts to break into the spotlight.

It was during Rasmussen's mountain bike career that he earned his ever popular, if unfortunate, nickname: Chicken. It doesn't stem from his skinny legs. Rather, there's a popular Danish children's television program called *Bamse og Kylling* (*Teddy Bear and Chicken*). On a trip to Canada for a 1994 mountain bike World Cup, one of Rasmussen's teammates was already being called Bamse. As Rasmussen recounts the story, he walked in for lunch after a hard training ride looking like "something the cat had dragged in" when someone piped up, "And here we have Chicken."

Rasmussen said he doesn't mind the nickname, even if it's not nearly as glamorous as the Killer or the Falcon. "I've had it for a long time, so I'm used to it," he said, though he griped to a French television reporter during the Tour, "One doesn't choose your own nickname."

There's one more thing he wants to make clear. "It's Chicken," Rasmussen points out. "Not *the* Chicken."

In 1999, Chicken was the surprise winner of the muddy men's cross-country race at the world championships in Åre, Sweden, beating pre-race favorites Miguel Martinez and Filip Meirhaeghe by a wide margin. He raced for Denmark at the 2000 Sydney Olympic Games and did two more mountain bike world's—he was in the winning break with winner Roland Green in 2001 when he flatted—but he'd already made the decision to make the leap back to the road scene.

"It's the Formula 1 of bicycle racing," he said. "As an athlete, you want to compete against the best."

Before leaving mountain biking, Rasmussen had a nice surprise at the world mountain bike championships in Spain. While out on a training ride, he met up with the Mexican national team and started chatting with one of its riders, Cariza Muñoz. She and Michael fell quickly in love.

After a long-distance affair, his Mexican sweetheart moved to Italy to live with him in 2001. Rasmussen and Muñoz were scheduled to marry in the fall of 2005 at the city hall in Tølløse, Denmark. On the same occasion, he'll be appointed an honorary citizen of the town. The couple was also expecting their first child in December.

ROAD TO THE TOUR

Rasmussen's road to the Tour de France wasn't easy. Midway through the 2001 season, after sticking a fork in his mountain biking career, he got a half-salaried contract to ride with fellow Dane Bjarne Riis's CSC team. "I had done everything I could do in mountain biking," he said. "I wanted to see how far I could go on the road scene."

Rasmussen was just one of a handful of mountain bike prodigies that were making the leap to the road. Two-time World Cup champion Cadel Evans, workhorse Dario Cioni, American Floyd Landis, and Olympic gold medalist Miguel Martinez would all make the crossover with varying degrees of success.

> **Rasmussen said his mountain biking background helped him with his time trialing, because a mountain bike race is essentially one long time trial.**

Rasmussen said his mountain biking background helped him with his bike-handling skills under sketchy weather conditions and with his time trialing, because a mountain bike race is essentially one long time trial. Learning his place in the peloton and adapting his body to the rigors of racing day-in, day-out took some time, but he managed to snag a win in his *stagiaire* season of 2001, taking a stage of the minor Tour of Croatia at Jadranska Magistrala while finishing the race in second overall.

By 2002, he was a full-time member of Bjarne's army at Team CSC. He finished 45th in his grand tour debut at the Giro d'Italia in June, and then won a tough climbing stage of the five-day Tour of Burgos in August.

"I felt I was the strongest climber in that period between the Tour and the Vuelta," he said. "There were some big names at that Burgos race."

The following season, Rasmussen became the first former mountain biker to win a stage in a grand tour at the 2003 Vuelta a España. After a long solo attack through the Pyrénées, Rasmussen won the seventh stage to Cauterets, France, and finished the Vuelta seventh overall.

That success raised his profile, and his contract price. Rabobank won the bidding war for his services. One reason he gave for joining the Dutch team was the unwavering support of its team manager, Theo De Rooj. "He's the first who really believed in my Tour potential," said Rasmussen. "They had some luck with some Danish riders before and he made me believe in myself for the Tour."

Rasmussen would later question that support when he was left off Rabobank's 2003 Tour team. Despite breaking a wrist in an early-season accident, Rasmussen said he was healthy enough to race, but a Dutch rider was given his spot instead.

The following year, after winning a stage of June's Dauphiné Libéré race, a healthy and ambitious Rasmussen finally headed to the Tour with a free hand to hunt for stage victories. The strategy irked Rabobank's team captain, American Levi Leipheimer, who basically had to fend for himself in the mountains as Rasmussen went on the attack along with just about everyone else on the team.

Rasmussen tried and tried again, but inevitably fell short in a Tour dominated by the overwhelming presence of the U.S. Postal team's Lance Armstrong, who won every mountain stage except for Ivan Basso's "gifted" stage to La Mongie.

The day after La Mongie, the epic, seven-climb 205.5km stage to Plateau de Beille looked to be ideal for a long breakaway. Rasmussen put everything into bridging out to two attacking riders already off the front over the day's first climb, the Cat. 3 Col des Ares. Through blazing heat, the Dane chased for 20km until he caught the leading duo on the day's second climb, the ultrasteep Cat. 2 Col du Portet-d'Aspet at 64km. The two other riders were Frenchman Sylvain Chavanel of La Boulangère and German Jens Voigt of CSC.

Once Rasmussen bridged up, Voigt suddenly stopped working. Chavanel was eventually dropped and Rasmussen could only watch the shadows of Voigt's front tire stuck on his wheel over the next four grueling climbs. Why was the CSC man not helping? Well, it was part of a hard lesson that Rasmussen was learning from the sometimes cruel world of bicycle road racing.

On his way to winning that stage of the Dauphiné Libéré the previous month, Rasmussen was sharing a breakaway with CSC star Ivan Basso on the mountainous stage into Grenoble. On the fifth of seven climbs, the Col de la Morte, Basso dropped his chain and his mechanic had a hard time fixing it. "I waited for him," Rasmussen said, "but he didn't come back, and I was 40 seconds ahead at the summit." The Dane wasn't going to wait around, as the highly technical 15km descent required all of his bike-handling skills and concentration. In the eyes of Basso and CSC team boss Riis, however, they saw Rasmussen look back and then just keep on going to eventually win the stage.

Flash forward to the Tour. It was payback time for CSC. "I told Voigt not to take one pull," said Riis. "We don't forget these things." And Voigt stayed stuck on Rasmussen's wheel for the remainder of the break's 130km run until they were caught by the U.S. Postal juggernaut on the lower flanks of the final climb.

FINAL PREPARATIONS

Before the start of the 2005 Tour, Rasmussen went to Mexico for a month—but he wasn't on vacation. Nursing a sore ankle that became infected during the Giro d'Italia and prompted his early departure from his second start in the Italian race, the Dane needed to recuperate and get ready for the Tour. He trained at altitude, first from his girlfriend Muñoz's family home near Durango in northern Mexico, then at over 8,000 feet in Toluca on a high plateau west of Mexico City. "It reminded me of my mountain biking career, when I would train at altitude in Colorado for three weeks and feel so strong," he said.

Before the Tour, there was talk of Rasmussen being a prime candidate for the King of the Mountains jersey or even finishing in the top ten, but his main goal was a stage victory. "This year's Tour is rather strange," he said at the start. "There's not just one stage you might be able to say you can win. Even in the Massif Central or in the Vosges, there could be chances. Winning a stage is a priority. If I can grab the polka-dot jersey or be in the top ten, great."

His chances for the overall seemed to take a blow right from the start, when he finished 174th, 3:14 behind stage winner Dave Zabriskie, in the opening 19km time trial. "I was already 1:20 back after 9 kilometers, so my sport director [Erik Breukink] told me to ride an easier gear to save the legs," Rasmussen said. "There's no point in cooking your legs for nothing."

In fact, there was one stage that Rasmussen particularly liked. It was the tricky six-climb stage from Gérardmer to Mulhouse through the Vosges that he had scouted during a trip following April's Flèche Wallonne classic. "It's an ideal stage for a breakaway," he said. "Even with the Ballon d'Alsace coming so far from the finish, it's still possible to try to make it."

It's now part of Tour history that Rasmussen won stage 9 in a long solo breakaway, took over the polka-dot climbers' jersey, and rocketed up the standings from seven minutes back to just 25 seconds behind Armstrong going into the Alps. Chicken would finally have to be taken seriously.

CHAPTER 14 | STAGE 10

Back in Charge:
Discovery Controls Climb to Courchevel

All around Grenoble on the first rest day of the Tour de France, team directors, riders, and race followers were guessing what might happen the following day in the crucial stage 10 through the Savoy Alps. There were two schools of thought: Either Lance Armstrong's team would take control and deliver the Texan to the mountaintop finish at Courchevel in perfect shape; or there would be so many attacks, especially by Jan Ullrich's T-Mobile squad, that they would stretch Armstrong's Discovery Channel riders to their limit and completely open up the race.

"Somebody *has* to attack," said CSC boss Bjarne Riis, talking at his hotel in Grenoble. Perhaps he was expecting that the man to do the attacking would be his protégé Ivan Basso, because Riis knew that Armstrong had to be challenged at Courchevel. One (small) advantage for CSC was that the yellow jersey was on the broad shoulders of its German veteran Jens Voigt, so the team could ride defensively in the flat opening half of the next day's stage. And, in theory, Basso would be able to wait for the right moment to counter-attack—if he were strong enough.

But Riis wasn't giving anything away. "We're strong, we're rested and we're ready to race," he stated, "but I'm not going to tell you our plan." Perhaps he was hoping that the stage to Courchevel would see a repeat of the opening alpine stage in the 1996 Tour, when red-hot favorite Miguel Induráin blew on the final climb to Les Arcs—a couple of ridges away from Courchevel—and Riis went on to win the Tour.

But Basso's teammate Bobby Julich, who had raced with or against Armstrong since their days on the U.S. national junior team in the late 1980s, wasn't expecting the six-time defending champion to show any weakness. "Lance has a minute or two over everyone already, and to get *that* back sounds like a monstrous task," he said, "and to actually get ahead of him is a totally different thing. So I definitely think that Lance is licking his lips for phase two of the Tour de France."

Julich, who was sitting only 1:07 behind Armstrong on overall time, said the upcoming stage would be revealing. "We'll know more of the 'pretenders versus the contenders' issue," he said, "I think it's going to be a much more close-fought battle [than people expect]." For the race to be close, of course, there would need to be a scenario similar to that on the first alpine stage of the '03 Tour, when Iban Mayo and Alex Vinokourov raced clear of Armstrong at L'Alpe d'Huez.

And Vinokourov was sure to attack, wasn't he? That was the near-unanimous opinion in Grenoble. With Vinokourov, Ullrich, and 2004 Tour runner-up Andreas Klöden riding together on the same Tour team for the first time, this was surely their moment.

Everyone remembered what happened when they got together at the Olympic road race in Sydney in 2000: The three broke away together and took all three medals, while Armstrong was left behind in the pack, not realizing that there was a break until he saw the jumbo TV screen with Ulle, Vino, and Klödi speeding away to victory.

The three broke away together and took all three medals, while Armstrong was left behind in the pack, not realizing that there was a break until he saw the jumbo TV screen with Ulle, Vino, and Klödi speeding away to victory.

On the road to Courchevel, though, Armstrong and his Discovery troops would be better informed, and they would surely jump instantly on any dangerous moves. But apart from the obvious favorites, no one yet knew which other riders to watch. The biggest question mark was Ullrich, who was not in top condition after his stage 9 crash, even though an MRI taken in Grenoble showed no broken bones.

The Spanish press was holding its breath in anticipation of some aggressive riding by homegrown stars Roberto Heras of Liberty Seguros, Francisco Mancebo and Alejandro Valverde of Illes Balears, Mayo and Haimar Zubeldia of Euskaltel, Carlos Sastre of CSC, and Oscar Pereiro of Phonak.

Many had expected that Saunier Duval, too, would play a major role, perhaps as the wild-card team in the mountains. "That's what I would say too," said team member Chris

Horner earlier in the Tour. "Once we get in the mountain stages, when the groups get really small, you're gonna see a lot more of us up there than any other team."

Unfortunately, Horner's assessment unraveled during the first part of the Tour. After climber Iñigo Cuesta didn't make the start because of injury, his Saunier Duval teammate Constantino Zaballa was forced to abandon in stage 5 with a strained left knee, and then José Gomez Marchante, an explosive young climber, crashed and broke his left collarbone on the stage to Mulhouse. This left the Spanish squad with its national champion Juan Garate, Italian climber Leonardo Piepoli, and Horner as its go-to riders.

None of the possible scenarios particularly bothered Armstrong, who after spending the rest day out of the public eye, said before the stage 10 start, "I have confidence in my team. Maybe it's possible to get the jersey today. I always think about the jersey, [but] what's important is that the team is strong again."

INTO THE ALPS

The indications were good for Armstrong when the peloton reached stage 10's first climb, the Cormet de Roselend, which marked the official entrance into the Alps for the '05 Tour. This two-part climb opened with a 10km stretch that kicked up at a 7-percent grade through a thick pine forest and past steep granite cliffs with waterfalls tumbling into a deep valley hundreds of feet below. On the latter part of this stretch, a sharp acceleration came from former Giro winner Stefano Garzelli of Liquigas-Bianchi, who was chased down by Liberty's Jörg Jaksche and Phonak's Pereiro. Illes Balears' Mancebo and Valverde quickly bridged, while another Spaniard, Oscar Sevilla, covered the move for T-Mobile.

This could have spelled trouble for Armstrong, particularly if the strong attacking group had joined forces with the seven riders from the day's early break who were still up the road. Instead, Discovery Channel massed at the front of the pack, with Manuel Beltrán, José Luis Rubiera, George Hincapie, and Benjamin Noval setting the tempo. They quickly closed down the Mancebo-Garzelli move, and any doubts raised by Discovery's stage 8 meltdown appeared to be ended. Armstrong's blue train was back.

The accelerations fractured the main pack, which numbered about 60 riders as it dropped down to a small mountain lake before tackling the second part of the climb to the rocky, 6,453-foot summit. Phonak and Liberty then jumped a second time, with Jaksche following the attacking Pereiro about a kilometer from the top. The pair gained

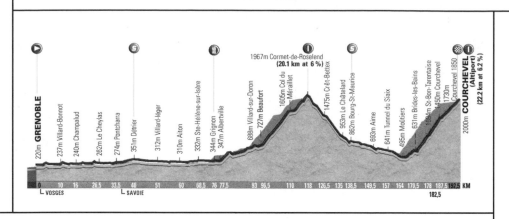

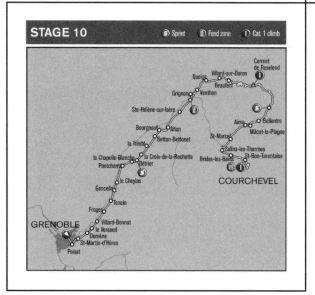

about 20 seconds before tackling the spectacularly fast 20km descent. Jaksche and Pereiro would eventually sweep up the seven in front to form a nine-man break, 4:30 ahead of the pack, with 41km to ride.

"We'll have a better chance with Jaksche," said Liberty team director Manolo Saiz, who knew that his leader, Heras, was not looking so good. "But Discovery is looking strong. We'll have to be patient."

The twisting Roselend descent has seen many spectacular crashes at previous Tours, notably in '96, when Swiss Alex Zülle and Belgian Johan Bruyneel both overshot irregular turns and landed in the trees. This time, a new crash involved Bruyneel, now at the wheel of Discovery's station wagon, when he careened into Team CSC's car on a sharp bend. Discovery's Yaroslav Popovych, who was slaloming his way through the line of team vehicles, clipped his own team car, fell, and cut his arm. He had a hard chase to catch the speeding pack.

Meanwhile, the leaders were approaching the day's major obstacle, the dead-end climb to the burgeoning ski resort of Courchevel.

WAR OF ATTRITION

Only two Tour stages have finished at Courchevel, which is a 20km climb with an average grade of 6.75 percent. There are several pitches approaching 10 percent on the smooth, zigzag road that ascends from a tight, wooded valley through four Swiss chalet–style villages, to a barren summit atop the resort's executive-jet airstrip, 6,562 feet above sea level.

In 1997, Richard Virenque was "gifted" the stage win by race leader Ullrich at the end of a difficult day that saw Ullrich saved by teammate Riis after Virenque's Festina team attacked en masse climbing the first of three monster peaks. And in 2000, the late Marco Pantani scored the last major victory of his career with a solo attack to beat Spanish climbers José Maria Jimenez (also deceased) and Heras, then a Tour rookie. That was the time when Armstrong, concerned about Pantani's attack, had Bruyneel call controversial climb coach Michele Ferrari to estimate the likely time gain of the Italian star.

No such assistance seemed necessary at this Tour's stage finale, which was resembling the climb to La Mongie in 2004, when favored rider after favored rider couldn't hold the pace set by Armstrong's blue train. With 20km to go it was race leader Voigt and Basque climber Mayo who lost contact. At 19km, Aussie hopeful Brad McGee and ambitious Austrian Georg Totschnig fell back. At 16km, Russian pretender Denis Menchov and Zubeldia were both dropped. Inside 15km, three-time Vuelta champ Heras and teammate Joseba Beloki couldn't hold the pace. They were quickly followed by Garzelli and '04 white jersey Vladimir Karpets, along with Americans Horner and Julich.

Most of this carnage happened while Discovery's Hincapie was sitting at the front of the train, pulling hard before handing the driver's seat to his new teammate, Popovych, who was smiling on the early slopes of Courchevel despite his earlier crash.

When the young Ukraine rider began applying the pressure, the Armstrong group soon passed Phonak's Pereiro who had broken clear in the valley with Liberty's Jaksche. Just before Perciro lost contact, Armstrong's closest rival, Vinokourov, was suddenly losing ground, meter by meter, to the fast-diminishing group. Vino went past the fading Spaniard, but he looked heavy-legged. There'd be no lightning attacks this time. His usual snap had deserted him.

Vinokourov was soon riding with CSC's Julich on their way to losing five minutes. "I could see the way he was turning his legs that he had big power," Julich commented. "I said, 'Gosh, why's he back here?' He must have been a little tired or blocked after the rest day." Vino later confirmed that observation, saying, "I trained for only two-and-a-half hours on the rest day, which wasn't enough."

Ahead, the eager Popovych was still churning away, carrying the leaders to the steepest, 9-percent stretch with 10.5km still left to race. Armstrong later said that "Popo was the man of the day" for coming back after his crash and then being his last remaining teammate. "When he was done, I told him to do a last acceleration," the Texan reported. "Man, he just sprinted!"

That final surge on the climb's steepest grade dramatically claimed the day's biggest victim. As Popovych pulled to the side, he looked across and saw that Ullrich was gapped. The German's Tour was slipping away.

"It was too much for my legs," said Ullrich, still in pain from his heavy fall on the previous stage. "My ribs were hurting today and it hurt a little to climb, but it didn't matter. I would have lost two minutes anyway."

The promising Kazakh, Andrey Kashechkin of Crédit Agricole, fell back with Ullrich. Also unable to hold the faster tempo, now being set by Armstrong, were American top-five candidates Leipheimer and Landis, along with the surprising Italian Eddy Mazzoleni of Lampre-Caffita and Tour rookie Cadel Evans.

Only five were now left with Armstrong: CSC's Basso, T-Mobile's Klöden, KoM leader Michael Rasmussen, and the Illes Balears twosome of Mancebo and Valverde. The five became four when Klöden was told to wait for team leader Ullrich. Then, with 8km still remaining, even Armstrong was shocked when he looked back to see Basso fall off the pace.

"My legs didn't feel as good as I had hoped," said Basso, "but I was able to limit the damage. I rode the final 8km alone, so I had to race smart and not risk blowing up."

The Italian's exit put Armstrong in a commanding position. He continued to push the pace, but then asked for help from Mancebo, Rasmussen, and Valverde. "I tried to get rid of those guys," Armstrong later said, "but perhaps I've lost some explosiveness. I'm 33, and at this age that's what happens. When I got the gap on Ullrich and Vino, I knew that the objective was just to put time into them. If you have to pull through with the guys that are with you, then *c'est la vie*."

Still, when the "boss" countered a couple of thrusts by Rasmussen, and then sprinted hard with 500 uphill meters left, it looked like he was going to win. But a lively Valverde managed to stay on Armstrong's wheel. And it was the exciting young Spaniard who had enough left to gap the champion and take the honors. "I really wanted to win the stage," said Armstrong, who was still winless in 2005. But what he and his team did at Courchevel put him much closer to the victory that mattered.

In the overall standings, Rasmussen was now in second at 38 seconds, while Basso, who lost another 1:02 to Armstrong, was in third overall at 2:40. "Everyone expected a lot from me today and so did I," said Basso. "It wasn't a great day, but it wasn't a bad day either."

For Armstrong, though, the stage went pretty much as he had hoped, even though he came in second to an extraordinary Valverde. "Days like this you have to look to [your rivals] . . . to hopefully take as much time out of them as you can. If you see them suffering, or on the limit, or on the ropes, you have to go. We weren't afraid to do that today. But it's not over. They'll come back and make life tough," he predicted.

STAGE 10: GRENOBLE-COURCHEVEL

1. Alejandro Valverde (Sp), Illes Balears 177.5km in 4:50:35 (36.650kph); **2. Lance Armstrong (USA), Discovery Channel, s.t.; 3.** Michael Rasmussen (Dk), Rabobank, at 0:09; **4.** Francisco Mancebo (Sp), Illes Balears, s.t.; **5.** Ivan Basso (I), CSC, at 1:02; **6. Levi Leipheimer (USA), Gerolsteiner, at 1:15; 7.** Eddy Mazzoleni (I), Lampre-Caffita, at 2:14; **8.** Cadel Evans (Aus), Davitamon-Lotto; **9.** Andreas Klöden (G) T-Mobile; **10.** Andrey Kashechkin (Kaz), Crédit Agricole, all s.t.

GENERAL CLASSIFICATION

1. Lance Armstrong (USA), Discovery Channel, 1,686km in 37:11:04 (44.92kph)

2. Michael Rasmussen (Dk), Rabobank, 00:38

3. Ivan Basso (I), CSC, 02:40

4. Christophe Moreau (F), Crédit Agricole, 02:42

5. Alejandro Valverde (Sp), Illes Balears, 03:16

CHAPTER 15
Valverde and Mancebo:
Study in Contrasts

Alejandro Valverde casually leaned against his Opera-brand bicycle beneath some shady trees before the start of the Tour's sixth stage from Troyes to Nancy. The 25-year-old Spaniard, whose smile is almost as quick as his finishing sprint, was clearly enjoying his first week at the Tour. He posed for pictures and signed a few autographs as he reflected on his recent past and much more urgent immediate future. "So far, so good," Valverde said. "We're just staying quiet the first week, following the wheels. The Tour for us starts in the mountains."

After three seasons in the professional ranks and 23 wins in Spain, the pressure was on Valverde to prove he could deliver on the hype that earned him an early reputation of being unbeatable. He had a quiet spring, which included winning the final stage of Paris-Nice, and then put his entire focus on the Tour. Officially, his position was to learn and help team captain Francisco Mancebo. But a week into the Tour, Valverde was a wide-eyed kid once again.

"The Tour de France is beautiful," he said. "The ambiance, the public, everything is very nice about this race. The amount of people lining the roads every day is amazing."

Most impressive for Valverde in his first Tour was rubbing shoulders with Lance Armstrong in his final Tour. "I've raced with Armstrong in other races, but to watch him at his highest level is something to see," he said.

What's surprising is that it had taken almost four years for Valverde to make it to the Tour, a fact that reflects some unexpected twists and turns in his otherwise impeccable rise through the professional ranks. His grand tour debut came in the 2002 Vuelta a España at age 22. He abandoned the race in stage 15, but only after confirming what observers of Spanish cycling already knew: Valverde had all the tools to be Spain's next big thing.

Born April 25, 1980, in the small village of Las Lumbreras in southcentral Spain near the regional capital of Murcia, Valverde caught the cycling bug from his family. His father, a truck driver, raced bikes on the masters' circuit, while his older brother, Juan Francisco, almost turned pro after a promising amateur career.

Contrary to legend, middle brother Alejandro didn't win his first race. He was the runner-up. The first victory came in his second race. After making a positive impression as a junior, he joined the Banesto amateur team in 1999 as an energetic 18-year-old, leaving behind any chance of university (his younger brother studied architecture) and devoting everything to cycling. He won three races his first year as an amateur, joined Kelme–Costa Blanca's regional farm team in 2000, and won 11 races in two seasons in the amateur ranks, including the *espoirs* national title in 2001.

Valverde was the best rider of his generation, and people were already calling him *El Imbatido*, the unbeaten one. "They started calling me that after I won a stretch of races," he said. "It's a funny name, but of course everyone loses sometimes."

In 2002, Valverde made the jump to Kelme's pro team and suffered through the only winless season of his career. That wasn't going to last very long, and Kelme's sport director Vicente Belda knew it. "We seem to be growing champions on this team," said Belda, referring to the string of stars that came out of the Kelme camp, including Roberto Heras, Oscar Sevilla, Santiago Botero, and Aïtor Gonzalez. "Next, we have Valverde."

THE GREEN BULLET

In 2003, Valverde burst onto the scene, quite literally. On the eve of the Spanish racing season, Valverde missed his flight to the Challenge Balears, a series of races on the Balearic Islands, and flew in the next morning. Just hours after stepping off the plane he won his first professional race. He ripped through the spring, winning the Clasica Primavera and a stage at the Tour of Aragon, and took third place at the semi-classic Luis Puig Trophy.

Valverde was deemed too green for that year's Tour de France and he reloaded for the second half of the season, winning two stages of the Vuelta and finishing third overall. He went straight to the world championships in Hamilton, Ontario, and came home with a silver medal to go with compatriot Igor Astarloa's rainbow jersey.

The next year was even more incredible for Valverde, as he racked up an impressive 15 victories. He was able to hit winning streaks not regularly seen in modern cycling, winning two stages and the overall at the Tour of Valencia in mid-February, coming back to win the Tour of Murcia in March, followed by three straight stages in May's Tour of Castilla y León, and then three consecutive stages and the overall in August's Tour of Burgos.

His winning streaks for Kelme, whose colors were green and white, earned Valverde his new nickname, *Balaverde*, the green bullet.

"The season was fantastic," he said, "but I failed in the Olympic Games road race. I was in good form, but I was dehydrated, and with cramps, there's nothing you can do."

Valverde's ticket to the 2004 Tour had been denied after his Kelme team became embroiled in the so-called Manzano Affair, in which former team rider Jesús Manzano, in a series of paid interviews for a Spanish sports daily, alleged the team was rife with doping. While an investigation into the allegations was dropped due to a lack of evidence, there was no way the Tour de France was going to allow the tainted Kelme team to start. The team also had trouble paying its riders, but Valverde escaped unscathed from the ensuing scandals and happily raced his way to the best season of his young career.

The 2004 Vuelta was meant to be his. The stars were aligned for a big victory and he won the Vuelta's third stage to set the tone for the rest of the race. His hopes unraveled, though, when he fell in a freaky, high-speed crash just after the start of stage 11, and moments after American Dave Zabriskie had gone on a solo flier. The American kept going to win the stage while Valverde was writhing on the ground, checking to make sure nothing was broken. "I don't like to make excuses about injuries, but I was just blown out," Valverde said. "When I lifted my head, my neck was totally twisted backward. The impact against my handlebars was intense." X-rays revealed Spain's latest big hope was still in one piece, but he wouldn't be able to race the final half of the Vuelta in top form. He finished a disappointing fourth.

After the tumultuous 2004 season, Valverde was happy to leave the troubled Kelme squad. He joined Illes Balears, a team with a solid foundation, which in its previous Banesto and Reynolds incarnations took Spaniards Miguel Induráin and Pedro Delgado to six Tour de France victories in a nine-year period. Valverde hoped that the team would be *his* ticket to Tour glory.

NO POKER FACE

The same day that Valverde was reflecting on his Tour destiny before the stage in Troyes, his teammate Mancebo woke up to the good news that his wife had given birth to a baby boy. There were smiles and backslaps all around in the Illes Balears camp, especially as the date was July 7, the start of the famous San Fermin festival in Pamplona, Spain. To mark the day, the whole Illes Balears squad wore the traditional red *pañuelos*, or neckerchiefs. Spirits were high.

The team has deep roots in Pamplona, which is the home of five-time Tour winner Induráin and the team's longtime team manager, José Miguel Echavarri. There's been a gap in the team's legacy since Induráin's retirement in 1996, and in recent years the team has had to set its dreams more modestly, taking satisfaction from the occasional stage victory or podium finish at the Tour.

Mancebo hardly seems the rider to pick up the mantle from the big stars that came out of the Reynolds-Banesto machine. Delgado, Induráin, Abraham Olano, and José Maria Jimenez all helped create the team's legacy, but Mancebo is the man the team was backing in its latest bid for Tour success.

"His most important attribute is his ability to be consistent in long stage races," said Eusebio Unzue, Mancebo's *directeur sportif* at Illes Balears. "When you look at all the great Tour champions, they were consistent. That's one quality Mancebo has in abundance."

Mancebo has another, more infamous attribute—his painfully distorted riding position. Hunched over the handlebars with his face twisted in contortions of discomfort, there's no hiding his suffering. "He wouldn't be very good at playing poker," Unzue said. "He suffers on the bike more than most. That's something everyone can see."

By his own admission, Mancebo is not the kind of rider likely to blow open a race, though that seems to be changing as he matures. "I finally had the experience to be aggressive in the race," Mancebo said, reflecting on his 2004 Tour. "I was able to attack rather than just follow the wheel. Of course, Lance Armstrong was too strong to be broken, but I reached a new level in my own riding."

Mancebo's strength in consistency manifested itself early in his career. At the 2000 Tour, he finished ninth overall to claim the best young rider's title. He was seventh in 2002, tenth in 2003, and sixth in 2004, confirming that he could stay close in cycling's most grueling race.

Less than 16km into the 2005 Tour's opening-day time trial, Lance Armstrong catches Jan Ullrich to lead the German by a full minute. That was Armstrong's *final* margin of victory over runner-up Ullrich at the 3,427km-long 2003 Tour!

TOP By riding too slow in the first half of the stage 1 time trial on Noirmoutier Island, Levi Leipheimer cost himself a place in the top five. **BOTTOM** On the first day of his first Tour de France, Dave Zabriskie celebrates with the yellow jersey following his remarkable time trial victory over Lance Armstrong.

ABOVE Belgian Tom Boonen raises two fingers for his second stage win in two days after out-sprinting Peter Wrolich (right) and Robbie McEwen (left). BELOW Floyd Landis powers Phonak to fifth place in the stage 4 team time trial.

ABOVE Proudly wearing the Australian champion's colors, Robbie McEwen wins the Montargis stage with his most impressive sprint. **RIGHT** After suffering through a viral infection in the opening week, Georg Totschnig becomes the first Austrian to win a Tour stage since Max Bulla in 1931.

OPPOSITE His right knee still scarred from a pre-Tour crash, Lance Armstrong leads Discovery Channel at a record speed of 57.324kph to a narrow victory over CSC in the stage 4 team time trial.

OPPOSITE, TOP Two years after his horrendous crash near Gap, Joseba Beloki is happy just to be able to climb again with the pack. **OPPOSITE, BOTTOM** Tour rookie Alejandro Valverde is exhausted but happy as he beats Armstrong for the mountaintop stage 10 win at Courchevel.

RIGHT After this fall on a steep alpine descent, his third crash of the Tour, Tom Boonen points to where it hurts; he won't start the next stage. **BELOW** Chris Horner (right) speeds toward the finish in Montpellier during stage 13 with French breakaway companion Sylvain Chavanel.

Eighteen minutes behind a break containing teammate George Hincapie, the Discovery team riders swarm to the front to escort yellow jersey Armstrong on the switchbacks of stage 15's Col de Menté.

ABOVE After repeated attacks in the Tour's toughest stage, Ivan Basso climbs with Armstrong toward Pla d'Adet: "I didn't have another attack in me, so we rode together to try to put time on Ullrich." BELOW Michael Rasmussen worked hard for his King of the Mountains jersey, reading the stage profiles carefully and gaining bonuses wherever possible.

TOP After this elbow-to-elbow tussle with Oscar Pereiro on the Pla d'Adet climb, George Hincapie (left) is about to win a Tour stage for the first time in his career. **LEFT** Discovery Channel is hoping that Ukrainian Yaroslav Popovych will upgrade from the white to the yellow jersey in future Tours.

TOP Australian revelation Cadel Evans leads Chris Horner up the ultra-steep Col de Marie-Blanque in stage 16's early breakaway group. **BOTTOM** Paolo Savoldelli just overtakes Kurt-Asle Arvesen before the stage 17 finish line in Revel. **OPPOSITE TOP** Stage 18's nasty closing climb at Mende fully challenged Basso, Ullrich, and Armstrong. **RIGHT** At 1,115 feet, the tallest pylon of the *Viaduc de Millau*, designed by British architect Sir Norman Foster, is higher than the Eiffel Tower.

RIGHT Oscar Pereiro earns the most combative rider award in his breakaway to Le Puy with Franco Pellizotti and Giuseppe Guerini.

ABOVE Kazakh champ Alexander Vinokourov crowns his Tour by beating Brad McGee for the final stage win and 5th place overall in Paris. **OPPOSITE LEFT** Despite this extraordinary effort, Jan Ullrich falls 23 seconds short of beating nemesis Lance Armstrong in the demanding stage 20 time trial at St. Étienne.

ABOVE Behind leader Lance Armstrong stand his team-time-trial winning Discovery Channel teammates (left to right) Paolo Savoldelli, Benjamin Noval, George Hincapie, José Azevedo, Manuel Beltran, José Luis Rubiera, Pavel Padrnos, and Yaroslav Popovych. **LEFT** It's the last day of the Tour, and Armstrong is ready to celebrate his historic win.

Of course, staying close and being on the podium are two different stories, but bolstered by his steady progression, the 29-year-old entered the 92nd Tour with new confidence and motivation. "After last year's Vuelta, when I finished on the podium despite an injury, I have new confidence," Mancebo said before the start. "I want to keep improving, and I think it's possible to be on the final [Tour] podium."

In the Armstrong era, staying close was becoming good enough for just about everyone.

CROSS-EYED

The tense mood following the stage 8 finish in Gérardmer was in stark contrast to the frivolity of a few days' earlier in Troyes. The team's performance in the stage finale over the Col de la Schlucht in the heart of the Vosges proved a missed opportunity, and no one was happy.

Their plan was to spring Valverde in the sprint finish, but the team didn't finish off the job of reeling in the attacking Pieter Weening and Andreas Klöden. The pair stayed away to contest the victory in Gérardmer, and Valverde had to settle for third place.

"We screwed up," Unzue said. "The break was just a few seconds from being reeled in and we let up at the wrong time. No one else collaborated, but that's no excuse. We failed."

"We screwed up. The break was just a few seconds from being reeled in and we let up at the wrong time. No one else collaborated, but that's no excuse. We failed."

A few days later, Valverde's goal of a stage win took an unlikely turn when the race entered the Alps on the stage from Grenoble to Courchevel. Somewhat surprisingly, after surveying the alpine stages in pre-Tour training camps, Valverde had handpicked this one as the one he wanted to win.

Valverde is the cycling equivalent of a *todo terrano*, an all-terrain vehicle. He's capable of taking sprints, making successful attacks, and winning on summit finishes. But he was unproven on the long-haul climbs of the Alps.

Courchevel was hardly the place you'd have expected Valverde to take center stage. He had won some mountain stages in the Vuelta, but the climbs south of the Pyrénées are nothing compared to the monsters in the Alps.

As the stage unfolded, Armstrong left a typical path of destruction—and found some surprising company in the final kilometers of the final climb: Valverde, Mancebo, and Dane Michael Rasmussen. Armstrong desperately wanted to win the stage, but even when he punched it at the finish, Valverde sprung around him to take the win. "I was almost cross-eyed and my legs were at their limit, but I saw the line and jumped," Valverde said. "I wanted to be first across the line more than any race in my life."

That victory catapulted Valverde into the best young rider's white jersey and fifth place overall, bringing on talk of an assault on the podium. "He's a natural-born winner," Unzue beamed. "He's been winning since he was 11. It's something instinctual for him, something you cannot teach."

That night in Courchevel, the Spanish celebrated Valverde's arrival and Mancebo's resistance. The flashy rising star and the hard-suffering diesel promised one thing: to attack Armstrong in the Pyrénées.

CHAPTER 16 | STAGE 11
Battle Stations in the
Highest Alps

Although Armstrong was on top, many felt that he was still vulnerable. Instead of a knock-out blow at Courchevel, he delivered body punches that allowed a dozen rivals to retain some serious hopes of reaching the still-distant Paris podium.

There were, of course, many surprises at Courchevel. When Bobby Julich posed his "pretenders versus contenders" question before the opening alpine stage, he didn't expect that his CSC team leader Ivan Basso would be among the men who would take a hit, and that the upstart Michael Rasmussen and Spaniards Francisco Mancebo and Alejandro Valverde would be the only riders able to stay with race leader Armstrong on the final climb.

Less surprised by reality was Phonak team leader Floyd Landis, who a year earlier was one of Armstrong's lieutenants and rode flat out for the Texan on every important climb. So after he placed 11th at Courchevel, 2:14 behind Armstrong in a seven-man group with Ullrich, Klöden, and Evans, Landis said, "I wasn't surprised at all. I knew exactly what Discovery's plan would be; it's what they always do. Lance has the ability to attack at the bottom of a hill and maintain it. That's how he's been able to win the Tour. The other guys can't do it. Even Ullrich can't do it. They try, and they expend too much energy and they pay for it later. When I saw that Lance was going to go 100 percent . . . I decided it was time to go my own speed."

American Levi Leipheimer adopted a similar policy, and he proved himself to be stronger than Landis and the other contenders in stage 10. He crossed the high-altitude finish line only 13 seconds behind Basso, to move into sixth overall, 3:58 back. "It was a super ride by Levi. He was strong like a bear," said Gerolsteiner sport director Christian Henn. "Because of the health problems with Totschnig, Levi is our lone leader now."

After reclaiming the yellow jersey, Armstrong recognized the sterling performance of Rasmussen, the solid KoM leader who exceeded his own expectations on the brutal Courchevel ascent by staying with the Armstrong-powered front group. "Rasmussen is riding strong," the Discovery leader conceded. "He's climbing very well and he's in second overall, and I don't need to add anymore. He's now a threat to the race. The other day he got how many minutes in a breakaway? We can't do that anymore, he's too close."

Armstrong also said he still regarded T-Mobile as his primary opposition, despite Ullrich dropping to 8th overall at 4:02, with Vinokourov in 16th, at 6:32. "T-Mobile may have had a bad day," said the race leader, "but as we saw, my team had a bad day a few days ago, and now they are back. So I suspect [T-Mobile] will be back."

BATTLE ON THE MADELEINE

The Discovery team riders "failed" on the stage into Gérardmer because they were surprised. At least, that's what their boss believed. "I think the boys were so focused on getting through the first week, getting through the Alps, all of a sudden this day popped up in the middle that was a lot harder than they expected, and they were caught off guard. I didn't like it, nobody liked it," Armstrong said. "But they were more upset than I was. You should have seen their faces that night; they were clearly disappointed."

The confidence of the Discovery riders had been restored by their performance at Courchevel, but they knew they would again have to be at their best to control the attacks on stage 11, a 173km trek through the High Alps that featured 12,600 feet of climbing. But they hadn't expected that those attacks would begin in earnest as soon as they had descended from Courchevel and started climbing the Madeleine, a 25.4km brute of a mountain pass that would take them back up to the same elevation, 6,562 feet, that they were at for the stage 10 finish.

Just after turning left out of the deep, wooded Isère valley, the aggressive Spaniard Oscar Pereiro of Phonak instigated the hostilities on the col's opening pitch. That was just what the incorrigible Vinokourov was waiting for. "You can't win the Tour by sitting on the wheels," said the Kazakh national champion, who chased after Pereiro with half a dozen other enterprising individuals: Pereiro's Colombian teammate Santiago Botero, Liberty's

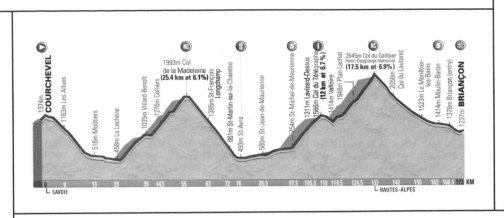

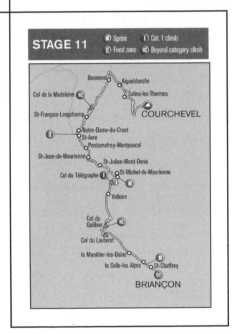

Roberto Heras, Illes Balears' Mancebo and José Luis Arrieta, Euskaltel's Egoi Martinez, and Saunier Duval's Chris Horner.

"It was my job to go with the first move, and I don't know if that was a good thing to do or not," said Horner. "We were going 100 percent. Look who we were with, I mean, we had the best climbers in the race outside of the top ten. And Discovery had to be going as hard as they could back there, too."

Horner was right about Armstrong's men having to ride extremely hard, but that was because of Mancebo, who *was* seventh overall, just four minutes back. The result was a wholesale destruction of the peloton while the break was pegged to a 35-second margin on the first half of the long, erratically graded climb.

In front, Vinokourov was riding the hardest, and his pace proved too much for Heras and Arrieta. When Mancebo realized his presence was dooming the break, he sat up 5km from the summit, where the grade steepened past high alpine meadows after a long flatter section. Horner, too, had to drop back. "That [climb] just put me in the red," said the fearless American, who had to watch Botero, Vinokourov, Pereiro, and Martinez disappear into the crowds lining the last few kilometers while he was swamped by the chase pack. Over the top, the leaders were 1:03 ahead of the peloton, which had been cut from 160 to fewer than 50 riders as a result of the brutal chase.

DROPPED AND DOPING

All those who had been dropped would finish the day at least half an hour behind the leaders, while CSC's second yellow-jersey leader, Jens Voigt, and Kevin Hulsmans of Quick Step would be eliminated on time. Sprinters Jean-Patrick Nazon, Kim Kirchen, and Stefano Zanini would quit during the stage. And one man, Dario Frigo of Fassa Bortolo, wasn't able to start the stage at all.

Earlier that morning, Frigo had been arrested at the Hotel Mercure in Courchevel by French police, who escorted him to Albertville where his wife Susanna was in custody. She had been stopped by customs inspectors on the Tour's rest day, apparently on her way to see Frigo, when they opened the trunk of her car to discover a dozen "suspect" ampoules stored in an iced vacuum flask. She was held under suspicion of transporting banned drugs (said to be erythropoetin, or EPO). Frigo, who finished the Courchevel stage in 77th place, 17:18 behind the leaders, was released on bail after being questioned as a suspected accomplice.

Frigo was the second rider to be excluded from this Tour, following Lampre-Caffita's Russian Evgeni Petrov, who provided an above-50-percent hematocrit result at a routine blood test during the Grenoble rest day. None of the other 162 urine and blood tests taken during the Tour were positive for banned substances. Those results tend to support riders' anecdotal evidence that doping, once rife in the European peloton, is a far-diminished problem.

When Française des Jeux's Aussie Olympic track champion Brad McGee wrote a missive on his Web site in 2004 denouncing riders who cheated, he received much appreciative support from fans and riders alike. He wrote: "I believe that given the right training, recovery, and mental approach that anything is possible in my profession. I have not, do not, and never will take performance-enhancing drugs or procedures to make this belief come true. And yet given recent estimates and accusations in the media . . . I fall into a category of 'must be' doped riders. F—k you."

That expletive is out of character in McGee, a mild-mannered Australian who's immensely proud of his "beautiful family"—wife Sharni and their young children Tahlia and Rory. McGee says he was surprised by the amount of positive feedback his Web story received. "I think it was important to say it how I see it," he said. "And a lot of people have appreciated that. I would rather the sport of cycling did not exist than to exist with doping."

Even so, McGee remains optimistic about pro cycling's future. "I've been feeling that the sport's just been cleaning itself up," he said. "What I'm most impressed with is that the mentality and feelings about [doping] have really changed. Keep that through another couple of years and the old thoughts, the dirty blood, will just about be wiped out. Look at this team [Française des Jeux] with an average age of something like 23 or 24. These guys are just young, talented hopefuls with their eyes on training hard, eating well, and progressing that way."

No negatives, right? "No, never. That's what I'm saying, the feeling is really good. There's none of the 'ah, yeah, but you know,' none of that anymore."

THE GALIBIER

For almost a century, the name "Galibier" has struck fear in the hearts of Tour de France riders. This highest mountain pass of the race has witnessed some of the greatest climbers in cycling history crest its barren 8,678-foot peak on their way to wonderful victories. Luxembourger Charly Gaul first emerged as a Tour contender here in 1958, spinning his way over the top more than ten minutes ahead of the field. Spaniard Federico Bahamontes made a long solo break over the Galibier in 1964, while an unforgettable attack by Italian Marco Pantani earned him a stage win and the yellow jersey in 1998.

The Galibier is not particularly steep; its toughest grade, in the final kilometer, is only 9.6 percent. But it's the culmination of a double-feature, started by the 12km Télégraphe, that rears up the steep side of a ravine in tight switchbacks. After an easy five-minute descent, the riders go straight into the 17.5km Galibier, which reserves its toughest stretch for the 5km at the top. The virtual 30km of climbing through 6,689 vertical feet remains one of the Tour's most forbidding challenges.

On reaching the foot of the Télégraphe, Vinokourov and his three breakaway companions had etched out a two-minute lead despite Armstrong's Discovery teammates driving the 42-strong chase group on the gradually rising valley road after the rapid Madeleine descent. "I was in the red the whole way through the valley," said Horner, "and I was in the red up the [Télégraphe], in the red to try to get back on, and I get dropped anyways [on the Galibier]."

Horner's tale wasn't much different from those of the others trying to stay with the Armstrong group, and only about a dozen were able to maintain the high tempo of the four teammates who set the pace for the yellow jersey in this vital phase of the race. That made Vinokourov's ride even more impressive. He spent most of the 90-minute climb at the front. First he shed Pereiro, then Botero lost contact as the two tackled the steeper switchbacks climbing away from the high valley at Plan Lachat, which marked the exact halfway mark of this Tour de France. Almost 1,800km completed; another 1,800km to go.

> **That was a tiny gain for a huge effort, but Vinokourov's feat earned the admiration of the whole peloton.**

At one point, the blond Kazakh stretched his lead to three minutes over Armstrong's armada, with Hincapie and Popovych doing the longest turns at the front. "We didn't want to give him too much time," said Hincapie, "so we kept him at two or three minutes the whole day. It was hard, *very* hard [on the Galibier]. We did an awesome job today."

Vinokourov was first over the high Galibier summit, 41 seconds ahead of the relentless Botero, and 2:23 ahead of Rasmussen, who picked up his KoM points 20 seconds ahead of the chase group. Botero fought back and caught Vino partway into the 40km downhill to the finish, but in the flat sprint at Briançon the Colombian had no answer to a very determined Kazakh.

Discovery did a team time trial from the Galibier summit, averaging almost 70kph for 35 minutes, to cut the gap to just 1:15 at the line. That was a tiny gain for a huge effort, but Vinokourov's feat earned the admiration of the whole peloton. CSC's Julich, who rolled across the line in fourth place, said, "That Vino's a bull, man. He just fights." As for the battler himself, Vinokourov said, "You have to risk something and that's what I did today. [The win] is great motivation for the whole team to keep attacking in the Pyrénées. It's a long race and anything can still happen."

STAGE 11: COURCHEVEL-BRIANÇON

1. Alexander Vinokourov (Kaz), T-Mobile, 173km in 4:47:48 (36.087kph); **2.** Santiago Botero (Col), Phonak, at 0:01; **3.** Christophe Moreau (F), Crédit Agricole, at 1:15; **4. Bobby Julich (USA), CSC; 5.** Eddy Mazzoleni (I), Lampre-Caffita, both s.t.

GENERAL CLASSIFICATION

1. Lance Armstrong (USA), Discovery Channel, 1,859 kilometers in 41:59:57 (43.902kph)

2. Michael Rasmussen (Dk), Rabobank, 00:38

3. Christophe Moreau (F), Crédit Agricole, 02:34

4. Ivan Basso (I), CSC, 02:40

5. Alejandro Valverde (Sp), Illes Balears, 03:16

CHAPTER 17
Never Say Die:
Kazakh Warrior Vinokourov

If Alexander Vinokourov wasn't already conspicuous enough with his hallmark attacking style and square-jawed determination, his rather loud sky-blue Kazakh national champion's jersey made him stick out even more during the 2005 Tour de France. But he wore the jersey with pride and, when asked about his plan for the race, he put it simply: "Attack and then attack some more."

It's a style that has served the 31-year-old well in his prolific eight-year professional career, delivering him more than 30 victories, including Liège-Bastogne-Liège, Paris-Nice, and the Dauphiné Libéré, along with an Olympic silver medal and other outstanding performances that include a stage win and third-place podium at the exciting 2003 Tour.

Vinokourov couldn't replicate his '03 Tour success because he dislocated his shoulder in a crash at the Tour of Switzerland, just two weeks before the 2004 Tour. But he was intent on returning for a podium shot in 2005, ideally with his close friend and T-Mobile teammate Jan Ullrich riding at his side.

Shy to the point of being almost reclusive, Vinokourov instinctively recoils in most public situations except when he's on his bike. "There's no emotion when you attack. That comes later," Vinokourov explained. "You just try to win, that's all." The blond-haired, blue-eyed Kazakh is obviously a man who prefers to let his legs do the talking. Or, to put it more accurately, do the attacking.

OUT OF ASIA

Back in faraway Kazakhstan, a landlocked nation half the size of the continental United States but with only one-tenth of the population, Vinokourov is a national hero. For his

Olympic silver medal at Sydney in 2000, he was promoted to captain in the Kazakh military and received various honors: a national pension, a furnished apartment, and a military escort when he and Ullrich venture to the rugged Altai mountains to hunt wild boar in the off-season.

Vinokourov's Tour exploits are followed daily on television, and a national cycling school bearing his name is in the works to help develop new young pros. Having bike fan Danial Akhmetov as Kazakh prime minister doesn't hurt things, either.

It wasn't always that way, of course. Little is known of Vinokourov's childhood, and he rarely broaches the subject in interviews. What is known is that Kazakhstan is a place that most people would be keen to get away from in a hurry. Temperatures soar over 100 degrees Fahrenheit in the summer and then plunge into a deep-freeze during the winter.

Proud, nomadic horsemen once roamed the barren steppes, but the country suffered for 200 years under the boot of Russian, then Soviet, domination. The Soviets deemed the semidesert expanses a perfect place to conduct nuclear testing. And during the 1950s and 1960s, millions of Soviet citizens immigrated to cultivate Kazakhstan's northern pastures in agricultural programs called "Virgin Lands."

With this stark background, Vinokourov was born in Petropavlovsk, just 60 miles from the Russian border, on September 16, 1973. His father worked on a poultry farm, earning the equivalent of $50 a month. After failing in other sports, Vinokourov took up cycling and one of his memorable early wins came in 1987 when he was just a scrawny kid, his blond hair sprouting up over his blue eyes. As he came in for the win against a field of riders much older than his 14 years, the confused race announcer yelled through the loudspeaker, "Hey, kid, get out of the way, the winner is about to come in."

The winner, of course, was Vinokourov and he snagged a new bicycle for the effort.

Exploits like that earned him a spot on the national team and he moved to the nation's capital, which was then in the faraway city of Almaty, on the other side of the country. Vinokourov described how he and his thirteen teammates would be forced to train three times a day: once at sunrise, then a three-hour training session after a midday meal, followed by another two-hour session before dinner. "In our clubhouse, we had a blackboard where we used to mark little crosses for every time we trained," he recalled. "When it was all tallied up at the end of the year, there were maybe just five or six days when I hadn't taken out my bike."

Like many pros now dominating the European peloton, Vinokourov was the best of the bunch, even as a youngster. He was soon the coach's favorite for his self-discipline and his fearless countenance.

Vinokourov's big break came in 1996 when Frenchman Gilles Mas, then the assistant sport director at the Casino pro team, bumped into the Kazakh national coach at Malaysia's Tour de Langkawi. The coach convinced Mas to take two of his promising riders to France.

Mas selected Vinokourov and one other rider, and sent them packing to St. Étienne, a gritty industrial city in central France, home of the EC St. Étienne–Loire amateur team. Trading the bleak steppes for France's hilly Massif Central, the 23-year-old Vinokourov showed up that spring with a backpack and a note from his national coach. His cycling adventure had just begun.

Vinokourov soon mastered French, and he quickly repaid Mas for the opportunity to race in western Europe. The quiet Kazakh ripped through the cutthroat French amateur scene, racking up an impressive eight wins in 1997. His success opened the door for more Kazakh riders. The next season, three more exotic-looking Kazakhs moved to St. Étienne, future pros Andreï Kivilev, Serguei Yakovliv, and Andrei Mizourov.

The Kazakh trio earned the nickname "The Three Musketeers," with the dashing Vinokourov playing the role of d'Artagnan—the older and more mature of these pioneers from another world.

STEPPING UP

The Casino team's management, led by manager Vincent Lavenu, made room on the roster for Vinokourov as a neo-pro for the 1998 season. Bumping shoulders with the likes of 1996 Olympic champion Pascal Richard and star sprinter Jaan Kirsipuu might have been intimidating, but not for an ambitious, self-confident rider like Vinokourov. He exceeded expectations, winning the Four Days of Dunkirk and five other races in his rookie season.

In 1999, he stepped even higher, winning the Dauphiné Libéré as well as the Tour of Valencia. Casino canceled its sponsorship at the end of that season, however, leaving Lavenu with too little money from new sponsor ag2r to keep his rising star.

Team Telekom (now T-Mobile) gladly scooped up this diamond in the rough. "Alexander was just our kind of rider," said team manager Walter Godefroot. "He immediately fit in well with the team and the others."

Vinokourov also settled in nicely to the French lifestyle, perfecting his French and marrying his hometown sweetheart. After leaving St. Étienne, he settled in Monaco on the Côte d'Azur and is now the proud father of three children, including twin boys.

At Telekom, Vinokourov traded quantity for quality in 2000. He quietly finished 15th in his second Tour, took the silver medal in the Sydney Olympics road race (after a three-man break with his Telekom teammates Ullrich and Andreas Klöden), and won a stage at the Vuelta a España.

Two more solid seasons followed with victories in the 2001 Tour of Germany and 2002 Paris-Nice. He was gaining more confidence in the grand tours and getting stronger in the big, longer climbs in the Alps, which were always his Achilles' heel.

Everything was going smoothly for Vinokourov when disaster struck in the second stage of the 2003 Paris-Nice. Kivilev, Vinokourov's best friend and blood-brother from the steppes of Kazakhstan, crashed face-first after coming off the lower reaches of an unrated climb near St. Chamond. Kivilev's pregnant wife was waiting at the stage finish in St. Étienne.

There wasn't anything particularly difficult about that 182.5km stage from La Clayette to St. Étienne. In fact, the narrow, twisting roads along the eastern edge of the Massif Central were where Kivilev and Vinokourov first cut their teeth in French racing.

Kivilev crashed with two other riders, but the Cofidis rider immediately went into a coma. He was taken to a hospital in St. Étienne, where he was diagnosed with a fractured skull and two broken ribs. Kivilev's condition worsened in the night and he died the next morning at age 29.

"I had just spoken to him in the morning. He said he wasn't feeling well and that he wanted to abandon," Vinokourov said. "I tried to lift his spirits, telling him to at least ride to Nice because he wanted to build a house near mine. We were all supposed to be together. That's all that's been in my thoughts, what Andrei said about stopping in St. Étienne."

The death of his best friend greatly affected this cold-faced man from the East. His first reaction was to quit the race in grief, and then he quickly changed his mind and vowed to win. "To lose one of my best friends is horrible," Vinokourov said. "We're such a strong gang, us Kazakhs. I thought about giving up, but now I have to win for him. I'm more motivated than ever."

The next day's stage was neutralized and then Vinokourov slugged through the 16.5km time trial in stage 4 to sit poised second overall, only 14 seconds off the pace going into the decisive summit finish at Mont Faron. The steep, winding climb is not very long, but it represents a severe challenge in March. Vinokourov poured all of his sorrow and fury into the pedals, dropping Giro d'Italia champion Gilberto Simoni to win the stage and grab the overall lead. On the podium, after taking the race leader's jersey, the normally unemotional man from Kazakhstan broke down in tears and pointed to the heavens in honor of his fallen comrade.

"His force was with me today," Vinokourov said. "I spoke to him during the entire climb. 'Kivi, I'm going to win this race and bring this yellow jersey and lay it on your coffin.'"

"His force was with me today," Vinokourov said. "I spoke to him during the entire climb. 'Kivi, I'm going to win this race and bring this yellow jersey and lay it on your coffin.'"

REBIRTH

Kivilev's death marked a sort of rebirth for Vinokourov. He lived up to his promise by winning Paris-Nice and putting the winner's jersey on Kivilev's coffin in an emotional funeral ceremony the day after the race ended. Vinokourov said he rode for two for the remainder of the 2003 season. He won for Kivi at the Amstel Gold Race, and he won for Kivi at the Tour of Switzerland, where he took a stage and the overall.

Vinokourov poured everything into the 2003 Tour de France. His fury and sorrow almost blindsided Lance Armstrong. The first sign that Vino was riding for two came on the Cat. 1 Col de la Ramaz, about 20km from the finish line of the opening alpine stage to Morzine. Vinokourov made two blistering attacks that caught everyone by surprise. Though he eventually was reeled in, the cards were on the table.

Basque rider Iban Mayo stole the spotlight in the next stage to L'Alpe d'Huez with his dramatic winning attack, but Vinokourov shot away again, with 6km to go up the Tour's most famous climb. This time he stayed away, finishing second and gaining 31 seconds on a haggard Armstrong.

Vino went on the attack for the third day in a row, this time shooting away from the bunch over the day's final climb, the Cat. 3 Côte de la Rochette, just 8km from the finish line in Gap. Armstrong and Joseba Beloki were giving chase on the descent when the Spanish rider dramatically crashed out of the race, and Armstrong narrowly avoided hitting him by riding across a bumpy field and bounding across a ditch before rejoining the astonished chase pack.

Vinokourov came across the finish line 36 seconds ahead of the Armstrong group to score yet another emotional victory. This time he wasn't winning for Kivilev. Instead, he rocked his arms back and forth like he was holding a baby in a cradle. In fact, he dedicated the win to two babies, his recently born twins.

Inspired by Kivilev and his growing family, Vinokourov eventually finished third at that Tour, one step below Ullrich, with the unbeaten Armstrong escaping with victory. Vinokourov returned home as a hero once more after becoming the first Kazakh to finish on the Tour podium. Ullrich and Vinokourov went hunting for wild boar that winter in the mountains of eastern Kazakhstan, plotting ways to dethrone the American.

Vinokourov's 2004 season started out optimistically enough, with three emotional stage wins at Paris-Nice a year after Kivilev's death, and a third-place podium at the Amstel Gold Race. His Tour hopes were shattered, though, when he dislocated his shoulder on the second stage of the Tour of Switzerland. With Vino on the sidelines, a demoralized Ullrich was out-gunned by Armstrong and the Texan roared to five stage wins and a record sixth Tour title.

Vinokourov salvaged his disappointing season with a bronze medal at the world time trial championships in Italy that fall, but that wasn't enough. "Winning the medal was great, but the Tour is the focal point of my season," he said. "I want to be back in 2005."

Vinokourov did return to his best form, winning April's Liège-Bastogne-Liège after a memorable break with another natural-born attacker, German rider Jens Voigt. At June's Dauphiné, Vinokourov attacked again, and won the prestigious Mont Ventoux stage.

Some seasoned observers question Vinokourov's attacking style, including Armstrong, who said the attacks need to be more tactically applied or it's just wasted effort. But it was obvious that Vinokourov wasn't listening to the naysayers.

Vino's aggression was paying some dividends at this Tour, starting with his bold attack on the rainy run-in to Nancy that almost netted him the stage win. But the expectation of Vinokourov giving T-Mobile a two- or three-pronged offense came unhinged at Courchevel, where he dropped five minutes and fell off the Discovery Channel team's danger list. Not one to rue his losses, the Kazakh champion bounced back with his immense stage win into Briançon.

In the context of T-Mobile's overall challenge to Armstrong, Vino's constant aggression was more of a distraction than a threat. But that's not to say that Vinokourov would give up on his dream of one day winning the Tour. With his seemingly endless reserves of strength and stamina, and once Armstrong is out of the way, Vinokourov will be one of the men to beat.

CHAPTER 18 | STAGE 12
One of Their Own

It was going to be a long, hot Thursday in Embrun, a town dating back to Roman times, built on *Le Roc*—a rocky bluff capped with ancient stone ramparts that once protected the citizens from marauding armies. The sun was already burning when its brilliant whiteness first appeared over the 10,000-foot peaks of the Queyras Alps, and filtered between the town's medieval houses into the main square, *le place Barthélon*. Street cleaners hosed down the rough granite cobbles while breakfast tables were set up beneath shady canopies and sun umbrellas. Guests at the Hôtel de la Mairie were soon buttering croissants and sipping café au lait, a sound crew was setting up a stage in front of the town hall for an evening concert, and townsfolk strolled to the Maison de la Presse to pick up their morning papers, the *Dauphiné* for local news and, especially today, the national sports daily, *L'Équipe*.

It was a big day for Embrun. Not only was this the Fourteenth of July, Bastille Day, but the twelfth stage of the Tour de France was coming through town around lunchtime. Mid-morning, a party of thirty or so English schoolchildren gathered around their teachers in the square. They were given instructions on things to see: the twelfth-century bell tower at the cathedral, the curio shops on the narrow medieval streets, and the splendid views from the ramparts across the valley of the Durance toward the snowy alpine peaks. The teachers' last entreaty to their students was: "Be back at 11, and don't be late! We don't want to miss the Tour de France."

On studying the sports pages in the morning papers, they saw that the Tour's publicity caravan was due to hit town at 11:30 a.m., while the race itself would be coming through a little before 1 p.m. for an intermediate sprint on the route nationale, the N94.

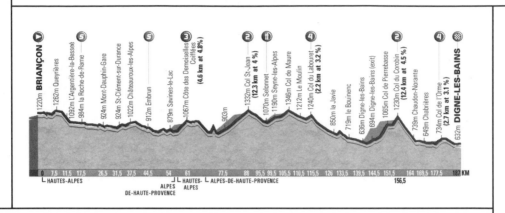

The stage itself, the third in the French Alps, bypassed the area's famed mountain climbs, the Izoard, Vars, and Allos. Instead, the 187km route stuck to the valleys and foothills. The (mild) sting in the tail was the Cat. 2 Col du Corobin, just before the finish in Digne-les-Bains.

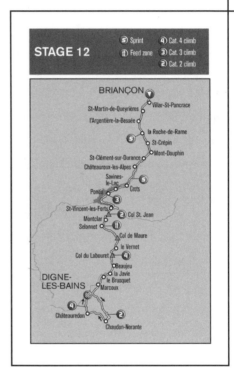

From Briançon, the opening 45km to Embrun were mostly downhill, including two intermediate sprints. These looked ideal for Tom Boonen to add to his lead in the green-jersey competition, but the young Belgian showed up at the start in a red T-shirt and casual black shorts, not his blue and white Quick Step uniform. His right knee was swollen from a heavy fall he took on the descent from Courchevel the previous morning; this, combined with the back and arms he injured in two crashes he suffered during opening week, added up to a DNS. The points classification would now be a battle between Thor Hushovd, Stuart O'Grady, and Robbie McEwen.

DAY FOR THE FRENCH

With half the field more than an hour behind solid race leader Armstrong, and with the prospect of a fast stage heading south through rolling hills into Provence, a breakaway looked certain on this first hot day of the Tour. And on their national holiday, the French would likely be heading the attacks. In the 91 Tours before this one, 24 Frenchmen had won on Bastille Day, from Louis Trousselier in 1905, via Jacques Anquetil in 1961 and 1964, to Richard Virenque in 2004.

It didn't take long for the locals to get into the action. After an early solo move by Aussie Brad McGee was squashed, two Spaniards, Juan Antonio Flecha and Alberto Contador, sparked a break climbing through Châteauroux-les-Alpes, 37km into the stage. Four of the seven riders who joined them were French. The 2004 Tour's yellow-jersey hero Thomas Voeckler and his Bouygues Télécom teammate Laurent Lefèvre were there, along with Française des Jeux's Sandy Casar and Cofidis's Sylvain Chavanel, who took the sprint at Embrun 8km later.

A dozen teams were *not* represented in the break, so they duly brought back the leaders on the early slopes of a Cat. 4 climb cutely named *Les Demoiselles-Coiffées* (the lace-hatted young ladies), after some sandstone-capped geological formations overlooking the stunning turquoise waters of Lac de Serre-Ponçon.

It was on this winding hill, after almost 51km were covered in the opening hour, that Discovery's Manuel Beltran touched wheels with another rider as they raced single file up the shallow incline. The Spaniard fell on his head. Beltran was forced to quit with a concussion, making him the first of Armstrong's teammates to leave the Tour since Christian Vande Velde broke his arm crashing into an iron lamppost in 2001.

The Spaniard fell on his head. Beltran was forced to quit with a concussion, making him the first of Armstrong's teammates to leave the Tour . . .

On the swooshing descent to a narrow arm of the Serre-Ponçon Lake, one of the biggest reservoirs in Europe, a new break of eleven riders from eleven teams gradually formed, including the highly motivated Frenchmen Casar, Patrice Halgand of Crédit Agricole, and David Moncoutié of Cofidis. After a fast chase in the valley, the leaders were joined by O'Grady and Hushovd, who were hoping to pick up more sprint points.

The thirteen men reached Digne-les-Bains with a 4:25 lead on the pack prior to a finishing loop of 47km that took the race over the narrow Cat. 2 Col du Corobin. This was the climb—raced in the opposite direction—where Armstrong and then teammate Tyler Hamilton broke clear on a stage of the 2000 Dauphiné Libéré to score a well-remembered one-two finish in Digne.

The Corobin was again the decision maker. This time, a first attack came from Davitamon-Lotto's Axel Merckx, perhaps knowing that his father Eddy was the last winner of a Tour stage finishing in Digne, when the five-time Tour champion outsprinted break companion Felice Gimondi over a course that included the Vars and Allos climbs in 1969. But within a kilometer of the summit, a strong counterattack came from Moncoutié, who made a similar move to win stage 11 into Figéac at the 2004 Tour. The 30-year-old French rider, who was enjoying the best season of his career, shot away up the steepest part of the climb, taking a 40-second lead at the top, still 30.5km from the finish. He then nursed a lead varying between 20 and 30 seconds to hold off seven chasers before dropping into Digne for a joyful Bastille Day victory.

The locals watching television back in Embrun probably let out a celebratory cheer before heading down to the place Barthélon for dinner with a bottle of chilled rosé wine, followed by the concert and a fireworks display over the ramparts, as the hot, bright day merged into a hot, dark night.

STAGE 12: BRIANÇON–DIGNE-LES-BAINS

1. David Moncoutié (F), Cofidis, 187km in 4:20:06 (43.137kph); **2.** Sandy Casar (F), Française des Jeux, at 0:57; **3.** Angel Vicioso (Sp), Liberty Seguros; **4.** Patrice Halgand (F), Crédit Agricole; **5.** José Luis Arrieta (Sp), Illes Balears, all s.t.

GENERAL CLASSIFICATION

1. Lance Armstrong (USA), Discovery Channel, 46:30:36

2. Michael Rasmussen (Dk), Rabobank, 00:38

3. Christophe Moreau (F), Crédit Agricole, 02:34

4. Ivan Basso (I), CSC, 02:40

5. Alejandro Valverde (Sp), Illes Balears, 03:16

CHAPTER 19

Beloki's
Long Road Back

Getting through the nervous transition stages between the Alps and Pyrénées is never easy. After nearly two weeks of racing at the Tour, fatigue, nerves, and stress can serve a dangerous cocktail. That's why on France's Bastille Day, while stage winner David Moncoutié was the happiest rider in the race, Joseba Beloki, who finished with the main peloton 10:33 later, was the most relieved.

The finish line in Digne-les-Bains marked a psychological barrier for the 31-year-old Beloki, the Spanish rider on Liberty Seguros. It was exactly two years to the day, on the nearby road over the Côte de la Rochette, that Beloki's career took a horrific tumble. Three consecutive Tour podium finishes were forgotten in an instant when he crashed on the road to Gap. Beloki was left with several broken bones, and his cycling future in tatters.

Simply being back in the 2005 Tour was a victory for Beloki. "I spent almost one year without riding, but I want to move on," Beloki said. "I didn't stop there," he added, referring to the crash.

At this midpoint of the Tour, Beloki knew he wasn't going to finish anywhere near the elusive podium. But his long journey back to the Tour was marked with a string of frustrations and setbacks that almost prompted the easygoing Basque rider to give up on cycling altogether. Now, simply arriving with the peloton in Paris would be victory enough.

He has learned that his way back to the top has to be taken in small steps. That's why he was so happy following the Tour's first climbing stage into Gérardmer a few days earlier. All it took was one glance at the smiling Beloki, after the high-charged sprint over the Cat. 2 Col de la Schlucht at the end of stage 8, to feel his joy.

"This is the first I've finished in the first group at the Tour [on a climbing stage] in two years," Beloki beamed. "After the horrible week I had in the Tour de Suisse, I was ready to quit for good. Now this Tour has given me the inspiration to keep fighting."

BASQUE ROOTS

Beloki's difficult and long road back to the Tour is in complete contrast to the quick, relatively unexpected rise he had as a Tour protagonist just five years ago. But ever since his earliest days on the bike, Beloki has been able to contest the conventional wisdom that said he'd never amount to much in the cutthroat world of professional bike racing.

Born on August 12, 1973, in Lazkao, Spain, deep in the heart of the cycling-crazed Basque Country, Beloki is the older of two brothers. His younger brother, Gorka, is also a professional, but he has never reached the level of success of Joseba. Beloki's uncle, Ramon Murillo, was an accomplished amateur rider and turned his young nephew on to the sport at a young age. Sundays were spent going to local races and, by his early teens, Beloki had already decided that he wanted to become a professional racer.

"I was never very good at any other sports and I was even worse at studying," Beloki said. "It was just as well that I could ride a bike because I'm not sure what else I could have done."

His family moved to Vitoria, the thriving capital of the Alava province of Spain's Basque Country set high on a plateau between the Pyrénées to the east and the Cantabrian Mountains to the north and west. There, Beloki was repeatedly eclipsed in his amateur days by another Vitoria rider, Igor Gonzalez de Galdeano, a future teammate who dominated the local competition.

"He beat me in every race," Beloki said. "I had to try to win when he was gone to other races. I gradually found my place, but Igor was always the reference."

Like many Basque riders, Beloki got his first break with Euskaltel-Euskadi, turning pro with the regional professional team in 1998. There wasn't much talk about Beloki in his early career and, at one point, one of his coaches urged him to reconsider his future as a racer. "We drove past a construction site and he said it might be a good idea to rethink my career," Beloki said. "He said I wouldn't be going anywhere as a pro."

But more than anything, Beloki had a dogged attitude to cycling. Although he was often overshadowed by the likes of Gonzalez de Galdeano and a flurry of stars at Euskaltel, Beloki kept plugging away.

Third place in the 1999 Spanish national championships got him noticed by Juan Fernández, the former Mapei team director, who was hustled in to right the troubled Festina ship after its notorious drugs bust in 1998. The Festina team's sponsor vowed to continue in the sport despite its name being implicated in the worst doping scandal in cycling history; meanwhile, the team was looking for new blood. Beloki joined Fernández, another of his Vitoria neighbors, at Festina for the 2000 season.

Beloki hit a nice streak in May that year, winning a hilly 24km time trial stage at Switzerland's Tour de Romandie and finishing second overall. Then he had a chance to show off his climbing legs at the Vuelta a Asturias in northern Spain, where he won a stage and the overall.

The wins earned him a spot in the 2000 Tour as a *domestique* to Festina team captain Christophe Moreau. Not much was expected of him, in part because he had never ridden a time trial longer than 25km and his only start at a three-week grand tour, the 1999 Vuelta, ended after only five stages.

"I told my parents if they wanted to see me [in the Tour], they'd better come to the Pyrénées," he said. "I didn't expect to make it to Paris."

But Beloki survived the first week, and then snuck into the top ten when he stayed close on the decisive Pyrenean climbing stage to Hautacam. He then followed Lance Armstrong and Jan Ullrich as best he could up Mont Ventoux and found himself sitting in third overall.

In the final time trial, he held off a challenge from Moreau to keep the third-place podium spot by a half minute. It was Spain's second Tour podium since Miguel Induráin won in 1995, but even Beloki had a hard time believing it.

"I don't remember much about that first Tour," Beloki said. "It was all kind of like a dream."

RIDING FOR SAIZ

Beloki found the team he was looking for when Spanish squad ONCE won the bidding war for his services following the 2000 Tour. Headed by sport director Manolo Saiz, ONCE had won just about everything in cycling but couldn't find the right leader for the Tour de France. Frenchman Laurent Jalabert and Swiss star Alex Zülle were never able to deliver the goods when it came to the world's biggest race.

Saiz, a cagey tactician whose ambition and fatherly instincts blend well with the Spanish contingent, was the perfect sport director for Beloki. By his own admission, Beloki requires a strong figure to keep him focused. "I need a firm hand and discipline," Beloki confirmed. "The only director who can do this is Manolo."

Things went well under Saiz's stern but loving watch. Beloki finished second at the Bicicleta Vasca and won two stages and the overall at the Tour of Catalonia, Spain's preferred warm-up race for the Tour.

Beloki returned to the Tour in 2001 with bigger ambitions and more pressure, yet he was able to confirm his 2000 performance with another third-place finish. The following year's Tour went even better, when he finished second overall and then placed third in the Vuelta a España later in the season.

Despite two grand tour podiums in one year and three straight Tour podiums, Beloki's cautious, calculated riding style evoked little excitement. His performances appeared flat when compared with the daring exploits from such compatriots as José Maria Jiménez, Roberto Laiseka, and Oscar Sevilla.

> "With Armstrong being so superior, it's impossible to attack," Beloki explained, echoing the laments of many rivals. "I tried to attack, but his blue train snuffed everything out. Then he flies past you like a motorcycle."

The hardworking Beloki was accused of being nothing more than a *chupareuda*—a wheel-sucker—about the worst insult anyone can throw at a Spanish rider. "With Armstrong being so superior, it's impossible to attack," Beloki explained, echoing the laments of many rivals. "I tried to attack, but his blue train snuffed everything out. Then he flies past you like a motorcycle."

By 2003, a newly confident Beloki had had enough of the critics. He vowed to be aggressive and risk everything rather than just follow wheels. "I'd rather attack and fail and finish 20th than just follow the others," Beloki said. "This year I will attack with everything I have."

Beloki demonstrated his new resolve with a string of sorties on L'Alpe d'Huez, forcing Armstrong to chase him down each time. It was another Basque, Iban Mayo, who tore away to take a dramatic stage victory, but it was Beloki who was poised in second place overall just 40 seconds behind Armstrong's yellow jersey. The next day's stage to Gap would mark the end of the first chapter of Beloki's career. Everything else beyond that fateful day would start from zero. Beloki doesn't like it when he's remembered more for his dramatic crash in the ninth stage of the 2003 Tour de France than the positive things he's accomplished in his career. "I don't want that to be the thing that people remember about me," Beloki said. "I want them to remember that I stood on the podium for three consecutive years. I realize I have to return to that podium for people to forget that image."

It might take more than that for the public to forget Beloki's horrific crash. In one of the decisive moments of the nail-biting 2003 Tour, the blond-haired Kazakh Alexander Vinokourov forced a 15-second gap over the Rochette when Armstrong and Beloki gave chase.

Soaring temperatures and overheated brakes on Beloki's carbon-fiber wheels spelled disaster. Beloki was driving the chase into the final two turns of the descent, before the back road joined the N94 highway for the short run into Gap, when he came hurtling into a sweeping right turn.

"I still remember it like it was yesterday," Beloki said. "People said I came in too fast, but it was my wheels that caused the problems. My brake pads weren't catching and when they did, my back wheel just locked up."

Beloki's rear wheel fishtailed and then his rear tire exploded as he tried to control the bike. Beloki "high-sided" over the bike, slamming hard on his right side, the impact breaking his right femur, elbow, and wrist.

"It was one of those moments that I relive in my mind," he said. "It happened very fast, but it was also very slow. I can remember watching the road come toward me as I fell. It was like slow motion."

Armstrong miraculously avoided crashing into Beloki and made a split-second decision to steer his bike to the left before picking his way across a field of stubble to safety. "Beloki could have been the spoiler here," Armstrong said. "He could have been better than Jan [Ullrich] and he could have been better than me. And I know that."

Beloki's teammates rushed to his side, and kneeled there helplessly as he screamed in agony. "There's no pain like that," he said later. "I still get shivers when I think about it."

DIFFICULT COMEBACK

Many race followers thought Beloki's career was finished the moment he smashed onto the hot, sticky asphalt on that Bastille Day in 2003. But he confounded the skeptics by vowing to come back. Beloki desperately wanted to continue with Saiz, but the ONCE trust was ending its longtime cycling sponsorship deal, leaving the team without a title sponsor at the end of the 2003 season.

Incredibly, despite his injuries and the prospect of a slow recovery, the French team Brioches La Boulangère signed Beloki to a two-year contract worth a million euros per year for the 2004 season. Beloki insisted he'd fully recovered, but he soon butted heads with the French team's management staff, who wouldn't allow him to use his preferred asthma treatment, Pulmicort, because high levels can trigger a doping positive for banned corticoids. Poor results followed and Beloki unhappily parted with the French team in June 2004. He quickly signed on with a new Spanish team, Saunier Duval, to race the Vuelta, but he pulled out early and was seriously considering retirement.

By this time, Saiz was back in the game with a big-dollar sponsorship deal with Liberty Seguros, the Spanish arm of American insurance giant Liberty Mutual, and he offered Beloki a rope at the end of the season. After a season in the wilderness, Beloki was happy to be back in the Saiz fold.

"Without Manolo, I'm not sure I would have been able to continue," Beloki said. "This is like home to me."

Beloki's 2005 comeback wasn't pretty. He didn't finish one major race the entire season, pulling out of the Giro d'Italia as well as the Tour of Switzerland. Saiz took a big gamble to bring Beloki to the Tour.

In that act of faith, Saiz was rewarding Beloki for his perseverance. And he was also hoping Beloki would pay him back with another Tour podium. Not in 2005, but perhaps '06 or '07.

CHAPTER 20 | STAGE 13

Horner and Chavanel
Go Down in a Standoff

Just after 5 p.m. on a torid, windy afternoon, Davitamon-Lotto teammates Johan Van Summeren and Wim Vansevenant were riding side by side, ten minutes behind the peloton, their jobs over for the day. The two Belgian *domestiques* had raced hard for most of the 173.5km stage from Miramas to Montpellier, helping to close a nine-minute gap on five breakaways. When the gap was inside 30 seconds, 20km from the finish, they sat up, exhausted.

As they rolled slowly toward the finish, they knew that their teammates were trying to put the finishing touches on the effort. They'd be reeling in the break and maneuvering team leader Robbie McEwen into position to get a shot at a third stage win. But via their team radios, Van Summeren and Vansevenant learned that the task wasn't that straightforward. Perhaps the prediction by their American teammate Fred Rodriguez was proving correct.

Before the day's start, Rodriguez said that a breakaway would take it to the line. "These stages between the climbing days almost always end up with a breakaway," the American said. "We'll be looking to see if we can set up Robbie, but I don't think it will come to that."

Rodriguez looked like a soothsayer when five riders went clear just 17km after leaving the start in the little town of Miramas, northeast of Marseille. Another American, Saunier Duval–Prodir's Chris Horner, was in the move with three Frenchmen, Ludovic Turpin of ag2r, Thomas Voeckler of Bouygues Télécom, Carlos Da Cruz of Française des Jeux, and a Spaniard, Juan Antonio Flecha of Fassa Bortolo.

Horner made it into the day's big break for the second time in three days not because he was told to cover it by his team—in fact, his instructions were exactly the opposite—

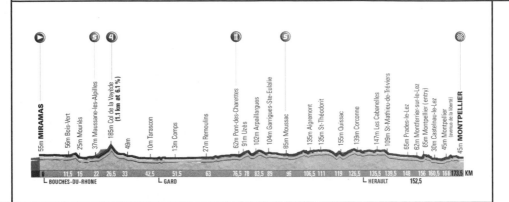

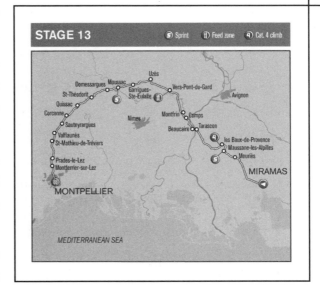

but because his sense of race tactics wouldn't let him do otherwise. "At the team meeting, they said don't do anything, just relax, recover, wait for Saturday and Sunday, try and recover," Horner said. "But Flecha went, and I was there. Saunier Duval had to have someone in the break, so I had to follow it."

Within 10km, atop the day's only climb, the Cat. 4 Col de la Vayède, twisting above the tawny stone houses and faded tile roofs of ancient Les Baux-de-Provence, the break had a two-minute lead. With Horner the highest ranked on general classification, starting the day in 29th, 15:22 behind race leader Armstrong, the field was content to let the gap stretch to 9:20 at the 50km mark.

That was when Davitamon team manager Marc Sergeant gave Van Summeren, Vansevenant, and their colleagues the order to start the chase. The sudden jolt in speed wasn't welcomed by everyone, particularly the Spanish rider wearing the best young rider's white jersey, Alejandro Valverde. His knee had been hurting ever since he had accidentally hit it against his handlebars during the team time trial. The pain wasn't too bad until he started climbing the Madeleine, the morning after his stage win at Courchevel. Now, his team doctor feared he had tendinitis, and agreed that he should pull out of the race if it didn't improve. So Valverde stopped at the feed zone and climbed into one of the Illes Balears team cars.

"It's better for me to stop now. The way my knee is, it's just not possible," Valverde said. "I'm sorry to be pulling out. The positive thing is I've won a stage, which has been enormous for me."

Meanwhile, McEwen's men drove the chase, steadily eating into the break's lead: 6:30 with 100km remaining, 2:30 with 55km to go, and one minute with 35km left. Finally, with only 20km remaining and the gap down to just 35 seconds, Da Cruz attacked the break. Though he was quickly brought back, the move by the Frenchman wasn't without incident, as Horner was later fined 200 Swiss francs for "incorrect behavior toward a rider" for reportedly throwing a water bottle at Da Cruz.

"I didn't throw the bottle," Horner claimed later. "I just sprayed it, and I didn't even hit him [with the water] because I knew they would fine me. I just sprayed it near him so he knew I was pissed off."

> "He was saying, 'No, no, we don't want any more time.' And I was like, 'We don't want any more time? We're going to need at least 12 minutes.' We only had nine . . ."

Why so angry? "When we're doing 50 kilometers an hour in the break, Da Cruz is pulling through at 43 and just killing our speed. He was saying, 'No, no, we don't want any more time.' And I was like, 'We don't want any more time? We're going to need at least 12 minutes,'" Horner said. "We only had nine," he continued. "He started doing those cheap little pulls and he was pulling the least and pulling the slowest, and then he was the first one to attack us . . . but everyone was either done or they just didn't want to commit 100 percent. I can't pull four guys around and still win."

With the gap under 30 seconds, Cofidis' Sylvain Chavanel jumped out of the bunch with 14km to go, and when he tried to race straight past the break, Horner was the only one able to follow. The pair held a lead of 20 seconds or less for the long loop through the hot streets of Montpellier, aided a little by Armstrong, who told his team to neutralize the chase a little "to help another American."

The gap held steady despite what was going on between Horner and Chavanel. "I figured he was fresher so he had to do the work," said Horner. "When he first caught us and attacked, I went with the move. Then he just kept attacking. I was like, 'Come on, we're 10 kilometers out, you can't do it by yourself!' I told him if he attacked me again I wouldn't pull, so he said okay."

The two were 18 seconds clear at the 5km-to-go marker, 15 seconds at 4km, and 10 seconds ahead at 2km. The gap was still 8 seconds as they sped into the final kilometer, and 6 seconds with 500 meters left. It looked as though all the work done by McEwen's teammates might be for naught. But Rodriguez was now at the front of the pack, racing as fast as he could to close the gap at a speed that McEwen later would call "amazing."

Just as amazing was the effort made by Horner, who had been at the front of the race for more than 150km, and was now going for the victory. But first, he and Chavanel had to stay clear. "He came through with 900 meters [remaining], and from there he was going to have to do the rest on his own," said Horner. "I mean, I was in the break all day; if he can't beat a guy that was in the break all day, it's not my fault. I could hear my director yelling 'Go! Go! Go!' but I played for the win. We both knew that one was going to lose if they led it out. I waited and he waited. I had to have him lead it out for me to beat him. If I had taken a pull he would have just sat on and beaten me. I'm not here for second; I'm only going for the win."

One of the ironies of the situation was the huge gulf in cycling status between Chavanel and Horner. The pampered Frenchman, 25, nicknamed Mimosa by his friends in the peloton, is paid more than a million dollars a year. Cofidis signed him to replace the EPO-suspended David Millar. To date, Chavanel had failed to deliver except for a stage win at the Four Days of Dunkirk in May.

In contrast, Horner was on the minimum wage for a UCI ProTour racer. Despite that, the Californian represented his Saunier Duval–Prodir team's best chance of winning something big at the Tour. He started this stage 48 places and 48 minutes ahead of Chavanel in the overall standings.

As Horner and Chavanel continued their standoff around the final bend, 200 meters from the line, Rodriguez was pacing McEwen toward a sprint with green-jersey rival Stuart O'Grady. But Horner hadn't given up hope. "When I was coming around Chavanel, I thought I might have the stage win. Then here comes Robbie and the gang: zoom, zoom, zoom!"

And just like that, with 50 meters to go, McEwen raced by Horner to take the stage win from O'Grady, with Rodriguez crossing in 3rd, Horner 10th, and Chavanel 16th.

McEwen paid a special thanks to his lead-out man. "My last guy, Rodriguez, practically delivered me to the line. Today is really a team victory. The amount of work today is absolutely incredible. They rode their hearts out all day. It's hard for anybody not in the race to realize how hard they worked today."

Two men who did realize were still 6km back down the road, riding side by side. Suddenly, as they were given the news on their radio receivers, Van Summeren and Vansevenant joyfully thrust their arms in the air. It really was a team victory.

STAGE 13: MIRAMAS-MONTPELLIER

1. Robbie McEwen (Aus), Davitamon-Lotto, 173.5km in 3:43:14 (46.633kph); **2.** Stuart O'Grady (Aus), Cofidis; **3. Fred Rodriguez (USA), Davitamon-Lotto; 4. Guido Trenti (USA), Quick Step–Innergetic; 5.** Thor Hushovd (N), Crédit Agricole, all s.t.

GENERAL CLASSIFICATION

1. Lance Armstrong (USA), Discovery Channel, 50:13:50

2. Michael Rasmussen (Dk), Rabobank, 00:38

3. Christophe Moreau (F), Crédit Agricole, 02:34

4. Ivan Basso (I), CSC, 02:40

5. Santlago Botero (Col), Phonak, 03:48

CHAPTER 21
A Renaissance Man:
Horner Makes His Tour Debut

Chris Horner doesn't pull any punches. Just listen to his immediate and perhaps too honest assessment of his ride in the Tour's second alpine stage from Courchevel to Briançon. "That was hard," said the 33-year-old Californian moments after crossing the line. "The team just used me up and killed me. I went with the early move and that just put me in the red. And I was in the red the whole way through the valley with Discovery driving it, and in the red up the climb, in the red to try to get back on, and I get dropped anyways. So basically every day I've been racing, and it'll take me five days of doing nothing now [to recover]."

It's difficult to imagine any other rider in the Tour saying that his team, in Horner's case Saunier Duval–Prodir, used him up and killed him. Riders on ProTour teams are more diplomatic. They say how strong their teams are, how much they appreciate the efforts of their teammates, and they frequently thank their sponsors. And they're always conscious of how their words might by written up by the press. Not Horner.

Despite being on a Spanish team, Horner doesn't speak Spanish. And because he was one of the best riders on its Tour team, the Spanish media was writing about him constantly. Sometimes, his quick-fire quotes didn't get translated quite right. Take the case of one Spanish journalist in the pressroom, who beamed, "Horner is my hero. He's sold his house, split with his girlfriend, sacrificed everything to live his dream of racing the Tour, and when he goes home, he'll be living with his mother."

That's a rough translation of what Horner had said, but it garbled a few key facts. In the spring of 2005, he did split with his longtime girlfriend, who was living in San Diego with the couple's three young children. And, in order to ride for his new team, he was working around a salary that was significantly lower than what he was accustomed to in the United States; the cut in pay forced him to sell his house in Bend, Oregon.

"I did a lot to get over here," Horner confirmed. "I sold the house. I wasn't making the same kind of money, and I couldn't afford to have a house that no one was living in back in the States. You come over and take half the pay, they end up taking taxes out, it ends up being a third of what I'm used to making. I don't need to tell anyone out there what it's like to go from making something to a third of it the following year."

And pursuing his dream of riding the Tour wasn't the primary cause of his split with his partner. "It had nothing to do with coming over to Europe," Horner said. "It had everything to do with cycling. I'm sure there are many women out there that know what it's like to have their husbands or boyfriends gone a lot, how difficult it is, and it was too hard on her that way. And that made it too hard on me."

BROKEN HIP

After three seasons spent atop the domestic rankings, and wondering what it would take to land a European contract, Horner placed an excellent eighth at the 2004 world road championship in Verona, Italy, and almost immediately landed a contract with Saunier Duval. He quickly proved his worth by placing 11th at the late-season Tour of Lombardy, the semi-mountainous Italian one-day classic where Horner was climbing alongside Ivan Basso and the race's eventual winner Damiano Cunego.

His 2005 season began with a broken hip, suffered at Tirreno-Adriatico in mid-March, and he wasn't able to race again until the Wachovia week of racing in Pennsylvania, in June. He rode strongly in all three of the Wachovia series races, but that did not earn him a spot on Saunier Duval's Tour team. So Horner flew to the Tour of Switzerland where, with less than ten days of racing in his legs, he won a stage in a mountaintop finish at Arosa in the Swiss Alps, battled with the likes of Jan Ullrich on the climbs, and ended up in fifth overall. With just two weeks to go to the Tour de France, Horner was in.

> **He won a stage in a mountaintop finish at Arosa in the Swiss Alps, battled with the likes of Jan Ullrich on the climbs, and ended up in fifth overall. With just two weeks to go to the Tour de France, Horner was in.**

If Horner's first half of the season was a struggle, it didn't show at the Tour. Though it was his debut, he showed time and again that he wasn't afraid to ride with the race favorites. On the Tour's first tough day, Horner stayed with the leaders in the Vosges Mountains when Lance Armstrong was isolated from his Discovery Channel teammates. Three days later, he finished 20th on the first alpine stage into Courchevel, four minutes behind the stage winner. And then, the following day into Briançon, he rode into a break-away that included the high rollers Francisco Mancebo, Santiago Botero, and eventual stage winner Alexander Vinokourov. On reflection, Horner admitted it was a stage full of rookie mistakes.

"As soon as Vinokourov came across I should have pulled out of the break," Horner said. "Experience should have told me not to pull even with those guys, which I was. Or I should have dropped back to the group, which would have been the wisest of the choices."

After coming out of the break near the top of the mighty Col de la Madeleine, Horner was caught by the field, and though he rode with the yellow jersey group on the long val-ley road and up the difficult Col du Télégraphe, he was again dropped 5km from the top of the Col du Galibier. "I made another mistake when I got dropped the second time, and I tried to get back on. I should have just dropped off and easily rode in. Instead, I rode the last 5 kilometers at 100 percent, trying to get back on. The writing was put on the wall mul-tiple times that day, and it was my own fault. Experience had told me not to do it, but being at the Tour told me to go ahead and try it."

LONG ROAD TO THE TOUR

Now that he was finally at the Tour, Horner must have wondered at times what might have been. Why was this talented athlete riding his first Tour de France at age 33? Why was he racing for minimum wage when his salary should have been in six figures? The answers are long and complicated.

Let's go back to 1997. Horner signed a two-year contract with the French team Française des Jeux after some promising results with the domestic Nutra-Fig team the previous season, including a victory at the First Union Classic in Lancaster, Pennsylvania, and fourth place at the USPRO Championship. Horner grew up in Southern California where he rode a bike to get around and later became one of the state's best junior racers. He became a typical early-nineties bike bum, and even beat Lance Armstrong in the 1991

San Diego Grand Prix, when they were both 19. While Armstrong turned pro the following year and won the world pro championship in 1993, Horner stayed on the domestic circuit and eventually turned pro with John Wordin's Nutra-Fig team in 1996.

At 5' 8" inches and 143 pounds, Horner doesn't have the power of an Armstrong, but he always showed all-around ability: a good climber, a pretty decent time trialist, and a not-bad sprinter. It was those qualities that attracted Marc Madiot, a French rider who at the end of his distinguished racing career (including two Paris-Roubaix victories) rode with the U.S.-based Subaru-Montgomery team. Madiot kept his eye on Horner and decided that he could be molded into a good Tour de France rider with Française des Jeux.

Once he moved to Europe in 1997, Horner's good results dried up. When a journalist called him in Nice, on the French Riviera, where he had moved into a small, rented apartment with his young family, Horner said he was sick and wasn't racing. A baby was crying in the background. He said life was hard. When he did race, he rode as a *domestique* for classics riders Davide Rebellin of Italy and Mauro Gianetti of Switzerland.

His health eventually improved and he started getting some better results in early 1998. In an important pre-Tour stage race, the Midi Libre, Horner took an excellent 8th place in the stage 3 time trial. He was starting to live up to Madiot's expectations and the French team director named the American, then 26, to his Tour de France squad.

It seemed that Horner's European career was about to take off, but shortly before the Tour he broke his wrist. That was a huge disappointment. Once the wrist was healed, though, Horner again showed signs of better form, taking 9th place in the prestigious Grand Prix des Nations time trial. It was enough to clinch a one-year extension on his contract, but after a mediocre spring in 1999, in which a 15th place in Italy's season-opener, the Laigueglia Trophy, was a "highlight," Horner's European experience was about to end.

Back home, Wordin had built up his small Nutra-Fig team into a program sponsored by the Mercury division of Ford. He offered a leadership role to Horner, who immediately repaid Wordin's confidence by winning Malaysia's Tour de Langkawi in February, followed by the Redlands Classic in March. Mercury then took a European trip, getting a starting slot in the Critérium International, a two-day, three-stage race run by the Tour de France organizers. Horner was 11th on the second day's mountain stage, finishing in a snow shower near the summit of the Col d'Aubisque, and later in the day placed 3rd in the concluding time trial at Pau. He finished 8th overall.

It looked like Horner was going to get back on track in Europe, but his team's major cosponsor went into bankruptcy and the team folded at the end of the year. In successive seasons, he stayed in the United States, joining the Prime Alliance team, then Saturn, and then Webcor Builders. Along the way, he picked up victories in most of the major U.S. races, including the Tour of Georgia and San Francisco Grand Prix in 2003.

Horner had nothing left to prove in North America. He had won USA Cycling's season-long pro series three years in a row; the USPRO Championship was the only big race not on his win list. So he headed to Europe for the 2004 world's, and met up there with his former Française des Jeux leader, Gianetti, who had become the manager of Saunier Duval–Prodir. Just like that, he was back on track for the Tour.

FINALLY, THE TOUR

Seven years after he should have made his debut, Horner approached his first Tour de France like a kid in a toy shop, testing all the different experiences, stopping to sign autographs for the fans, happily answering questions thrown at him by journalists, and just relishing the magic of the race. "So far it's been exciting, it's been fun," he said. "I've just been taking in all the crowds and the energy of the race itself too. It's been great."

When the CSC team put on the pressure on the Tour's first real climb in the stage into Nancy, Horner was right there. "Yeah, I was third wheel going over that thing," he said at the rain-drenched stage finish. "I didn't want to take any chances. As soon as we got on the hill, I was like, 'Uh-oh, better get to the front in case there's five of these or something.' I just heard the finish was really hard, really hard. I didn't know whether there was going to be multiple hits like that—I didn't expect the hill to be so long and so steep. But that was the only hard hill."

By riding at the front of the peloton, Horner was able to see and join a series of promising moves, and it looked as though his aggressiveness was finally going to pay dividends on the stage into Montpellier. After breakaway companion Sylvain Chavanel pulled through with 900 meters remaining, Horner decided that would be the last pull for the day. It was a finish reminiscent of the final shootout at the USPRO Championship in June, where in a three-man break, Chris Wherry attacked and won as Horner waited vainly for Danny Pate to chase Wherry down. Still, Horner said if he could relive that final kilometer in Montpellier with Chavanel, he wouldn't change a thing.

"I've seen it happen to many other riders and I knew it was going to happen to me sooner or later," Horner said, still smiling about the day's dramatic outcome. "Too bad it had to come at the Tour. Still, it was a spectacular day. The only reason we got caught is because Chavanel didn't want second and I didn't want second. I would have loved to have won it, but I had a blast, and all said and done, it was a great experience. If I don't get another shot at winning a stage, that was a pretty good feeling. I'm just ecstatic to be here."

Likewise, Horner said he had no regrets about what it took for him to get to the Tour. "No way, you've got to do it," he said. "I'm just so happy to have been a part of the Tour. I didn't want to finish my career without winning a big race in Europe, and I did that at the Tour of Switzerland. I certainly didn't want to finish my career without doing the Tour de France. That doesn't mean my career is done, but that means when it is done, I've done everything I needed to do."

CHAPTER 22 | STAGE 14
Armstrong Purges His Demons at Ax-3 Domaines

Every year since Lance Armstrong first won the Tour de France, his rivals said they'd come back the following year and go on the attack. They said they would eliminate Armstrong's teammates, and then, like vultures, they'd pick off the team leader.

The closest anyone came to fulfilling those predictions came in 2003, the day after dehydration caused Armstrong to lose more than a minute and a half to archrival Jan Ullrich in a baking-hot time trial at Cap'Découverte. The heat wave continued the next day on the first Pyrenean stage that ended with two vicious climbs: the 15km, 8.1-percent Port de Pailhères and the 8km, 8.3-percent climb to the Ax-3 Domaines summit finish. Perhaps this was the moment that everyone was waiting for. Armstrong was vulnerable, and it looked as though Ullrich, then racing for Bianchi; Alex Vinokourov of Team Telekom; or Ivan Basso, then with Fassa Bortolo, would go on the attack.

That was the expectation, but no one made a truly aggressive move on the awesomely difficult Pailhères climb. It wasn't until the second half of the second climb, only 3 or 4km from the finish line, that Vinokourov finally accelerated. Ullrich immediately counter-attacked, and Armstrong was struggling. But there wasn't enough climbing left for major time gains, and the race leader kept his yellow jersey by a handful of seconds.

Two years later, and two weeks into this Tour, the same two mountain climbs awaited the riders at the end of stage 14 on another day of 95-degree temperatures. Armstrong's team had shown signs of weakness, and his lead over runner-up Michael Rasmussen was only 38 seconds. So, once again, there was speculation that the opposition would attack.

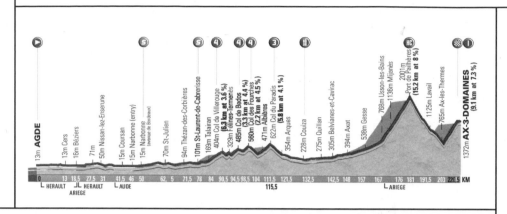

That speculation grew into a strong expectation partway up the deep, narrow limestone canyon of the Aude River as the peloton headed toward the base of the Port de Pailhères.

"It's scary when you see, five kilometers before the bottom [of the climb], an entire team go to the front and start riding as fast as they can," Armstrong later said, describing a mass breakout by Ullrich's T-Mobile team. "You see what's going to happen, the order they're in. You see what they're setting up for. So in that situation you either fight back, or you run away. I was motivated at the time to not be necessarily put down by such strong tactics. But, I have to say, I think it was the right thing to do. They did a good job. If I was the director, that would have been my call too."

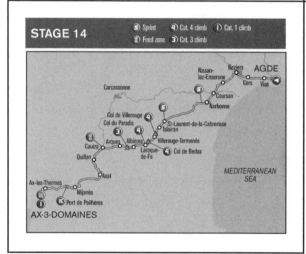

Seeing T-Mobile's tactics so clearly meant that Armstrong would not be taken by surprise. But his team was still thrown off balance by an all-out attack by five members of the German team on the steep initial slopes of the Pailhères. Within moments, and with the toughest 40km of the stage to go, Armstrong suddenly had no teammates to cover the moves about to be launched by Vinokourov, Basso, and Ullrich.

"[My team] is not made to do those all-out sprints," Armstrong said when asked about his isolation. "T-Mobile was all-out sprinting. The Discovery team was made to ride a medium-fast tempo for a long time, to take the lead group from 50 to 30 to 15 guys. They disrupted our plan. Their tactics were fine; I was left alone, but when you ride like that, no one stays around long. You not only eliminate your rivals, you eliminate your teammates as well."

DESTRUCTIVE CLIMB

A factor that Armstrong didn't mention in his team's annihilation was the mountain pass they were climbing. This wasn't a smoothly graded boulevard like that leading to Courchevel in the Alps. The Port de Pailhères was rated *hors catégorie* after the organizers mistakenly gave it only a Cat. 1 designation in 2003. The climb is so narrow, and the switchbacks near the top so tight, that the publicity caravan vehicles were diverted around it, a rare happening at the Tour. The grades switch wildly between 4 and 12 percent, with some pitches close to 15 percent on the hairpins. That's not the sort of climb where a team like Discovery can ride a steady 20 to 25kph tempo. In places, even the leaders were riding at closer to 15kph.

"The first 5 kilometers of the Pailhères was very difficult," said one of those leaders, Levi Leipheimer. "A little bit too much for me. I think I will always suffer when we come into the bottom of climbs like that; the [speed] is just too hot for me."

A different perspective came from Chris Horner, who had been in the previous day's stage-long break and knew he would have to ride conservatively on these climbs in order to survive. "As soon as it started going up," Horner said, "I just dropped off and rode my own pace. It's funny, because honestly when you're going up with the leaders, it doesn't even seem that steep, but when you go up there like I did, you're just like, 'Huh, this is *crazy*.'"

While Horner rode at the back, doing the best he could on the steep grades, Leipheimer was trying to pace himself back to a break formed by Ullrich, Basso, Armstrong, and Phonak's Floyd Landis. "I just rode my own race, and it took me awhile but I came back," said Leipheimer. "And at the top I felt fine. By then, I think they'd kind of taken it out of their legs with all the accelerations, and I never once did an acceleration. So that was good."

Leipheimer did well to pull himself back in contention on this monster climb, especially when KoM leader Rasmussen, and contenders like Vinokourov, Mancebo, Evans, and Klöden, were all dropping a minute or so back. Basso was perhaps the strongest on the Pailhères, but his repeated bursts weren't strong enough to dislodge Ullrich, Armstrong, or the two other Americans.

TOWARD DESTINY

After withstanding the onslaught by Basso and the T-Mobile riders, Armstrong was happy to top the Pailhères alongside Basso, Ullrich, Landis, and Leipheimer. As they raced through a tunnel of flag-waving fans at the 6,565-foot summit, the five were still some four minutes behind the day's solo breakaway rider, Georg Totschnig.

The Gerolsteiner coleader almost quit the Tour before the Alps because of a heavy cold. "I had no energy and wanted to go home," Totschnig admitted. But he felt better coming into the Pyrénées and was one of seven men who split from a 15-strong group that raced clear on the flat, straight roads leading away from the start at the port of Agde on the Mediterranean coast. A couple of hours later, on leaving the chasmlike Aude canyon, the seven had a 7:15 lead on the pack. That didn't seem enough to hold off the leaders with 23km of tough climbing in the final 44km, so Totschnig quickly left behind the other six, all of whom were eventually caught and passed by the Armstrong group.

The Austrian conceded half of his advantage on the Pailhères climb, but held his own on the long, winding descent. With a headwind on the downhill, none of Armstrong's rivals wanted to make a premature effort, and they were caught by Mancebo, Rasmussen, Evans, Klöden, and Euskaltel's Haimar Zubeldia. The resultant ten-strong group was 4:10 behind Totschnig at the 15km-to-go point, and about to be joined by a rapidly approaching Vinokourov. The Kazakh exploded into the picture in the streets of Ax-les-Thermes in the valley bottom, and then he was the first to attack on the steep early slopes of the final climb.

It seemed that T-Mobile, with three riders, could finally put the solo Armstrong on the ropes. Klöden and Ullrich followed teammate Vinokourov in his attack, but they couldn't dislodge the yellow jersey. And when Basso lent his power to the acceleration, Klöden and Vinokourov were both dropped, while Mancebo, Rasmussen, Evans, and Zubeldia all fell back again.

The gap to Totschnig was down to two minutes halfway up the final climb, where Armstrong surprised his companions by putting in a strong surge that only Basso and Ullrich could follow. Landis and Leipheimer trailed at a short distance.

"Floyd and I hung for half of it, and then we both went steady," said Leipheimer. "Floyd was kind of dragging me along. It was all I could do to follow. But it was great because we could always see the three in front of us."

Among those three, Ullrich tried one more attack, but Basso and Armstrong followed him immediately. "[Ullrich and Basso] were both stronger than we saw in the Alps," Armstrong said later. "Ivan seemed to be the stronger of the two, working more. When he was on the front he was riding fast. He was doing most of the attacking. But at the same time, Jan was there also. He's a tough dude. He kept following the attacks and kept following regardless. He was immediately on the wheel, which is an indication that he's strong too."

Not strong enough though. When the six-time champion again went hard inside 2km to go, atypically dancing on the pedals to maximize his speed, Ullrich finally lost contact. "When Armstrong went I had nothing left," Ullrich told Eurosport. "We had to go on the attack, but it just didn't work out. Armstrong matched everything we did."

Ahead, Totschnig looked to be in a desperate situation. His head and torso were covered in sweat, and his legs were starting to buckle. "I couldn't see myself matching Armstrong on the final climb," Totschnig said. "I just went as hard as I could, ignoring the heat. I didn't believe I could do it until I crossed the line. I didn't even zip up my jersey; I hope my sponsor will forgive me."

"I just went as hard as I could, ignoring the heat. I didn't believe I could do it until I crossed the line. I didn't even zip up my jersey; I hope my sponsor will forgive me."

Besides the relief of holding on to win, the 34-year-old veteran knew that he had just become only the second Austrian to take a stage of the Tour, seventy four years after Max Bulla, who raced without a team when the Tour was contested by nations, not trade teams. By outsprinting small breakaway groups at Dinan, Marseille, and Aix-les-Bains, Bulla won three stages of the 1931 Tour. Totschnig was ecstatic with taking just one.

He crossed the line 56 seconds ahead of Armstrong, who sprinted clear of Basso in the final meters. Without really extending himself, Armstrong put time into all of his opponents, and pushed his lead on Rasmussen to a more comfortable 1:41.

It wasn't hugely exciting, but it was all the Texan needed to do to consolidate his grip on the yellow jersey, and purge those dehydration demons from two years earlier. Asked if his struggles in that difficult stage in 2003 had crossed his mind, the Tour champ said, "Yeah, for sure, but I kept trying to remember my training day here six weeks ago versus the 2003 Tour, because I felt better then."

Armstrong was feeling even better now. He had taken everything that Basso, Ullrich, and the T-Mobile team had thrown at him. But as dominant as his day had been, his opponents wouldn't be giving up quite yet. "As I have said all along," Ullrich stated, "we will fight the whole way to Paris."

STAGE 14: AGDE–AX-3 DOMAINES

1. Georg Totschnig (A), Gerolsteiner, 220.5km in 5:43:43 (38.491kph); **2. Lance Armstrong (USA), Discovery Channel, at 0:56; 3.** Ivan Basso (I), CSC, at 0:58; **4.** Jan Ullrich (G), T-Mobile, at 1:16; **5. Levi Leipheimer (USA), Gerolsteiner, at 1:31; 6. Floyd Landis (USA), Phonak, s.t.; 7.** Francisco Mancebo (F), Illes Balears, at 1:47; **8.** Michael Rasmussen (Dk), Rabobank, s.t.; **9.** Andreas Klöden (G), T-Mobile, at 2:06; **10.** Haimar Zubeldia (Sp), Euskaltel-Euskadi, at 2:20.

GENERAL CLASSIFICATION

1. Lance Armstrong (USA), Discovery Channel, 55:58:17

2. Michael Rasmussen (Dk), Rabobank, 01:41

3. Ivan Basso (I), CSC, 02:46

4. Jan Ullrich (G), T-Mobile, 04:34

5. Levi Leipheimer (USA), Gerolsteiner, 04:45

CHAPTER 23
Gerolsteiner's Tough Guys:
Leipheimer and Totschnig

On the eve of the 92nd Tour de France, Levi Leipheimer sat in the shade of a tent along a sandy beach in Fromentine, the small Atlantic resort town that was being invaded by Planet Tour. As windsurfers frolicked in the choppy waters off the Pointe Notre-Dame-des-Monts, beneath the bridge that the Tour riders would follow in the next day's time trial to Noirmoutier-en-l'Île, Leipheimer was sounding more confident than ever.

He was also more cautious than ever. This race was make or break for Leipheimer's Tour ambitions, and he wasn't going to risk getting too cozy the day before it all started.

"I can't shake your hand," Leipheimer apologized to a small group of journalists who showed up for Gerolsteiner's pre-Tour soirée. "I don't want to pick up anything."

Germs aside, this was a new Leipheimer: more focused, more determined, more assertive. "I am definitely more ambitious," he said. "When I finished the Tour last year, the last few days was when it really sparked something in me. It opened my eyes and I realized that I needed to work a little harder."

After twice placing top ten in three Tour starts (his 2003 Tour ended in a stage 1 pileup), the 31-year-old revised everything in the off-season. Changes included a new diet ("no dessert, no wine, no coffee for four months"), a new team (Gerolsteiner), a new and improved position on the bike (thanks to close work with bike sponsor Specialized), and a new trainer (ex-Motorola team doctor Massimo Testa).

His collaboration with Testa was probably the most crucial change. The California-based Italian specialist helped fine-tune Leipheimer's training schedule, giving him precise power-meter measurements to aim for during his training rides. "I know what I have to do," Leipheimer said. "It's a training program more specifically tailored for me. It's helping me getting closer to the goals I want to achieve."

More than anything, Leipheimer wanted to prove that he deserved his status as a Tour team captain. And after a strong third-place finish in the 2005 Dauphiné Libéré, including two days in the race leader's jersey, Leipheimer knew his time had come. "When I finished the Dauphiné, I was like, man, I should have won that race. I felt like I was the most consistent, strongest rider there," he said. "So now I think, hey, with good luck, why can't I stand on the podium in Paris?"

NOTHING GOOD COMES EASY

Leipheimer's arrival as the Gerolsteiner team captain capped a hard-fought trajectory that took the American from the long shadows of the Rocky Mountains to the highest levels of professional cycling. It was never easy and always marked by a fierce independent streak and laserlike focus on improving.

"I am never fully satisfied with my performance," he said. "When you are, it's time to give up, because there's always something that you can improve on."

Unlike Lance Armstrong and George Hincapie, who were nurtured by their respective Motorola and U.S. Postal Service teams, Leipheimer had to carve his own path toward the Tour de France. And it's that self-sufficient, no-nonsense character that has helped him innumerable times throughout the nine years of his professional career.

Perhaps it's no coincidence that Leipheimer hails from the West. His family has been a stalwart fixture of Butte, Montana, since the 1930s, when Levi's grandfather moved to what was still very much a frontier town. Born on October 24, 1973, Leipheimer was the younger of two brothers and part of an active, outdoorsy family.

The ranch life was good, but when Leipheimer was just two years old a horse kicked him in the stomach and ruptured his intestines. He managed to recover, but the injury came back to haunt him nearly thirty years later. In August 2002, while he was racing in the Tour of the Netherlands just weeks after finishing eighth in his Tour de France debut, Leipheimer had intense stomach cramps after an evening meal. Hours later he was in a Dutch hospital bed. Scar tissue caused by the horse kick three decades earlier had blocked his intestines. An emergency three-hour surgery saved his life, but Leipheimer spent nearly two weeks on his back recovering.

"I think to most people it looks like a normal rebound, but it was pretty difficult," said Leipheimer, who lost 20 pounds as his muscles atrophied over the course of his hospital stay.

LEARNING FRENCH

The hospital time must have been difficult for Leipheimer, who grew up in a household where being outdoors was part of everyday life. Along with his older brother by seven years, Rob Leipheimer, who now runs the family business called The Outfitter, young Levi trekked to the mountains and soon took up ski racing.

By his early teens, Leipheimer was an accomplished skier and he went to high school in the prestigious Rowmark Ski Academy, a boarding school in Salt Lake City, to hone his skills. Among the school's alumni are Olympic skiing champions Hillary Lindh and Picabo Street.

At age 17, while downhill racing on the steep trails in Jackson Hole, Wyoming, Leipheimer crashed horribly and seriously injured his back, crushing some vertebrae. Doctors ordered him to ride a bike to rebuild his strength during the lengthy rehab. Leipheimer, who had already done some serious bicycle training, couldn't have been happier. He liked the speed, self-discipline, and hard work cycling demanded, and slowly his passion turned from skiing to cycling.

The Leipheimer brothers often trained together, racing up the 600-foot ascent on Butte's Main Street, something the pair dubbed, "the toughest mile in Montana." The efforts drew Leipheimer to the mystique of European bike races, and he started taking French classes. He dreamed of racing one day in Europe. "I knew someday if I wanted to race bikes, I would need to learn French," said Leipheimer, who impressed journalists at the 2005 Dauphiné by easily slipping into their language at news conferences.

Leipheimer started racing in local events in Montana and met up with Jason Van Marle, another local racer who shared Leipheimer's growing passion. Two years older than Leipheimer, Van Marle ventured to Belgium to try his luck in the amateur ranks.

According to a story from one of Leipheimer's teachers at the Rowmark school, Leipheimer was determined to make his dream come true. During the summer vacation between his junior and senior years in high school, Leipheimer took his savings and went to Belgium to try his hand with an amateur team Van Marle had contacted on Leipheimer's behalf. When the team manager found out Leipheimer was an American high school student on summer break, the incredulous Belgian informed Leipheimer there was no room for a part-time dreamer.

A distraught Leipheimer begged the manager for a shot. Touched by Leipheimer's passion, the manager caved in and let the American race for the weekend. Leipheimer promptly won a race. "When he has a goal, Levi is the most single-minded person I know," said his wife, ex-pro Canadian cyclist Odessa Gunn.

After graduating high school, Leipheimer and Van Marle returned to Belgium and chased their Tour de France dreams. For three years, they bounced around between amateur teams, winning the odd race, honing their French, sharing an apartment, and having the time of their lives.

"Nothing I do now is as hard as those days in Belgium," Leipheimer would later say. "I really learned to race the bike there. That was hard."

Leipheimer returned to the United States and took an important step in 1997 when he turned pro with Comptel Data Systems at the age of 23. In 1998, he joined Saturn and won a stage and the overall in Canada's Tour de Beauce. The next year, Leipheimer won the national time trial championship and got noticed by U.S. Postal Service. The team had just won its first Tour with Armstrong and was keen to add some American riders to its roster. Leipheimer fit the bill. But he wasn't about to get anywhere near the Tour.

SECOND STRING

When Leipheimer began racing with U.S. Postal in Europe, he realized his professional career was just starting. Like most of his new American colleagues, he quickly settled into Gerona, Spain, eventually buying a home with his wife and their growing horde of dogs and cats.

Being on Postal's so-called second string made life complicated, however. Riders that were part of the Tour squad garnered all the attention and energy of the staff, while the other riders were often left on the fringes of the team. "You never knew which races you were doing." Leipheimer said. "It was hard to get any sort of form to get any results."

Leipheimer made the most of his meager chances, picking up a few top ten finishes, and learning as much as he could from each race. He even bagged a victory, taking a time trial stage in the Circuit Franco-Belge. In 2001, he enjoyed a strong spring in California, winning a stage of the Sea Otter Classic and another at Redlands, but the Tour remained a distant dream. With experienced pros such as Tyler Hamilton and Viatcheslav Ekimov protecting Armstrong's flank, Leipheimer's Tour hopes seemed slim at best.

As the 2001 season drew to a close, Leipheimer was tapped to race the Vuelta a España as a support rider for former race champion Roberto Heras. The event changed his career. The stages of the three-week Vuelta are not nearly as long or hard as those in the Tour, but Leipheimer raced them with the tenacity of a Tour veteran.

He finished a strong third in the opening 12.3km time trial, just six seconds off David Millar's winning time. He showed resilience, hanging tough through the Pyrénées with another strong performance in the climbing time trial to Arcalis that kept him in fourth overall at the end of the second week.

Leipheimer entered the final stage, a 38km time trial, poised in fifth overall, just 1:35 behind third-place Heras. The American rode what was his best-ever flat time trial in Europe, finishing just 14 seconds behind stage winner Santiago Botero. Heras didn't do badly, considering the flat course in Madrid, but the climbing specialist could only muster 15th at 2:46, meaning Leipheimer leapfrogged into third place.

Support riders aren't supposed to outshine their leaders, of course, and Leipheimer admits the pair didn't even speak in the final days of the race. Heras thought the unknown American should simply work for him, while Leipheimer was told by team manager Johan Bruyneel to ride his own race.

Leipheimer became the first and only American among the top three at the Spanish tour. That achievement, even when compared to his solid top ten finishes in the Tour, still stands apart. "I got to stand on the podium, that's something," he said. "When you talk about the physical aspects between the Tour and the Vuelta, if you can put apples to apples, maybe eighth place [at the Tour] is a bigger achievement. But I still think standing on the podium is a good thing; it outweighs an eighth place."

TOUR DREAMS

Leipheimer's dream of riding the Tour came true the following season, after he penned a contract with Rabobank to lead the team's general classification (GC) efforts at the Tour. In Leipheimer's eyes, his move to the Dutch squad was the next step in his patient evolution as a professional racer. His stated aim was the top ten as he rolled into the 2002 Tour, but friction soon developed within the team.

The Rabobank squad was desperate for a strong GC rider after it became obvious neither of its two stars, Erik Dekker and Michael Boogerd, had the all-round skills to fight for a three-week Tour crown. But the two Dutch riders soon let it be known there was no way they were going to subjugate their stage-winning aspirations to help an unproven American go for all the glory. As a result, Leipheimer was left to fend for himself in the key moments of the mountains.

While Leipheimer is friendly with the American media, the Dutch press found him somewhat standoffish and unapproachabile after a big race. Things were exacerbated when the quiet American seemed unable to unleash attacks like Dekker or Boogerd. Leipheimer was equally frustrated that the press never seemed to understand that just staying close to Armstrong's wheel was pretty damn good for a Tour rookie.

"I felt the negativity. It caught me by surprise," Leipheimer admitted. "I got roasted because they said I never attacked, but what they didn't understand is that I am trying to stay in the race to where it's down to the main players and it's a real race."

> **"I felt the negativity. It caught me by surprise."**

Despite the behind-the-scenes struggles, Leipheimer soldiered through the 2002 Tour, and finished a promising eighth, the third-best Tour debut ever for an American. The following year, Leipheimer lined up, intent on aiming for the top five, but his Tour ended even before it started. In the same crash that left Tyler Hamilton with a broken shoulder, Leipheimer was out with a fractured sit bone.

The 2004 season started nicely when Leipheimer won a mountain stage of the Setmana Catalana, a race he likely could have won had he not conceded more than a minute in the opening stage when he lost contact with the main bunch after being zapped by rain and cold. That year's Tour saw Leipheimer once again aiming for the top ten, but he struggled on the epic stage to Plateau de Beille, and an off-day on the climbing time trial to L'Alpe d'Huez saw him finish ninth.

After two top ten placements in three Tour starts, Leipheimer felt he had yet to show his true potential. So when Gerolsteiner boss Hans-Michael Holczer made contact with Leipheimer's agent in the summer of 2004, Leipheimer was more than ready for a new start. "I was looking to make a change," said Leipheimer, who turned down a one-year contract extension with Rabobank. "In this sport, change is good. It brings new motivation, new perspective. Start over with a clean slate and take all your experiences and put them into a new way of working, a new structure."

ONE LAST RUN

Leipheimer's Gerolsteiner teammate Georg Totschnig was also staking everything on the Tour. But the dreams of the 34-year-old Austrian began to unravel even before the start. Following the Tour of Switzerland in late June, a nasty cold left him flat on his back for a week. It became obvious Totschnig wasn't going to recover in time for a 100-percent shot at a top-five Tour finish.

"I got the flu. I was on my back shivering despite it being summer," Totschnig said. "I did hope to become better in the first week, but in these fast stages, it's not possible to come back." With his overall chances in ruins, Totschnig decided to push through the Alps to reach the Pyrénées, if for no other reason than to help Leipheimer as much as he could. A strong climber who can do well in a hilly time trial, Totschnig was hoping to ride side by side with Leipheimer in the high mountains.

Raised in Meierhofen, Austria, in the Alps of Tyrol, where skiing is to Austrians as football is to Nebraska's corn-fed farm kids, Totschnig was right to be disappointed. At 34, this might be his last run at the Tour in top shape.

Much like Leipheimer's early sporting career, Totschnig's started with ski racing. Young Georg didn't take bike racing seriously until it was obvious he wasn't going to be able to make it as a skier. By the time he was 16, he started winning local amateur bike races thanks to his ability to go uphill fast.

In the 1980s, cycling in Austria was about where it was in the United States—an exotic sport better practiced on the roads in faraway France. In Austria, the only sports that mattered were skiing and, as everywhere in Europe, soccer. But, said Totschnig, "For a small country, we don't have a bad cycling history, especially at the amateur level. When I first turned pro, there were maybe two of us. Now there are 15 to 20 Austrian pros between the small and bigger teams."

Totschnig quickly made a name for himself in the pro ranks as a climber and, in 1996, he finished in the top ten at both the Giro and the Vuelta. His consistency didn't go unnoticed by Telekom, a team anxious to bring on riders to help its protégé, Jan Ullrich. The Austrian decided to ride for the German team, though he realized that meant the end of his personal ambitions. "I felt then that I stopped in my evolution as a rider because my job was to help Jan," he said. "Now that I look back at it, I lost some years for myself. That's a lot of time in a professional career, time that I had to later use to rebuild my strength."

By 1999, he was chafing under the Ullrich yoke. Gerolsteiner was a small, young team, but Totschnig liked the freedom it offered. "I came to Gerolsteiner with the opportunity to develop my characteristics as a leader," he said. "It was a smaller team, they were patient for me to get results, but it allowed me to get better and improve."

In 2003, Gerolsteiner earned a wild-card bid for the Tour and Totschnig placed 12th in Paris, after finishing 5th at the Giro. Twelve months later, his determination helped him deliver an impressive 7th place overall. Totschnig said that finishing 3rd behind Armstrong and Ivan Basso on the Tour's hardest stage to Plateau de Beille was his finest professional moment.

"I almost stayed with them, but [José] Azevedo did one more pull [for Armstrong] and I lost the wheel. But it was still one of my best days as a pro," he said. "It was a big mountain stage, there were millions there to see it. These are the moments you train for as a professional."

By the spring of 2005, Totschnig was emboldened with Leipheimer by his side. They went into the Tour with shared ambitions. Fate dictated that the Austrian would lose his chance at overall glory, but win a stage, while his American buddy still had a shot at the podium.

CHAPTER 24 | STAGE 15

The Lieutenant
Stands Tall

After outclimbing his main rivals on the first of two mighty days in the Pyrénées, Lance Armstrong talked to journalists at the Ax-3 Domaines ski resort about his preparations for the upcoming stage. "It's just a question of getting out of here as fast as possible, starting to hydrate, starting to eat, starting to rest and recover," he said. "We had a very early start to the day once again, an hour and a half in the bus to get to the start, and I'm sure [my teammates] will have an hour and a half to get to the hotel tonight. It doesn't make it any easier . . . and we have an early day tomorrow."

Armstrong pointed out that Sunday's stage would be the toughest of the Tour, 205.5km in six progressively difficult climbs, starting with the Cat. 2 Portet d'Aspet, followed by four tough Cat. 1 climbs before the grind up the *hors-catégorie* Pla d'Adet. It would all add up to more than 16,000 feet of climbing in temperatures forecast to be in the mid-80s.

Armstrong won a similar stage in 2001. That year, French star Laurent Jalabert split from an early breakaway on the Portet d'Aspet descent and rode solo over the remaining humps toward what looked like a daring stage win. But after Armstrong's teammate Roberto Heras set a fierce pace on the first part of the final 10.3km climb, the Texan went ahead on his own, passing Jalabert and seizing victory by a minute over Ullrich.

As for Ullrich, cycling's biggest enigma was rounding into form as this Tour entered its final week, while Basso was showing the best climbing form of his career. Both men vowed to continue their attacks in an attempt to dislodge the American superstar from his perch. Basso's CSC team manager Bjarne Riis even went so far as to say that he had never seen Armstrong as vulnerable as he appeared to be at this point in the Tour. Riis's smack talk

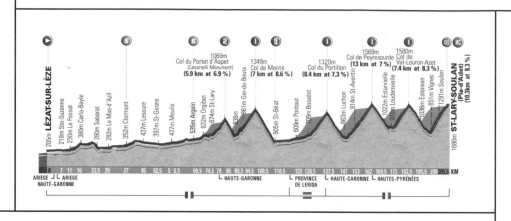

may have been more for the benefit of his lead rider, although Armstrong did admit that his team couldn't follow the rapid tempo set by Ullrich's T-Mobile squad on the Port de Pailhères in stage 14, although the champion himself looked as strong as ever. But if Basso took Riis's bait, the upcoming mountain stages would be even more exciting— especially the one to Pla d'Adet.

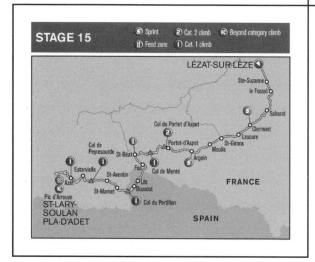

In eight Tour stages finishing on the Pla d'Adet climb in thirty years, the most decisive were the Tour-winning solo attacks by Lucien Van Impe in 1976 and Armstrong in 2001. The Discovery Channel team leader said he would dearly love to win there again, not only because this would be the final mountaintop finish of his storied career, but also because this was the tenth anniversary of his Motorola teammate Fabio Casartelli's fatal crash on the Portet d'Aspet descent.

HONORING CASARTELLI

The white marble Fabio Casartelli Memorial is an ornate carving, intertwining stylized bicycle wheels, elements of the Italian rider's career, and the time and date of his death. The ten-foot-high monument sits on a small patch of grass about 100 meters above the spot where Casartelli died. On the Aspet's 17-percent descent, the 24-year-old Italian cyclist was involved in a terrible high-speed pileup that sent a couple of riders over a parapet wall into the trees. Casartelli, the 1992 Olympic road champion in Barcelona, was left curled in the middle of the road. He had cracked his unprotected head on the pavement and fractured his skull. Efforts to save his life were unsuccessful. He was only the second participant in Tour history to die from a crash.

Casartelli had been the final rider selected for Motorola's 1995 Tour squad. "We could only take nine guys," Armstrong remembered, "and the last place, the ninth guy, was between Fabio and George [Hincapie]." The selection meant that Hincapie would not make his Tour debut until the following year, but he did race with Casartelli in some of the spring classics, and the sweet-natured Italian and the New Yorker had become friends. So the tenth anniversary of the tragedy was, according to Armstrong, "special for me *and* for George."

By the time this year's race passed the memorial at kilometer 89, Hincapie was in a front group of fourteen riders that had been away for 60km, and had carved out a 14-minute lead. Of this group, the best-placed rider in the overall standings was Phonak's Oscar Pereiro, 24th at 24:40.

Hincapie's instincts as a classics rider helped him get into the early break. "There were so many attacks," Discovery team director Johan Bruyneel said later, "the team just couldn't control it, and George decided to follow one of the attacks." With the American in the move that formed through the village of Mas d'Azil after 29km were several other classics specialists, including Dutchmen Erik Dekker, Michael Boogerd, and Karsten Kroon of Rabobank, Frenchmen Laurent Brochard and Jérôme Pineau of Bouygues Télécom, and Italian Alessandro Bertolini of Domina Vacanze.

Powered by Kroon and Dekker, who were banking on Boogerd winning the stage, the break averaged almost 42kph for the first two hours along swerving valley roads and over the first climb, the Portet d'Aspet, in the eastern Pyrénées. When the gap topped 18 minutes over the next pass, the ruggedly steep Col de Menté, Bruyneel called ahead to Hincapie on the team radio. "Listen, George, you're probably not going to come back," Bruyneel decided. "You can do your own race." A green light from Bruyneel? That sometimes happened in the classics, of course, but in the Tour it was a rare and unusual opportunity. Hincapie listened in disbelief, and then put his head down and accelerated into the group. His legs felt strong, and he could only hope that his form would hold through the rest of the day's climbs.

ATTACKS AND CHASES

By the time the race made a brief excursion into Spain to tackle the Col de Portillon, the breakaway had accumulated a lead of 18:45. With four climbs and 80km to go, Riis decided it was time to make Armstrong's teammates work harder and step up the peloton's lethargic pace. So he instructed his CSC team to step on the gas on the Portillon and split open the peloton. Their acceleration cut the gap to 15 minutes by the foot of the day's fourth climb, the Col de Peyresourde, where the breakaway began to crumble after Kroon attacked; he was hoping to shatter the group and launch teammate Boogerd toward the finish. And indeed, by the time the leaders reached the wide, open descent, with a daunting view across the green Louron valley toward the next crowd-lined climb, only six escapees remained: Hincapie, Pereiro, Boogerd, Brochard, Oscar Sevilla of T-Mobile, and Pietro Caucchioli of Crédit Agricole.

Meanwhile, CSC continued a furious tempo on the Peyresourde before Armstrong's Discovery team took over and further split the pack. Only twenty or so riders were left with the yellow jersey when they topped the climb 11:30 behind the break.

Basso knew he had to attack early if he wanted to make up any of his overall 2:46 deficit on Armstrong, so as soon as they started climbing the day's fifth *col*, the difficult Val Louron-Azet, he stormed away from the group. The race was now on the line, and Armstrong jumped forward to match the Italian's impressive acceleration. Ullrich was slower to react, but then chased hard, relentlessly pounding a stiffer gear than his two rivals, more diesel than racehorse, and eventually joined them. Now the Tour's power trio began to overtake stragglers from the breakaway, gathering momentum as they rode. With a collective high-horsepower effort, they reached the summit only 7:40 behind the six leaders. Another minute passed before the "best of the rest" came into view: Rasmussen, Leipheimer, Landis, Vinokourov, Mancebo, and company.

"I don't even know what happened," said Landis at the end of the day. "I was dropped on the second-to-last climb. It was just Lance and Ullrich and Basso, and the rest of us trying to get back on in the descent. Nothing anybody can do then. [The speed] was out of hand. I was cross-eyed the entire last mountain."

Landis wasn't the only one who struggled on this final monster, which opens like a wall, straight out of the flat streets of St.-Lary Soulan. After six hours in the saddle, everyone except for Armstrong was dropped when Basso made a furious attack 10km from the finish. It was his final attempt to shake the American and gain precious seconds, but to no avail. "I gave everything today," Basso said later. "I want to leave my mark on this Tour de France. I attacked as hard as I could, but Armstrong was able to follow. I didn't have another attack in me, so we rode together to try to put time on Ullrich and the others."

END GAMES

At the head of the race, when T-Mobile's Spanish climber Sevilla put in a tentative attack on the long 10-percent pitch starting the climb to Pla d'Adet, Pereiro immediately countered with a much more powerful surge. Sevilla and Brochard fell back, while first Boogerd and Hincapie, and then Caucchioli fought back to join the aggressive Spaniard. Just inside 5km to go, Pereiro went again. Neither Caucchioli nor Boogerd could follow this time. Only Hincapie had the strength to go after the Phonak rider.

"I covered attacks all the way up the climb. I tried to conserve as much as possible," said Hincapie, who found himself fighting for a Tour stage win for the first time since 1998 when he placed third in stage 3 from Roscoff to Lorient. Back then, he ceded his chance of victory to two opportunists on the run-in to a flat stage across Brittany; this time, he seemed to have the reserves he'd need to battle Pereiro on a mountaintop.

The Spaniard later said that he and Hincapie spoke and agreed to share the work and then sprint out the stage win.

> **"Making agreements to work together to stay away, that never works, unless the agreement is you can win."**

But as Landis pointed out, "Making agreements to work together to stay away, that never works, unless the agreement is you can win."

Hincapie explained that the crowds, including tens of thousands of Basque fans swathed in orange, were so thick that it was impossible for him to come past Pereiro to make a pull. It was a frustrating situation for the Spaniard, but he knew that his main hope of winning the stage was to outclimb his American opponent. "If he was going to win, we knew that Oscar would have to finish on his own," said Phonak *directeur sportif* Jacques Michaud. "But Hincapie was a surprise."

In other words, the Phonak camp was pretty much resigned to what happened next: At the top of the mountain, where the spectator fences began and the roadway was finally clear of fans, Hincapie was able to make his move. With 300 meters left, Hincapie lifted his long legs out of the saddle, sprinted hard, and left Pereiro in the dust. The 32-year-old American, Armstrong's most devoted teammate, riding his tenth Tour, was finally a stage winner. He shook his head in disbelief, raised his arms in triumph, and then placed his hands over his face as he crossed the line. How many times had he dreamed of victory in the Tour de France?

It was fitting that faithful lieutenant Hincapie was the first of Armstrong's support riders to win an individual stage. It wasn't a surprise for Armstrong though. After the yellow jersey rode in with Basso five minutes behind Hincapie, Armstrong said, "What he's done [this year] is incredible. He almost won Paris-Roubaix, he was still with me at the top of the Galibier, and he's just won the hardest stage of the Tour. Nobody has done that since Merckx or Hinault."

Lofty praise, but Armstrong's pride seemed boundless. When asked if Hincapie could perhaps one day *win* the Tour, Armstrong said, "I've been thinking that for a couple of days. He's an excellent time trialist and now a very good climber. So why not?" Hincapie as Armstrong's designated successor—was that to be the legacy of this Tour?

For now there was a stage win to savor and another long ride in the team bus to the hotel. "This last week has been very, very hard," Hincapie confirmed. "I'm going to take a well-deserved rest day tomorrow. I have family that lives in France and I'm glad they are here to watch this [victory]. I have a French baby, Julia Paris, and my wife Melanie is French, and this is for them." The faithful lieutenant toweled his face and then, as usual, headed off to look after the needs of others.

STAGE 15: LÉZAT-SUR-LÉZE–PLA D'ADET

1. George Hincapie (USA), Discovery Channel, 205.5km in 6:06:38 (33.630kph); 2. Oscar Pereiro (Sp), Phonak, at 0:06; **3.** Pietro Caucchioli (I), Crédit Agricole, at 0:38; **4.** Michael Boogerd (Nl), Rabobank, at 0:57; **5.** Laurent Brochard (F), Bouygues Télécom, at 2:19; **6.** Ivan Basso (I), CSC, at 5:04; **7. Lance Armstrong (USA), Discovery Channel, s.t.; 8.** Oscar Sevilla (Sp), T-Mobile, at 6:28; **9.** Jan Ullrich (G), T-Mobile, s.t.; **10.** Michael Rasmussen (Dk), Rabobank, at 6:32.

GENERAL CLASSIFICATION

1. Lance Armstrong (USA), Discovery Channel, 62:09:59

2. Ivan Basso (I), CSC, 02:46

3. Michael Rasmussen (Dk), Rabobank, 03:09

4. Jan Ullrich (G), T-Mobile, 05:58

5. Francisco Mancebo (Sp), Illes Balears, 06:31

BELOW Lance Armstrong's professional cycling career spanned thirteen years, including eleven Tours de France. He starts his second Tour in the rainbow jersey as the defending world champion as a hefty 22-year-old, and chats with three-time Tour champion Greg LeMond, who is riding his final Tour at age 33.

ABOVE Only two and a half years after emerging from debilitating chemotherapy and surgery to overcome testicular cancer that had spread to his lungs and brain, Armstrong is back at the Tour. He earns the yellow jersey by winning the first two time trials, then shocks the Europeans by breaking away on the first alpine stage to Sestriere. **BELOW** After winning the Tour for the first time, Armstrong's the homecoming hero on his "Vive Le Lance" parade through the streets of Austin, Texas.

ABOVE With tougher opposition at the 2000 Tour, Armstrong has to bide his time before taking the yellow jersey in the Pyrénées. Then, on the mythic climb to Mont Ventoux, he needs all of his newfound climbing skills to thwart 1998 Tour winner Marco Pantani as they race toward the 6,263-foot summit.

RIGHT It is July 17, 2001, stage 10 of the 88th Tour de France starting at Aix-les-Bains, and the Alps are on the horizon. Over the *hors-catégorie* climbs of the Madeleine and Glandon, Armstrong pretends that he's suffering on the hot, six-hour stage. He bluffs Jan Ullrich and his Telekom team into thinking he is about to explode. Then, a kilometer into the final climb, to L'Alpe d'Huez, Armstrong attacks.

On this first alpine stage of the 2001 Tour, after attacking an astonished Ullrich (previous page), Armstrong puts two minutes into his rival in a solo 12km break to the Alpe d'Huez summit. Before him, only the legendary Fausto Coppi, in 1952, won at the Alpe and went on to win the Tour.

LEFT With an injured Ullrich absent from the 2002 Tour, Armstrong's main opponent is Joseba Beloki, who placed third at the previous two Tours. **BELOW** After Beloki tries an attack halfway up the 22km finishing climb of Mont Ventoux, the feared Giant of Provence, Armstrong counterattacks to ride the last 8km alone. He leaves Beloki 1:45 back, but Armstrong is only third on the stage behind two riders who started the climb with a huge lead.

It's 2003. Armstrong has started the Tour's thirteenth stage with an overall lead of only 34 seconds on Ullrich. The previous day, Armstrong was dehydrated and lost a vital time trial to the German. Here, on the day's final climb to Ax-3 Domaines, Ullrich is attacking. Armstrong, Haimar Zubeldia, and Ivan Basso are all struggling to hang on.

ABOVE A despondent Armstrong finishes only fourth at Ax-3 Domaines. His overall lead over Ullrich is down to 15 seconds and the future is uncertain. **BELOW** The next day in the Pyrénées (below), he rides at the head of the pack with his closest rivals Ullrich (left) and Alexander Vinokourov (right), who are waiting to profit from any signs of weakness.

The final climb of the fifteenth stage to Luz-Ardiden has just started. Armstrong has attacked, while Basque rival Iban Mayo (in orange) and Ullrich try to follow. Suddenly, the strap of a fan's Tour souvenir bag gets entangled in Armstrong's bars. He's heading for the tarmac. Is the yellow jersey about to slip from his grasp?

TOP After picking himself off the floor and winning the stage at Luz-Ardiden by a minute, Armstrong cruises to his fifth consecutive victory, thus joining the other living record holders (from left) Bernard Hinault, Eddy Merckx, and Miguel Induráin, as well as the deceased Jacques Anquetil. **ABOVE** Tour director Jean-Marie Leblanc congratulates Armstrong from the sunroof of his car on the final stage of the exciting 2003 Tour.

ABOVE Armstrong has already won four of the five major mountain stages at the 2004 Tour when he chases after the modest Italian rider Filippo Simeoni on the rolling stage 18. After the pair joins a small breakaway group, Armstrong forces Simeoni to return with him to the peloton. Simeoni's crime? He has sued Armstrong for telling an Italian magazine that Simeoni lied in testifying that he had been supplied with the banned drug EPO by the Texan's training consultant Dr. Michele Ferrari.

TOP Even after he has been interviewed by television and radio reporters, and given a press conference, Armstrong is still pursued for one more quote before being driven away in a U.S. Postal team car to his hotel. **ABOVE** In his final Tour, now in Discovery Channel colors, Armstrong chats with Johan Bruyneel, the man who created the strongest team in Tour history, making Armstrong's seven victories possible.

ABOVE Armstrong was determined to have fun at the 2005 Tour, whether he was signing autographs for the fans, or
BELOW enjoying a quiet moment with faithful lieutenant George Hincapie on one of the rest days.

ABOVE Armstrong has always had the ability to raise his game for the Tour's races against the clock. In 2005, he guides the Discovery riders to victory in the team time trial, here following Hincapie and racing ahead of Yaroslav Popovych and Paolo Savoldelli.

BELOW Armstrong summons all of his mental and physical resources to win the final time trial at St. Étienne by a twenty-second margin—taking the final stage win of his career.

NEXT PAGE Worth his weight in . . . gold maybe, but on this occasion, a French wine region has awarded the yellow jersey his weight in vintage wine. That's just about seven cases, one for every victory.

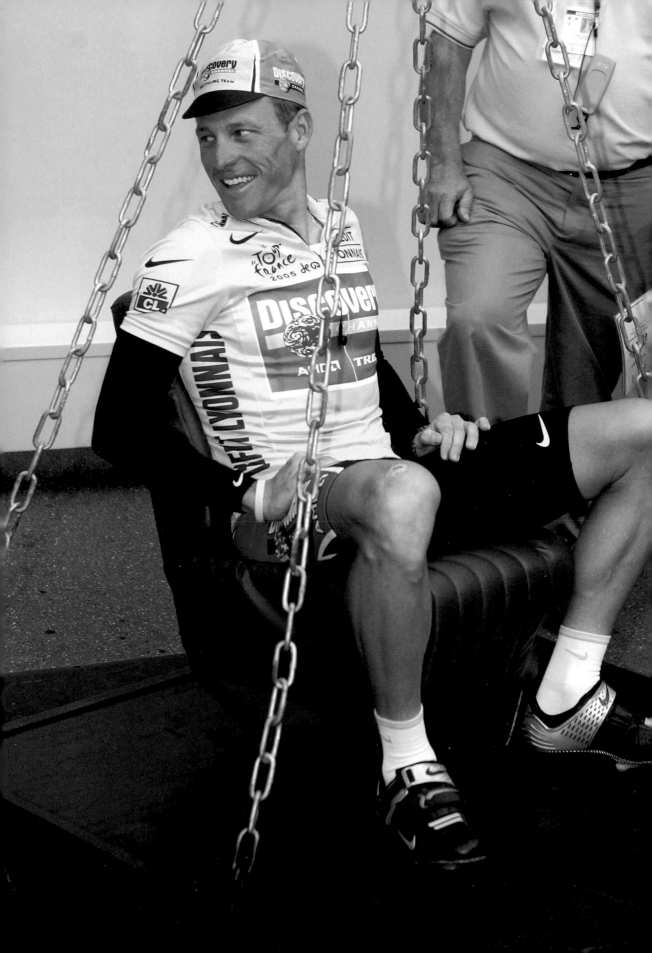

CHAPTER 25
The New Hincapie:
Sprinter Turned Climber

When George Hincapie shot across the line victorious at Pla d'Adet ahead of Spanish rider Oscar Pereiro, even the 32-year-old native New Yorker acted surprised. After all, it was the first victory by a teammate of Lance Armstrong in seven Tours. And there was a reason for that drought: To earn a spot on Armstrong's nine-man Tour team meant unequivocal sacrifice for the leader, and anyone who dared challenge this unwritten edict assured himself of a one-way ticket *off* the Tour team.

If anyone was deserving of such a rare victory, it was Hincapie, the only rider to be a member of every one of Armstrong's Tour-winning campaigns. "This is the biggest win of my career," Hincapie beamed. "This Tour I've felt so strong, stronger than ever before."

The first to congratulate him was Armstrong, the man that Hincapie worked so hard for every July since 1999. "George is my best friend in the team," Armstrong said. "We have been friends for a long time, from the time we were juniors. We've spent 17 years together on the bike. It's his first stage victory on the Tour and to do that in the mountains is incredible."

The bond between Hincapie and Armstrong dates back to the late 1980s. The two have long been inseparable, with Hincapie being one of the few riders that Armstrong trusts and confides in. "The relationship that Lance and I have has been amazing. He's one of my best friends," Hincapie said. "I owe everything to him."

It was hard to tell who was happier at the finish line in Pla d'Adet, stage winner Hincapie, team leader Armstrong, or Discovery Channel's assistant sport director Dirk Demol. The modest Belgian team official, an ex-Paris-Roubaix winner, has been especially close to Hincapie, helping him develop into one of the strongest classics riders of today's generation. "He's making progress every year in his climbing. If you work hard like he's doing, it pays back with the biggest stage in the Tour," Demol said. "It's been another George [in 2005] because he's won all year. Today his confidence will go up even more."

Hincapie's victory wasn't without controversy. Phonak's Pereiro stewed that the American did little of the work in their breakaway. "The strongest man didn't win," Pereiro said at the finish line. Hincapie admitted that sitting on the back of the breakaway made for an easier day in the saddle than if he were in his more familiar role, pulling at the front of the peloton for Armstrong. Almost as an aside, he also noted that on the upper slopes, the crush of spectators had narrowed the road to a barely discernable path, making it all but impossible to pass anyway.

Once Discovery Channel had Hincapie in the day's major breakaway, it meant that Armstrong had someone up the road to help him if he needed it later in the race. "That's why I didn't work in front," Hincapie said. "But we ended up getting 18 minutes and once Johan saw that, he said, 'Listen, George, you're probably not going to come back here now, you can do your own race.'"

That meant marking the moves on the final climb to Pla d'Adet, and when Pereiro couldn't drop him in the final kilometers, Hincapie knew the win was his.

METAMORPHOSIS

Hincapie's victory in the hardest mountain stage of the 2005 Tour de France started long before that 205.5km trek across the Pyrénées began. Ever since Armstrong's miracle comeback from cancer in 1998, Hincapie saw the writing on the wall. "It was obvious if I wanted to be on the Tour team each year, I'd have to improve in the mountains," Hincapie said. "I've worked hard to control my weight and improve my strength on the climbs."

Hincapie started his professional career in 1994 with Motorola. He possessed a quick finishing sprint, but he soon morphed into a classics powerhouse after he fell in love with Paris-Roubaix. "I rode my first Roubaix when I was 21. It was snowing, raining, cold, and I was one of only about forty guys who finished. I just loved it from that day on," he said. "I always dreamed of doing well in that race."

The spring classics became Hincapie's focus, resulting in fourth-place finishes at Roubaix in 1999 and 2001, and capped by an even more impressive second place in 2005.

At the same time, the chance to help Armstrong chase history soon prompted him to broaden his focus. He wanted to be at his friend's side, but he knew he'd have to earn his spot in the mountains.

"This team gives me a lot of freedom for the training, allows me to prepare 100 percent for the classics and then take the month of May off and prepare for the Tour," Hincapie said. "I am able to change my training around from the winter to the summer and prepare for those specific events."

Once the spring classics are over, Hincapie gladly sacrifices the remainder of his season to help Armstrong. Hincapie's relaxed, laid-back style blends well with the natural-born aggressor inside Armstrong, and the pair clicked even back in their junior racing days on the U.S. national team.

"Lance and I met when I was 14 and he was 16," Hincapie said. "Even then he was amazing to me. The first race we did together I asked him, 'What's your tactic today?' and he told me, 'I'm going to go from the gun and I'm going to win.' I said, 'You can't do that,' and he did it. He's been doing that ever since."

By 2001, Hincapie had made impressive improvements in the mountains. The duty of protecting Armstrong's flanks in the middle flats was transferred to such bulldogs as Pavel Padrnos and Viatcheslav Ekimov, while Hincapie started to help the team's Spanish climbers in the medium mountains.

By 2003, Hincapie was strong enough to carry Armstrong up the lower flanks of the steeper climbs. That progression continued into 2005, when Hincapie led the peloton on the *hors-catégorie* Col de Galibier, the highest peak of this Tour, in stage 11 to Briançon. "I know that climb well. I knew if there weren't any big attacks I could do it," Hincapie said. "It was hard in the last kilometer, but I made it."

Hincapie also looked around to see who was there and who wasn't. Two faces he didn't see were those of Pereiro and Michael Boogerd—another of the riders in the breakaway to Pla d'Adet. "I knew Pereiro was strong and that Boogerd was a good climber, but I also knew that the day I was pulling on the Galibier they weren't there," Hincapie said.

PROLIFIC JUNIOR

Hincapie's road to the top of the Pyrénées began in the most unlikeliest of places: New York City. Hincapie's father, Ricardo Hincapie, now 62, raced as an amateur in Colombia before moving to New York. His two sons, Rich, older by four years, and George, soon took up their father's passion and started to compete in local events.

"I raced Central Park and in New Jersey, raced against older guys," Hincapie recounted. "I had big support from my family. I had the right support and it got me to where I am now."

Hincapie enjoyed one of the most prolific amateur racing careers in American cycling history. As a junior, he won 16 medals at nationals, including ten national titles, and two world championship medals. In 1991, he graduated from Long Island's Farmingdale High School; the following year, he participated in the Barcelona Olympics, the first of four Olympic Games that Hincapie would attend.

> **Hincapie enjoyed one of the most prolific amateur racing careers in American cycling history. As a junior, he won 16 medals at nationals, including ten national titles, and two world championship medals.**

After turning pro with Motorola in 1994, Hincapie snagged four victories in his first three seasons. His 1996 Tour debut ended when he pulled out in the fifteenth stage, the day after he'd been injured in a crash. He returned the next year with the upstart U.S. Postal Service team.

Bilingual in Spanish and English, Hincapie was one of the "original Gs" to move to Gerona, the bustling college town in Spain's Catalonia region that most of the American racers now use as their European base. "I love it there, the roads are great for training," said Hincapie, who used to share an apartment with Tyler Hamilton. "I live right downtown and I love to be able to go out of my door and have a coffee. It's also great to have the good riding just ten minutes away."

Hincapie and the other Americans were encouraged to move there by Johnny Weltz, the former Danish pro who was Postal's sport director. He noticed the Americans were having a hard time adjusting to life in Europe. "For the European racers, it's easy. They could just go home after the race," Weltz said. "I saw the Americans missing things from home. I thought it would be good for them to be all in one place."

During the winters, Hincapie would return to Charlotte, North Carolina, where his brother, Rich, studied at university. A few years later, Rich relocated to Greenville, South Carolina, where Hincapie bought a house on nearby Paris Mountain before moving to a downtown apartment.

Hincapie acts as a technical advisor to Hincapie Sportswear, a company started by his brother that sells activewear bearing the family name. The rapidly growing business has seven full-time staffers and uses Hincapie's images to promote the product line.

The newest additions to the Hincapie clan came in 2004 when George married a French podium girl he met at the 2003 Tour, Melanie Simmoneau; in November, they became the proud parents of a baby daughter, Julia Paris.

In his early Tours, Hincapie was the American team's best chance for a stage victory, his closest attempt being a third place at Lorient in 1998. Those were more modest times, when the team's primary objective was simply to arrive in Paris with all nine riders. That changed dramatically when Armstrong returned to the Tour in 1999. Hincapie's role changed as well, becoming one of Armstrong's reliable motors in the flats.

Hincapie's success in both the Tour and the classics reached a new level in the new century, both with his improved climbing abilities and increasing confidence in the mean streets of Belgium and northern France. In 2001, he won the Ghent-Wevelgem classic and placed fourth at Paris-Roubaix; he took fourth at the Tour of Flanders the following year. A viral infection derailed Hincapie's classics season in 2003, but he came back to win Belgium's Three Days of De Panne in 2004.

In the spring of 2005, Hincapie won the semi-classic Kuurne-Brussels-Kuurne and finished second at Roubaix. In June, he won the prologue time trial and the final mountain stage of the Dauphiné Libéré. By July, Hincapie was stronger than ever.

FUTURE LEADER?

Two weeks before Hincapie's win at Pla d'Adet, Jim Ochowicz, the former Motorola team manager, quietly put forward a notion that many found to be outlandish: Hincapie could take over the team leadership when Armstrong retired on the Champs-Élysées. "I haven't heard about that," Hincapie laughed when asked about it after stage 6 in Nancy. "I don't know about that."

But moments after his dramatic victory in the Tour's hardest mountain stage, the proposal was suddenly gaining legs. Adding fuel to the fire was Armstrong himself, who said it wasn't such a crazy idea after all. "We always have these dreamers who say they're going to win the Tour, so why couldn't George Hincapie be in that position?" Armstrong said. "He's a complete rider."

Armstrong talked about the possibility with his friend, but insisted Hincapie would have to give up on his beloved classics if he wanted to focus his entire season on the Tour. Johan Bruyneel, sport director at Discovery Channel, suggested Hincapie might be better suited for weeklong stage races, but he didn't discount the idea altogether. "It's difficult to say. George is a great rider; he's never been in a position where he's a leader of the team in a stage race," Bruyneel said. "I'm sure if he could focus on it he could be one of the great riders."

For Hincapie, all the talk about taking over where Armstrong left off was a bit overwhelming, especially coming on the heels of his unexpected mountain victory. "I've been working for Lance for a long time, and for him to say stuff like that is pretty amazing. If they want to give me a shot, I'll do what I can," he said. "But right now I want to soak all this in. This is the biggest win of my career!"

CHAPTER 26 | STAGE 16
Payback Time

A few minutes before the start of stage 16 in Mourenx, George Hincapie was chatting with a journalist when the man he outsprinted atop Pla d'Adet rode over to the American, gave him a big smile, and shook hands. Hincapie, who speaks fluent Spanish, acknowledged the Spaniard's nice gesture. It ended any bad feelings that may have remained after Oscar Pereiro had taken out his frustration at losing the previous stage by criticizing Hincapie for not sharing the workload in their mutual breakaway. The gesture also showed that Pereiro was ready to move on in his quest for a stage win, while Hincapie would return to his first-lieutenant duties for race leader Armstrong.

Pereiro rode off to the start village, which was set up on the infield of an outdoor velodrome named after the legendary five-time Tour champion Eddy Merckx. Why Merckx? Well, Merckx rode triumphantly into Mourenx, a small town at the foot of the Pyrénées, to climax the most remarkable breakaway in his Tour de France career. The year was 1969 and the Belgian was already wearing the yellow jersey In his first Tour. After some infighting between the leaders up the Col du Tourmalet, Merckx was the first over the summit. The finish was 130km in the distance, but the race leader blazed down the long descent to find himself a couple of minutes ahead of the others, and then decided to continue solo for the next three hours over the Col du Soulor, Col d'Aubisque, and a couple of lesser climbs to arrive in Mourenx eight minutes ahead of the chasers.

Such gargantuan exploits are rarely seen in modern grand tours, especially from a race leader, but the young Merckx was never afraid of taking huge risks to achieve victory. If there had been a most combative rider in Merckx's day, the Cannibal would have won it hands down every year.

At this Tour, a panel of judges (all of them French) decided who would receive the daily award for most combative rider. The winner wears a red number in the following stage, which is usually an honor, but if the peloton feels the title is unjustly awarded, it is more likely an embarrassment. That was the case when Frenchman Carlos Da Cruz was chosen in stage 13 into Montpellier. "That was a joke," commented Chris Horner, who was in the same break as Da Cruz and said the Française des Jeux rider made shorter, slower pulls than the others. "I'd have been embarrassed to put on the number."

Two days after the Da Cruz mistake, the most combative race number went to the worthy Pereiro. The solid Spanish rider, in his fourth season with Phonak, finished tenth at the 2004 Tour, and he hoped to improve upon that finish. But after crashing in the team time trial, he shifted his ambitions to helping the other team leaders, Floyd Landis and Santiago Botero. "The first week I could tell I didn't have the legs to fight for the GC," said Pereiro. "Floyd and Botero were better than me, so I put my energy into trying to win a big stage."

EARLY BREAK

Like Alexander Vinokourov on the T-Mobile squad, Pereiro had been serving his team by attacking rather than defending. That policy nearly paid off on the Galibier stage when Pereiro went into the red for Botero, who was just beaten for the stage win by Vinokourov. Pereiro was again in the successful break on the stage to Pla d'Adet, where only the inspired Hincapie denied him the win.

Pereiro, wearing the red number, looked fresh and eager in Mourenx. He was still searching for that big stage victory. Perhaps this would be the day. His young Belgian team manager John Lelangue even said he'd shave his head of thick black hair if a Phonak rider won a stage.

Pereiro wasn't the only one eager to break out on this final stage in the high mountains, where the pièce de résistance was the *hors-catégorie* Aubisque, which would be climbed in the opposite direction to that taken by Merckx in his famous 1969 exploit. "I thought today might be an opportunity for an early break," said Aussie revelation Cadel Evans, who started this stage in 11th place, 12:57 behind Armstrong. "But I didn't know if the GC guys would let me go."

Apparently, Evans was far enough back on GC that when he initiated the day's main break after 25km on narrow roads in rolling terrain, there was no serious chase from the

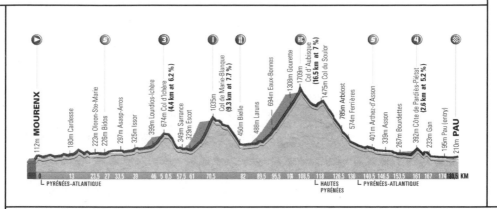

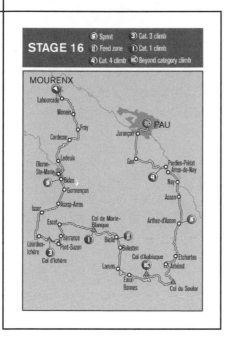

field. Following Evans's wheel was a small crowd including his Davitamon-Lotto teammate Fred Rodriguez and a second American, Saunier Duval's Horner, along with German Jörg Ludewig of Domina Vacanze, Belgian Philippe Gilbert of Française des Jeux, Spaniards Xabier Zandio of Illes Balears and Juan Antonio Flecha of Fassa Bortolo, and Frenchmen Cédric Vasseur of Cofidis, Ludovic Turpin of ag2r, and Jérôme Pineau and Anthony Geslin of Bouygues Télécom.

The French and Spanish riders in the lead group tried to persuade Evans to go back to the peloton to give them a better chance of succeeding. But Evans was firm. He said he would ride conservatively on the opening two climbs, and have his Davitamon teammate Rodriguez work on the flats, until they reached the Aubisque, where the stage would probably be decided.

Just before the eleven-man breakaway formed, the T-Mobile squad was put on the defensive when tenth-placed Andreas Klöden was involved in a small pileup. The team helped him return to the peloton, but after the stage he was taken to a hospital in Pau, where a small fracture was spotted in his left wrist. The injury would force the 2004 Tour runner-up to pull out of the race the next morning.

On the approaches to the day's second climb, the ultrasteep Col de Marie-Blanque, 70km into the 180.5km stage, no one knew whether the T-Mobile team was going to continue its declared policy of constant aggression. The answer came when the main pack was halfway up the 10km climb, 6:10 behind the Evans breakaway.

Suddenly, the tireless Vinokourov made a strong attack. He was followed by Levi Leipheimer and Crédit Agricole's Andrey Kashechkin. Seeing an opening, Pereiro was quick to join these three, while Lampre's Eddy Mazzoleni and a hopeful Basso also jumped on the chance to put Armstrong under pressure. Eventually, Discovery Channel's Hincapie came through with the yellow jersey on his wheel to set a tempo that initially only Basso, Mazzoleni, and Ullrich could follow.

As Hincapie controlled the pace, Rasmussen, Landis, Leipheimer, and Julich caught back to the group, and then Pereiro came dashing through to make a bold solo attack. When that attempt was foiled, Pereiro went again. This time, the Phonak rider went clear on the steepest, 12-percent pitch near the top of the climb, pursued by Mazzoleni. Over the Marie-Blanque summit, Pereiro was only 2:50 behind the Evans break, while Hincapie led the yellow jersey group at 3:13.

"We talked about going on the attack today because we knew the big favorites would be watching each other," Pereiro said. "It was difficult to try to bridge out to the front group. I had to go really hard."

THE AUBISQUE

Mazzoleni linked up with Pereiro, and they set about chasing the breakaway along a broad valley before reaching the Aubisque. As the Italian and Spaniard continued to close in, the front group started to break up on the easy, early slopes of the 16.5km climb. The peloton arrived at the Aubisque 7:35 later, at which point Vinokourov attacked again, and he was joined by a revived Roberto Heras.

T-Mobile then put Kessler, Klöden, and Ullrich on the front of the bunch, and their acceleration soon splintered the yellow jersey group. Halfway up the climb, the only riders remaining with Armstrong were Hincapie, Rasmussen, Ullrich, Basso, Kashechkin, Mancebo, Landis, and Leipheimer.

Ullrich wasn't done yet and he made a strong surge as the course pushed high above the pine trees. He reeled in Heras and Vinokourov with his acceleration and spit Mancebo out the back. "I tried today again and I showed that I haven't given up," said Ullrich, who was in fourth overall. "Lance has beaten me again, but the podium motivates me now. I didn't like finishing fourth last year and to be on the podium again is important to me."

While Ullrich's team was making life hard for Armstrong, Evans saw the perfect opportunity to carry out his team manager Marc Sergeant's encouragements to attack. The Aussie took off 7km from the top, where the ascent steepened to 10-percent, and he was soon out of sight of the break. As Evans headed clear, Pereiro and Mazzoleni bridged to the remnants of the lead group.

Over the 5,607-foot Aubisque summit, Evans was 47 seconds ahead of Pereiro, and a minute clear of Mazzoleni and Zandio, the only other member of the early break able to stay with the Italian. More stragglers from the original break slipped over the crest until Rasmussen led the pack at 4:08, with Horner getting

"I tried today again and I showed that I haven't given up," said Ullrich, who was in fourth overall. "Lance has beaten me again, but the podium motivates me now. I didn't like finishing fourth last year and to be on the podium again is important to me."

caught right on the summit. Hincapie, Sastre, Klöden, and Kashechkin came through 5:14 back and then Popovych topped the pass another 15 seconds slower, giving Armstrong some help on the run into Pau.

The front four riders joined forces after the fast curving descent to ride the remaining 50km of hills en route to Pau. Evans, the one most interested in making time on those above him on GC, did the longest pulls, especially on the run-in through the streets of Pau. He was still charging hard down the finish straight when an incredulous Pereiro flashed by to edge out Zandio and claim Phonak's first Tour stage win after two runner-up spots.

Evans, after being at the front for 155km, crossed in fourth place, 3:24 ahead of the 50-strong yellow jersey group, to jump into seventh overall, 9:29 behind Armstrong. It may not have been a performance on par with the incomparable Merckx, but it was just reward for a hard day's work by the Tour rookie.

As for Pereiro, he said, "It's a thorn that I've taken out of my back. I'm happy with the big win today. It makes me forget the disappointment of Sunday." Besides taking the stage, the genial Spaniard was awarded another red number. And Lelangue did keep his word and shave his head.

STAGE 16: MOURENX-PAU

1. Oscar Pereiro (Sp), Phonak, 180.5km in 4:38:40 (38.864kph); **2.** Xabier Zandio (Sp), Illes Balears; **3.** Eddy Mazzoleni (I), Lampre-Caffita; **4.** Cadel Evans (Aus), Davitamon-Lotto, all s.t.; **5.** Philippe Gilbert (B), Française des Jeux, at 2:25.

GENERAL CLASSIFICATION

1. Lance Armstrong (USA), Discovery Channel, 66:52:03

2. Ivan Basso (I), CSC, 02:46

3. Michael Rasmussen (Dk), Rabobank, 03:09

4. Jan Ullrich (G), T-Mobile, 05:58

5. Francisco Mancebo (Sp), Illes Balears, 06:31

CHAPTER 27

Cadel Evans Embarks on a
Great Adventure

There's a much-used expression in English soccer to describe a hot new player: "The boy's a bit special!" Cadel Evans is no longer a boy, but he's always been a bit special. The soft-spoken Aussie zipped to the top ranks of mountain bike racing as a teenager, converted successfully to road racing in his midtwenties, and he was now being talked about as the revelation of his first Tour de France.

After solid rides in the Alps and Pyrénées, Evans emerged from the mountains in great shape. "I can't remember my middle name right now," said an exhausted Evans on finishing fourth in stage 16, after breaking away on the legendary Aubisque climb and pulling the winning break into Pau. "I have to choose my moments carefully. The other mountain stages were for the big GC guys, and I'm not there yet. This is just my first Tour, but I wanted to make up some time today if I could. It worked out great."

By moving into the top ten overall, Evans was right where he wanted to be at his first Tour, and he was looking ahead to achieving some of the results that many had predicted for him when he left mountain biking in 2001. And it's at the Tour that the former mountain bike World Cup champion really wants to leave an impression, especially as his debut had come a few years later than he had hoped.

Evans made his grand-tour debut at the 2002 Giro d'Italia, which he started as a *domestique* for the mighty Mapei team's Stefano Garzelli, and ended as the race leader. Evans was wearing the *maglia rosa* on the final mountain stage, and lost it almost solely due to inexperience. "I did a big build-up in December and January that year, which in retrospect was too much," Evans reflected. "And I had a heavy racing schedule leading up to the Giro that really made me tired before I started the race; and for that reason I had the bad day."

Despite falling to a final position of 14th at the 2002 Giro, Evans had a string of suitors when Mapei ended its sponsorship at the end of that season. The successful bidder was ultimately Germany's T-Mobile, who wanted Evans as a Tour prospect. But a twice-broken collarbone prevented him from riding the *Grande Boucle* in 2003, while team management pulled him from the squad at the last minute in 2004. They said he was too fragile to survive the speed, echelons, and crashes of the Tour's opening week. Evans answered such criticism in the best possible way at his last race with T-Mobile, the semi-mountainous Tour of Lombardy, by placing fourth in a break behind Italian studs Damiano Cunego and Ivan Basso, and Dutch star Michael Boogerd.

That performance helped him get noticed by a bunch of other teams looking for a rider of his caliber. "I just want to forget about the last two years and learn from the experience," said Evans.

NEW BEGINNINGS

When Evans heard that Davitamon-Lotto was calling, he shook his head. He told his agent, "What, me, on a Belgian team? No." But after meeting with Davitamon company boss Marc Coucke and hearing from team manager Marc Sergeant that Davitamon was planning to hire an Australian, Allan Peiper, as one of its *directeurs sportifs,* Evans softened his stance. It also helped that Cadel's big hero is a Belgian. No, not Eddy Merckx, but Tintin, the adventure-seeking cartoon character created in 1929 by Belgian artist and writer Hergé.

"I have a big collection of Tintin books and memorabilia," said Evans, who has read every Tintin book "over and over" since he discovered the character twenty years ago when he was growing up near Melbourne, Australia. "I like Tintin because he's young, he's intelligent, he's brave, he's kind, he's everything that you could want to be. He's the only idol I've ever had."

Evans revealed that in all the Tintin books there are only two images of the hero riding a bicycle. "I have one framed at home," he added. "He's the only bike rider that gets put up on the wall of my house."

Evans then proudly showed off a Tintin key ring and other items he was given by a Belgian collector during this year's spring classics. That gift may have been a small gesture, but it's the small things that have made Evans feel at home with his Belgian team.

Davitamon's confidence in signing Evans as its Tour de France leader—even though he had yet to ride the Tour—gained credence at the last of the spring classics, Liège-Bastogne-Liège. That was where the 28-year-old Aussie made a ferocious uphill attack on the second-to-last hill to leave behind a chase group that was a minute behind the two leaders, Jens Voigt and Alexander Vinokourov. In the chase group were such international stars as Paolo Bettini, Davide Rebellin, Boogerd, Cunego, and Basso.

On the Côte de St. Nicolas, a veritable wall of a climb that has a 13-pitch amid four steep curves near the top, Evans's solo attack left the strongest riders struggling behind, and the only men to catch him (on the descent) were an inspired Boogerd and Italy's Olympic champion Bettini. These two veterans did outkick Evans in the end, but the Aussie's fifth place was confirmation that he was among the world's elite climbers.

Right after finishing the Liège race, Evans needed a few seconds to catch his breath before quickly reviewing his performance. "I tried," he said modestly. "I gave it everything. It's really my first go at Liège, so I can't complain. I came here with hopes, wanted to do something and be part of the race. I'm a lot calmer in the races now. I think that also comes from time and maturity. And I feel that I'm now back at the level I was at [in 2002], back in the swing, back at the front of the peloton, where all the action is.

"I saw that I was climbing pretty good compared to the others, so I thought, 'Oh, if I'm feeling good on St. Nicolas, I have to have a go.' And, of course, I had my directors in the car encouraging me, so I figured with the [one-minute] gap to the breakaway, it's all or nothing.

"Apparently, when I'm climbing, they always say that I look as though I'm about to be dropped. I *was* on the limit on St. Nicolas, but then again I was on the front, so it's not so bad. Right at the end, I was giving my all. Then I tried to attack and do the sprint; it was a long day on the limit."

Asked about his new team, Evans said, "Fantastic. For me, Davitamon-Lotto is the perfect team. They look after me so well, give me so much confidence, and they have confidence in me, which is really what I needed at this point in my career. I couldn't be happier with the directors, the staff, the riders."

That "feel good" confidence has been emphasized by the support of his two young Belgian teammates, Christophe Brandt and Johan Van Summeren, who also rode for Evans at the Tour. "I have to calm those guys down," he said. "They get a bit excited, Summie especially. They think I'm asleep and I've got to calm them down. No worries, though. Christophe is like my left leg in these races."

SWISS HOME BASE

With his new team, Evans feels also that he has become better at focusing on his goals in racing and training. He still works closely with Aldo Sassi, the Italian coach from his Mapei team days. To make that task easier, the easygoing Aussie bought an apartment near the southern Swiss city of Lugano, just across the border from Italy, "because I speak Italian and it's close to my coach and girlfriend Chiara."

Chiara, a concert pianist, takes a keen interest in her boyfriend's cycling career. She visited him at Grenoble on the Tour's first rest day and gave him a beautiful blue bracelet that Evans wore for good luck during the rest of the race. The couple became engaged once the Tour was over.

He reinjured the collarbone he broke three times in 2003, and though the crash came on Friday the 13th, it was not a full break and he was able to start light training within a few days.

Evans's main European home is in Lugnorre, a small lakeside town in Romandie, the French-speaking part of Switzerland. "I was planning on going to the Tour de Romandie [in May]," he said. "That's my home race and I only want to go there to win, but it's a long way before the Tour." Evans explained that his preparation in 2005 was aimed at being 80 percent by early-April's Tour of the Basque Country, 95 percent at the Ardennes classics (including Liège), and 100 percent at the Tour.

As final preparation for the Tour, Evans had scheduled Spain's Tour of Catalonia and France's Dauphiné Libéré, but while scouting the Tour's Pyrenean stages in May, he crashed on the descent of the Col d'Aubisque while pacing behind his team car. He reinjured the collarbone he broke three times in 2003, and though the crash came on Friday the 13th, it was not a full break and he was able to start light training within a few days.

The injury prevented Evans from racing Catalonia and pushed his return to the peloton to the Tour of Switzerland in mid-June. The Swiss race saw him back in the swing, finishing in the top twenty in the long time trial and arriving with the front group on the opening mountain stage.

But his collarbone wasn't fully healed by Tour time—though he never complained about it affecting his performance. On finishing the first Pyrenean stage at Ax-3 Domaines, Evans said, "It's held together with gaffer tape, that's all. No, that's not my problem. It's the legs that are the problem at the moment. The shoulder's hanging in there."

A SMOOTH TRANSITION

Evans switched from mountain biking (two overall World Cup titles and an Olympian in 1996 at Atlanta and 2000 in Sydney) to road racing in 2001, and quickly made an impact. Riding for the Saeco–Cannondale team (the American bike manufacturer was also his mountain bike sponsor), the then 24-year-old Aussie won the Tour of Austria by taking the toughest mountain stage that finished atop the Kitzbüheler Horn. "I had a mechanical at the bottom and started the climb dead last," Evans recalled. "Two of my teammates took me to the back of the group and I won by two and a half minutes. In retrospect, that was pretty good, as last year I won [the Tour of Austria for a second time] with about 18 seconds."

The current vogue in climbing is the high-cadence style that Lance Armstrong first developed in 1999 and used throughout his long reign at the Tour. But Evans claims that he was already using that technique in the mid-90s: "If you see any videos on me, you'll probably notice that I always rode a much higher cadence than everyone, even in the mountain bike races, and so that's something I brought with me to the road. It's something that's always suited me better.

"So when I look at Lance I don't say this is something I've got to do. For me, Lance is not a climber. He's a time trialist who can time trial uphill. I just ride my own style."

Knowing that he is a world-class climber and a better-than-average time trialist (he won the Commonwealth Games time trial in 2002), what did Evans expect to achieve at his first Tour? "A lot of people have been asking me: How am I going to go? Can I get in the first ten? I'm not interested in that," Evans said. "I'm not interested in battling with Lance, but I *am* interested to see what my level is at the Tour. I want to get there at my best. I might have a fantastic Tour, and if I'm [only] 20th I have to say, 'Well, I'm not going to win the Tour.' But from what I do [this year] I can say what type of Tour rider I'm going to be."

By Pau, he had already shown that he was growing into the role of a true contender. A big part of what Evans was achieving at the Tour was his new squad. "I'm very happy with the team," he said. "I've never had Aussie teammates before, and having Robbie [McEwen] as a teammate has turned out to be great. I'm motivated. And the Belgians are so passionate about cycling. It's part of their culture. So I'm very happy with the team."

And the team is very happy with Evans. After he finished in the Jan Ullrich group at Courchevel on the first alpine stage, the Davitamon officials at the finish line were shaking their heads, congratulating themselves, and they kept on repeating, "Fantastic, fantastic!"

Like his hero Tintin, Evans is an adventurer, and he was now showing his capabilities to the world.

CHAPTER 28 | STAGE 17
The Longest Day

With only five stages remaining in the 2005 Tour and with ten teams still without a stage win, competition was bound to be fierce on this rolling 239.5km jaunt from Pau to Revel, the longest stage of the race. As on virtually every other road stage, a scramble of attacks and probes tangled the front of the race until the right combination of riders and teams came together.

The successful move began after a half hour of attacks and counterattacks when French national road champion Pierrick Fédrigo of Bouygues Télécom jumped away 25km into the stage. The first to catch him was CSC's Norwegian Kurt-Asle Arvesen, quickly followed by inveterate Dutch aggressor Erik Dekker of Rabobank and Carlos Da Cruz, the Frenchman who had a knack of getting into long breakaways.

Thirteen others soon joined the leaders, to make a break of 17 riders representing 14 different teams. It was a perfect combination, as none of the escapees was any closer to the yellow jersey than T-Mobile's Oscar Sevilla, who started the day 38:51 down. The three teams with two riders apiece in the break were Discovery Channel, with Paolo Savoldelli and José Luis Rubiera, Française des Jeux with Da Cruz and Thomas Lövkvist, and ag2r with Sammy Dumoulin and Simon Gerrans.

Once the break established a two-minute lead, the peloton slowed to a club-ride pace, enjoying the expansive views across the wheat fields of the Haute Garonne. The last two times that a Tour stage finished in Revel, two men arrived together after a long breakaway to contest the finishing sprint. In 1995, it was Sergei Uchakov who outwitted a youthful Lance Armstrong, while in 2000, on an almost identical course to this one, Erik Dekker got the better of Santiago Botero. With 50km still to race on this stage in 2005, with the 17 leaders 20 minues clear, the first move to break things open came from Dekker, whose uphill surge prompted a number of other attacks. But when another Dutchman, Bram Tankink of Quick Step, spearheaded the eventual winning move, Dekker was unable to follow.

Seven riders made it across to Tankink: the Australian rookie Gerrans, Spanish veteran Sevilla, Giro d'Italia champion Savoldelli, the eager Frenchman Hinault, and Norwegian sprinter Arvesen, along with Ukrainian Andriy Grivko of Domina Vacanze, and Italian Daniele Righi of Lampre-Caffita. These eight men quickly moved clear, their former companions defeated not only by the high-speed tactics, but by the marathon distance and the afternoon's oppressive heat.

When the peloton reached the same point on the course, the T-Mobile team went to the front and began setting a 48kph pace in a bid to retain its overall 22-minute lead over Discovery in the team competition. The 138-strong pack disintegrated and was down to fewer than 50 riders when they reached the 10km finishing loop at Revel.

TWO CLIMAXES

This loop is the famed circuit of St. Ferréol, often used for French national road championships and the site of a significant time trial battle at the 1971 Tour between the two protagonists, Eddy Merckx and Luis Ocaña. At this Tour, the 2.7km Cat. 3 climb to St. Ferréol would produce the decisive moves in both the break and the bunch. The hill isn't particularly steep, averaging only 5.1 percent, but a long, false flat continues the climb after the summit, and then comes a twisting 2km descent on a narrow back road leading into the final flat 3km back into town.

When the eight riders left from the all-day break reached the climb, Tankink again started the attacks, quickly followed by Grivko. They moved 50 meters clear until Frenchman Hinault, normally a lead-out man for his Crédit Agricole sprinter Hushovd, burst past both of them.

"The hill wasn't really my thing. But I decided to put everything into my move," Hinault said later, even though well-known climbers Sevilla and Savoldelli were also in the group. Only Savoldelli had the strength to chase and catch Hinault, who admitted he went deep in the red just to hold the Italian's speeding wheels. "Hang on, this is the Tour," Hinault said to himself.

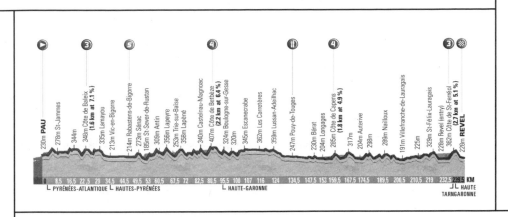

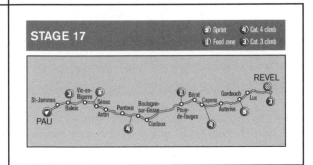

More than 20 minutes later, when the first part of the disintegrating pack arrived on the St. Ferréol hill, many others went into the red. A pileup entering the streets of Revel compounded the splits, and then the inevitable Vinokourov sprinted away on the climb. Ready for some fun, Armstrong then punched it, followed by Ullrich, and suddenly ten riders were clear. The only GC guys to miss the sudden acceleration were Evans, Kashechkin, Landis, and Moreau.

Some later suggested that comments made by Landis to *L'Équipe* about the uneasy climate at U.S. Postal during his tenure there might have spurred Armstrong to drive the select group over the St. Ferréol climb in the final kilometers, knowing that Landis had missed the split. Landis would lose 20 seconds by the end of the stage, dropping to ninth, 15 seconds behind Vinokourov in the overall standings.

Armstrong and his teammates Hincapie and Popovych pulled hard in the move, aided by T-Mobile's Ullrich and Vinokourov, whose colleague Klöden had pulled out early in the stage because of the broken wrist he sustained the day before. Much was made of Armstrong wanting to push "enemy No. 1" Landis down the standings, but their push also helped Discovery snatch the prestigious overall team lead from T-Mobile by 37 seconds, and also bolstered Popovych's white jersey lead over Kashechkin.

When the leaders tackled the twisting descent into Revel, French team rider Hinault managed to latch onto Savoldelli's wheel and wouldn't budge as the pair reached the final kilometers. Hinault's refusal to work certainly frustrated Savoldelli, judging by his repeated attempts to slow up, sit up, and urge him to take a pull. In any case, their pace slowed enough that Arvesen and the upstart Gerrans, riding his first Tour, had time to catch the two leaders with 2km still remaining.

Once the four were together, Arvesen caught his breath and 600 meters later bolted up the road, to force Giro champ Savoldelli into a long, grinding pursuit. Discovery's other miracle man—back to the top after two years of painful crashes and injuries—chased and chased, then caught and passed his prey 50 meters from the line. It was probably the longest finishing "sprint" of the Tour, and Savoldelli's first-ever Tour stage win.

The fans in Revel had just witnessed two races for the price of one, and Discovery came out top in both.

STAGE 17: PAU-REVEL

1. Paolo Savoldelli (I), Discovery Channel, 239.5km in 5:41:19 (42.102kph); **2.** Kurt-Asle Arvesen (N), CSC, s.t.; **3.** Simon Gerrans (Aus), ag2r, at 0:08; **4.** Sébastien Hinault (F), Crédit Agricole, at 0:11; **5.** Andriy Grivko (Ukr), Domina Vacanze, at 0:24.

GENERAL CLASSIFICATION

1. Lance Armstrong (USA), Discovery Channel, 72:55:50

2. Ivan Basso (I), CSC, 02:46

3. Michael Rasmussen (Dk), Rabobank, 03:09

4. Jan Ullrich (G), T-Mobile, 05:58

5. Francisco Mancebo (Sp), Illes Balears, 06:31

CHAPTER 29
Paolo Savoldelli:
Another Miracle Man

Lance Armstrong wasn't the only miracle man at the 2005 Tour de France. While Armstrong's revival after cancer remains one of sport's all-time great comebacks, the 92nd Tour was full of stories of riders who had beaten the odds in one way or another. For instance, there was Alberto Contador, a 22-year-old Spanish rider who collapsed on a roadway in the 2004 Vuelta a Asturias with a cerebral blood clot. Contador slipped into a coma and nearly died, but 14 months later he was starting his first Tour.

Another rider making a return was Santiago Botero, the 2002 world time trial champion, back in top form after two forgettable seasons with T-Mobile. The classy 32-year-old Colombian suffered a litany of ailments, problems, and nuisances. One of them was the team's insistence that he train and live in Europe most of the year. Botero said it affected his performance because, as he put it, "I'm very Latino; I miss my family and I don't like cold weather." His new team, Phonak, was smart enough to let him stay in Colombia's hot and humid Medellin until the heart of the racing season, and Botero promptly erased his two-year winless spell at the Tour de Romandie, and followed that with a stage win and second place overall at the Dauphiné Libéré.

Paolo Savoldelli was a more reluctant comeback kid. The two-time Giro d'Italia champion was back at the Tour for the first time since 2000, when he finished 41st to Armstrong's second maillot jaune. Unlike most riders, Savoldelli wasn't exactly aching to return to the Tour. Being a good Italian boy who lived at his mother's house until he was 30, Savoldelli simply didn't like to stray too far from home. "I'm an Italian; the Giro is the race that counts for us," Savoldelli said. "I've always centered my season around the Giro. This year, things have changed a little bit."

If Savoldelli appeared the reluctant lieutenant, he was nevertheless ready to do the job. What brought him back to the Tour was the chance to help Armstrong win for a seventh time in his final Tour. When Discovery Channel team boss Johan Bruyneel came calling on Savoldelli with a lifeline after the Italian suffered two frustrating, crash-ridden years at T-Mobile, he was more than happy to take the chance with a new team. "The opportunity to help Armstrong motivates me more than ever," he said. "I don't know him well, but I respect his actions on the bike. I will do everything I can to help the American win the Tour again."

Before the Tour, however, Savoldelli had some unfinished business with the race he loves most. Savoldelli's love affair with the Giro isn't dissimilar to that of most Italian pros, who get hooked on the color and excitement of the Giro at a young age. If the Tour is cycling's greatest race, the Giro is its most beautiful. As the Tour has grown in importance and evolved into the gargantuan international beast it is today, the Giro has retained the charm and emotion that make it the race of choice for many in cycling's inner circle.

WORKING TOWARD THE GIRO

Born on May 7, 1973, Savoldelli was lucky enough to grow up near Bergamo, a bustling city along the edge of Italy's beautiful lake country. It's the center of one of the hotbeds of Italian cycling that has produced men like world champion, multi-Giro winner, and 1965 Tour champion Felice Gimondi, and many more since.

The oldest of three brothers, Savoldelli became enamored with bikes after watching pros train and race on the local roads. "My father was also a young racer, not great, but good," he said. "He would take us to the races. I always liked to ride a bike, but I never took it seriously until I turned 14."

While he was a serious young man, Savoldelli wasn't very serious about his homework. He was the kind of kid who liked to get his hands dirty, a trait that continues to this day. "I always preferred to go to work, to do my training on the bike, rather than stick my nose in the books," he said. "I could see I could make a living with it, so I worked harder than most."

Sidelined for one year of required military service, Savoldelli jumped to the pros in 1996 with Roslotto–ZG, and it's somewhat ironic that his first signs of success would come at the Tour de France, not the Giro. That first year, he finished 10th on the Tour's longest mountain stage, a 262km trek across the Pyrénées into Pamplona, Spain, and he ended up 33rd overall. Not bad for a rookie.

In 1997, he finally got his wish to start the Giro. He took third in the 15th stage and finished 13th overall. "I always like a race that's at least five days; it takes me that long to get my legs warmed up," he said. "I don't like one-day races at all."

The Giro result got Savoldelli picked up by Italian superteam Saeco–Cannondale for 1998. Riding alongside megastar sprinter Mario Cipollini, he snagged his first major victory, winning a stage and the overall classification at a Giro warm-up race, the Giro del Trentino. And at the Giro d'Italia, he moved into the top ten at ninth overall. People started calling him a future winner of the *maglia rosa*.

They also started calling him other things, including Baby Face, Savo, and *Il Falco*, the Falcon, for his already legendary descending skills. "Where [Savoldelli] gains is when the corners aren't so tight and he can carry a lot of speed; a lot of other guys start braking," said Sean Yates, the ex-pro who joined Discovery Channel as a sport director for the 2005 season. "The man has no fear."

Savoldelli has also earned a reputation as being a stickler for his equipment. He still rides with the 175mm cranks he first experimented with in 1999, and continually nags his mechanics to try new things to make his bike lighter.

Watching his own weight, though, was a problem. Savoldelli admitted he had a hard time staying away from his favorite dishes during the off-season. "Weight is the determining factor to going fast in the mountains, so I never eat chocolates, cheeses, or heavy meats," he said. "I never like to get more than 2 to 3 kilos from my optimum weight. It takes too much to lose that weight."

His appetite has impressed many. Yates was amazed at how much Savoldelli would pack away during the Giro. "It's crazy the amount he gets through in the race," Yates said. "It's like a catering service. Six sandwiches, six bars, twenty-eight gels. It's unbelievable. We just have to carry everything we got. He gets the menu out and checks off what he wants."

RACES LOST AND WON

By 1999, Savoldelli was one of the favorites to challenge Marco Pantani at the Giro. Though Il Falco won the 14th stage, Pantani was on cruise control, holding a lead of 5:38 over Savoldelli going into the final weekend. Then came the bombshell before the penultimate stage: Pantani tested above the 50-percent hematocrit level and was unceremoniously kicked out of the race. Savoldelli refused to wear the *maglia rosa*, but he ultimately lost it when he couldn't follow an attack that included Gilberto Simoni, Roberto Heras, and eventual winner Ivan Gotti.

"When things are going well, I can ride and ride and ride, but when things are bad, everything is harder for me. Things get too heavy," he said.

In 2000, Savoldelli won Switzerland's Tour de Romandie and was the heavy favorite for the Giro, but he took a hard fall and finished a disappointing 24th. He hoped to rebound for the Tour, but rode an uninspired 41st and vowed never to return.

Despite his again winning the Tour de Romandie and finishing 14th at the 2001 Giro, Saeco wasn't interested in retaining Savoldelli's services. Incredibly, neither did any of the bigger Italian teams and he settled for the Division 2 Index-Alexia squad in 2002. The team's riders weren't receiving their checks on time and morale was bad, but Savoldelli surged in the final week of the Giro. Going into the last mountain stage, he was quietly sitting in sixth, 46 seconds behind race leader Cadel Evans.

The Australian's powerful Mapei team seemed to have things under control in the seven-hour stage until the final climb up Passo Coe. One by one, riders ahead of Savoldelli in the standings flamed out until an attack by Tyler Hamilton dropped Evans. The wily Savoldelli counterattacked, surged into the *maglia rosa*, and fended off Hamilton's challenge in the closing time trial.

At last, the Giro was his. "I'm not one of these natural-born champions," he said. "All my victories have come through hard work and sacrifice. If the race is decided on who works hardest, I win every time."

Savoldelli went on to sign a million-dollar contract with Germany's Team Telekom, where, with fellow new arrivals Bobby Julich, Botero, and Evans, he started to train alongside Jan Ullrich, Erik Zabel, and Alexander Vinokourov. "When I joined the German team, I thought I was going to be the top stage-race rider in Italy," Savoldelli said.

But a string of injuries and frustrations in two humiliating, winless seasons totally derailed Savoldelli's big plans, if not his career. His first setback came during a training camp in Tenerife in February 2003. Savoldelli was struck by a motorcyclist and suffered severe facial injuries that required major plastic surgery, and he had to wear a neck brace for six weeks. He missed the Giro and a viral infection sidelined him for the Tour.

His return in 2004 for T-Mobile was short-lived when he crashed in his first race back at the Tour of Cologne, where he suffered a concussion, facial cuts, and a broken wrist. The injuries kept him out of both the Giro and the Tour and he didn't return until August's Tour of Britain, where he placed sixth overall.

With the advent of the ProTour, Discovery Channel was looking for a rider to lead the team in its first Giro. Team manager Bruyneel guessed correctly that Savoldelli might be ready for a change, and the Italian happily closed the book on his T-Mobile adventure. His luck didn't change immediately, however, when he fell and broke his collarbone at the team's January training camp in California. Luckily, the recovery was short enough to allow him to start the Giro, but even he didn't know what to expect.

"He came into this Giro saying he was fit, but up until that point, he hadn't really done anything to back it up," said Yates, who was behind the wheel for Discovery Channel at the race. "There was a certain amount of trepidation among us all about how good he was really going to be. We didn't imagine he was going to win the Giro, let's put it that way."

Savoldelli seemed content enough with a stage win ahead of the apparently superior Ivan Basso, but the Team CSC leader was weakened by a chronic stomach infection and lost more than half an hour over the Stelvio Pass; Savoldelli slipped into the *maglia rosa*.

The race finally came down to an epic mountain stage over the giant Finestre climb. At 18km, the climb held an average grade of 9.2 percent with 5,558 feet of climbing to reach its spectacular 7,146-foot summit. His main rivals, Danilo Di Luca, Gilberto Simoni, and José Rujano, isolated Savoldelli on the grinding climb, dropping him by

This was when *Il Falco* lived up to his reputation as one of the best descenders in the game, dropping like a rock down the backside of the climb. Just like that, he clawed his way back into the *maglia rosa*.

two minutes to put Simoni into the virtual lead at the summit. This was when *Il Falco* lived up to his reputation as one of the best descenders in the game, dropping like a rock down the backside of the climb. Just like that, he clawed his way back into the *maglia rosa*. But he still had to resist Simoni's challenge on the climb to the finish in Sestriere.

Ahead, Di Luca's heroic effort collapsed after his legs cramped on the tortuous descent. Rujano then played his card with 4.5km to go, standing out of the saddle to turn the screws on Simoni. The man from Trentino was cooked and threw a bottle of water on his face, dousing his chances for the upset. Even so, at the line, he was only a half minute short of defeating Savoldelli for the overall victory.

"Paolo doesn't say a lot, but he rides very cleverly the whole time," Yates said. "He has gauged his efforts. He's raced very intelligently in this race. The cycling gods were definitely on our side. We won it—that's what counts."

Savoldelli's final 28-second margin was the closest at the Giro since 1976 when his fellow Bergamo citizen, Gimondi, beat Belgian Johan De Muynck by 19 seconds. "I don't feel like I am a champion because a champion used to attack on the climbs and make the difference," said Savoldelli. "I am a regular rider and I think a lot and know my limits."

Armstrong wanted that same wisdom and composure as he went under fire in his final Tour. And the Italian was more than willing to oblige. "Mentally, I was ready to help Lance, and quite simply, Lance was a lot stronger than me," Savoldelli said. "He motivates everyone on the team."

By the time Savoldelli slipped into the breakaway on the stage to Revel, there was already talk he might be the team's new leader in 2006. But he shrugged off the notion and said he might not be the right guy for the job. "It's so difficult to win the Tour. The last Italians to do it were Gimondi and Pantani, so that's the level you need to be at," he said. "For me, the Giro is really important. I don't know if I'm prepared to give up the Giro for the Tour."

And regardless of the role he will take for Discovery, Savoldelli has let it be known that he has no interest in hanging around the cycling world after he retires. He has started a construction company, which he'll dedicate himself to full-time once he hangs up the cleats. "I like to work; that's always been my passion," he said.

For Savoldelli, true fulfillment will always be found close to home.

CHAPTER 30 | STAGE 18
Finish Line
Surprise for Armstrong

Temperatures were stiflingly hot at the stage 18 start in Albi, a handsome city set around a pink-bricked, oval-ended Gothic cathedral set on the Tarn River. The high mountains were long gone, but still ahead lay the nagging climbs of the Massif Central. This stage served up another difficult course, with the day's five climbs capped by the infamous Côte de la Croix-Neuve at Mende. It was one more day of punishment in a Tour that had already taken a heavy toll on the peloton. "All the riders are tired, everything hurts," said Discovery Channel team boss Johan Bruyneel. "It's more mental suffering at this point of the Tour. Everyone has their job to do, but everyone is glad the suffering is almost over."

Despite the heat, it didn't take long for the attacks to begin. A flurry of moves ebbed and flowed until Carlos Da Cruz of Française des Jeux jumped clear after 39km. He was soon joined by nine riders from nine different teams: two more Frenchmen, Cédric Vasseur of Cofidis and Thomas Voeckler of Bouygues Télécom; three Spaniards, Egoi Martinez of Euskaltel, Xabier Zandio of Illes Balears, and Marcos Serrano of Liberty Seguros; German Matthias Kessler of T-Mobile; Aussie Luke Roberts of CSC; Belgian Axel Merckx of Davitamon; and Italian Franco Pellizotti of Liquigas-Bianchi.

"I've been trying to get into some breaks during this Tour, so it was fun to be out there," said Roberts, a 2004 Olympic gold medalist in the track team pursuit. "I knew I didn't have much of a chance against all the climbers, but this Tour has been good for me."

Under the sticky conditions, the peloton was content to let the leading ten enjoy their day in the sun. "The team has been working hard at the front the entire Tour, so when the

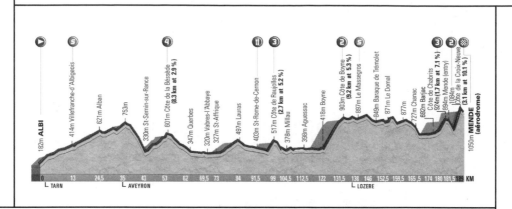

break went away, it wasn't our responsibility to bring it back," said Bruyneel. "Maybe Lance could have won the stage, but the breakaway had too much time. It was more important to save the legs for the final."

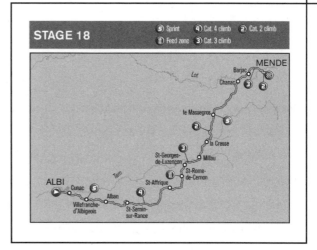

By the 100km point, where the leaders passed beneath the world's newest and highest highway viaduct, the spectacular 1,225-foot-high Viaduc de Millau, the gap was 12 minutes. And by the time they'd scaled the Côte de Boyne, climbing a side valley out of the Tarn Gorge, the gap was still growing as they reached a grassy plateau 3,000 feet above sea level.

STEEPEST CLIMB

Just like the day before, separate races for the stage and GC would take place in the final hour of the 189km stage through the rocky gorges and across the high, windswept meadows of the Massif Central.

In front, the break had 15:20 on the main bunch when Da Cruz reopened hostilities on the penultimate climb, the Cat. 3 Côte de Chabrits. Merckx, inspired by this being Belgium's national day, joined Da Cruz, as did the other Frenchmen Voeckler and Vasseur, and the Spanish riders Zandio and Serrano. The quintet hit the base of the final climb together with no clear favorite.

The Croix-Neuve climb is a Cat. 2 "wall" that's only 3.1km long but it has a 10.1-percent average and 15-percent pitches on its three switchbacks. It was the steepest and most challenging hill of the three weeks, which was confirmed by the all-out battles that took place between the men in front and the podium contenders behind.

Some 20km before reaching the base of the climb, Basso's CSC team stepped on the gas and trimmed the peloton to about two-dozen riders before Discovery's Hincapie, Popovych, and Armstrong surged into the climb from Mende's shady, medieval streets. Basso then made a ferocious attack on the Croix-Neuve's rugged steeps. Only Armstrong, Evans, and Ullrich could follow the Italian, while a weary Rasmussen fell off the pace with Leipheimer.

Basso put all of his energy into the attack. "I tried to drop Armstrong," he said, "but he was on my wheel the entire time. It was the last summit finish. I went 100 percent, but Armstrong is too strong." In turn Armstrong said, "I knew the attacks would come. It was the last chance for them to try to get some time. Ullrich was trying to drop Rasmussen, and Basso was trying to drop Ullrich. I just had to follow."

Ullrich, who was getting lighter and stronger as the Tour progressed, was momentarily gapped when Armstrong got out of the saddle to show his rivals that he could still make them hurt, but the German was able to claw his way back. Vinokourov couldn't quite follow and drifted back to join Rasmussen and Leipheimer.

Evans was more than comfortable in this elevated company, confirming his opinion at Courchevel that he is best on grades of 10 percent or steeper. "A climb like that was made for me," said Evans, who was showing impressive reserves in the Tour's final week and moved back into seventh overall. "After yesterday, I would have been happy to get through without losing any time, but it's a bonus to get some back before the final time trial."

FOLLOWING HISTORY

Long before the leaders sped upward through the thickest crowds of the 2005 Tour, Merckx made the first move from the five breakaways, but Serrano soon passed him. The 32-year-old Spanish rider, whose best victory in a 13-year pro career came at the 2004 Milan-Turin classic, didn't really attack. He just kept grinding at a steady cadence while his opponents buckled one by one. Serrano then zipped down the short descent to the finish on an airport landing strip high above Mende, a half minute ahead of Vasseur and Merckx.

"It's unbelievable. You try hard, you work hard all year, and all of a sudden, it works out," said Liberty's Serrano, who had scored top ten finishes in all three grand tours. "I almost quit in 2003. The results weren't coming. I kept saying I was going to quit but at the bottom of my heart, I don't think I really meant it."

What helped Serrano were some pre-stage words from his team manager Manolo Saiz. "At the team meeting today, Manolo told us the story of '95, and said this was a stage for our team. That was an inspiration." Saiz, who directed the ONCE team of Laurent Jalabert in the 1990s, recounted how Jalabert won here by breaking clear on the Croix-Neuve climb after leading an all-day breakaway that almost deprived then Tour champion Miguel Induráin of the yellow jersey.

> **"I almost quit in 2003. The results weren't coming. I kept saying I was going to quit but at the bottom of my heart, I don't think I really meant it."**

There were no such fears for Armstrong when, some 11 minutes after Serrano won the stage, the Texan led Basso, Ullrich, and Evans into the flat finish straightaway. It looked as though the race leader wanted to cross the line first, and he was somewhat upset when Evans made a late spurt to take the stage's 11th place. "Why did you have to do that?" Armstrong asked with a glare. "Sorry, mate," replied a feisty Evans.

Had it been Armstrong's first Tour and *he* had been the only rookie able to stay with the likely podium finishers on the steepest climb of the race, would he not have sprinted too? "Armstrong was pissed at me that I sat on and sprinted for the group," explained the Aussie. But, he continued, "You put a finish line in front of me and I've got to sprint for it, I'm sorry."

As for the other overall contenders, Rasmussen, Mancebo, Leipheimer, and Vinokourov lost 27 seconds to the Armstrong group, a fading Landis conceded 39 seconds, Moreau and Pereiro gave up 1:10, and white jersey Popovych came home at 1:26. Those were big gaps for such a short hill. If more such challenges were included in the Tour, then climbing specialists like Basso and Evans would have a much greater chance of fully challenging power riders like Armstrong and Ullrich.

The fading Rasmussen officially sewed up the King of the Mountains title on the climb, but he admitted he might have trouble holding off Germany's big diesel on the upcoming 55km time trial at St. Étienne. "I'm satisfied I finally won the jersey," said

Rasmussen, who was seeing a late challenge from Pereiro. "It was too bad Ullrich got away, but I have no excuses. I am feeling the third week in my legs and I just couldn't follow."

The skinny Dane wasn't the only one who was suffering. And there was yet another hot, hilly stage through the Massif Central coming up the next day.

STAGE 18: ALBI-MENDE

1. Marcos Serrano (Sp), Liberty Seguros, 189km in 4:37:36 (40.850kph); **2.** Cédric Vasseur (F), Cofidis, at 0:27; **3.** Axel Merckx (B), Davitamon-Lotto, s.t.; **4.** Xabier Zandio (Sp), Illes Balears, at 1:08; **5.** Franco Pellizotti (I), Liquigas-Bianchi, s.t.

GENERAL CLASSIFICATION

1. Lance Armstrong (USA), Discovery Channel, 3254.5km in 77:44:44 (41.664kph) 2. Ivan Basso (I), CSC, 02:46 **3.** Michael Rasmussen (Dk), Rabobank, 03:46 **4.** Jan Ullrich (G), T-Mobile, 05:58 **5.** Francisco Mancebo (Sp), Illes Balears, 07:08

CHAPTER 31
Ivan *il Terrible*: The Charmed Life of Italy's Hottest Star

Ivan Basso was all smiles on the Tour's first rest day in Grenoble. He had survived the harrowing first week with nary a scratch. Now the mountains were looming and Basso was preparing to step center stage. As he lounged by the swimming pool at the Alpexpo Vgeral Hotel, he fielded softball questions from a press corps anxious to make inroads with the man everyone expects to win the Tour de France someday. It was a good day to be Ivan Basso.

"I'm feeling good physically, but we still don't know how the opponents are," Basso said. "Everybody says the Alps will be decisive, but I think that the Pyrénées will decide the winner. There are two summit finishes with a lot of climbs. That's going to be really tough, especially after the stages here," he decided.

Basso's CSC team was riding a wave of optimism and good vibrations. Jens Voigt had been the team's second rider to wear the yellow jersey, following Dave Zabriskie's early capture of the coveted prize, and even the young American's early departure from the race couldn't dampen the team spirit. The upcoming Courchevel stage loomed high in everyone's thoughts, especially those of Basso and CSC team boss Bjarne Riis, who had worked seven hard months to get ready for this moment. The world would soon find out if Basso had what it took to dethrone Armstrong. "I am not pessimistic," Riis growled. "I am optimistic."

There was plenty to be optimistic about. Over the years, Basso had taken one positive stride after another on his steady, methodical approach to his Tour career. First came the best young rider's jersey in 2002, then a strong top-ten finish in 2003, followed by 2004's impressive third-place finish and a stage victory ahead of Armstrong at La Mongie.

At that Tour and in the months that followed, Basso soldiered through the painful experience of watching his mother suffer from pancreatic cancer. He had kept his deepest thoughts private during the off-season until the news broke just before the start of the 2004 Tour. Armstrong, calling on his connections to the cancer community, offered to help Basso find the best doctors, but nothing could stop the deadly tumor. His mother died in January 2005.

Basso carried that burden into the new season, where, surprising everyone, he set his sights on the Giro d'Italia—not the Tour de France. Even the normally unshakeable Riis was thrown for a loop. But Riis had to agree that Basso's reasoning was convincing, if unconventional: Focusing on the Giro before tackling the Tour was a fresh challenge, the latest of many goals Basso has set for himself since he was a junior racer.

"I did a very nice Tour last year, but I still lost six minutes to Lance. That's a lot of time," Basso said. "I decided to race the Giro because it's a new challenge. The Giro is a different race. I can win the Giro."

As the Italian tour began, Basso did indeed appear to be on a winning trajectory. He grabbed the *maglia rosa* after the opening climbing stage in the Dolomites, riding with a command and a rhythm that appeared unbeatable. But he caught a stomach bug before the next tough stage, and he barely survived the fearsome climb up the Stelvio. He lost 45 minutes on the unrelenting, 25km mountain climb and it looked like his Giro was over.

Basso showed his class by bouncing back to win a mountain stage and then the final time trial ahead of eventual winner Paolo Savoldelli and teammate Dave Zabriskie. The stage victories erased his disappointment and brought a smile back to his face. In that way, at least, the Giro fit in nicely to the pattern of Basso's amazing cycling career. Since a very early age, everything has been onward and upward, almost without interruption.

"This is what we work for," Basso said while sitting poolside at his hotel in Grenoble. "This is what's great about cycling. Win or lose, these moments are magical."

AMATEUR DAYS

Basso's pro career has been marked by steady, methodical progress, but his amateur days were full of prodigious leaps that made him one of the hottest amateurs to come out of

Italy. Born November 26, 1977, at Gallarate in northern Italy, Basso was raised in a family with deep bonds to cycling. His father was a passionate lifetime fan who taught Ivan the joys of bike racing at a very young age.

In fact, by age six, bright-eyed Basso was already winning local events. He was a natural-born attacker who rode so hard and so fast that he often finished solo, the other kids trailing far behind. In 1993, he won Italy's top junior race, the Coppa d'Oro, putting him in the company of such homegrown cycling stars as Gianni Bugno and Giuseppe Saronni. Basso earned the nickname Ivan *il Terrible*. He took that aggression into the 1995 world junior road championship, but an unlucky puncture with about 10km to go cost him the victory.

Encouraged by his results, Basso dreamed of a professional career, but his parents insisted that he finish school. He complied, putting his burgeoning cycling career on hold until he finished his prep studies in technical geometry. "I could see their point," he said. "Racing bikes is a hard profession, so they wanted what was good for me."

Basso began to keep meticulous notes of each training ride, the distances, heart rates, conditions, and routes. That attention to detail and self-discipline paid off handsomely in 1998. With his studies behind him and his focus squarely on racing at the elite amateur level in Italy as part of the Zalf team, Basso won 11 races and entered the world championships in the Dutch city of Valkenburg as one of the favorites for the under-23 road race. On a cold, windy day, Basso rode alone across the line to win the rainbow jersey, making up for his disappointment three years earlier.

He would then demonstrate the loyalty that has come to characterize his career. Despite wearing the rainbow jersey as the under-23 world champion, Basso delayed turning pro for half the next season out of gratitude to Zalf, the amateur team that stuck with him during his time in school. He bagged four more wins with Zalf before accepting an offer from pro team Riso Scotti–Vinavil in May 1999, just in time for his debut at the Giro d'Italia.

Basso described the transition as a passage from Earth to Mars, saying, "The two greatest memories from those days were winning the world title and starting my first Giro. It still gives me goose bumps." Basso abandoned that Giro, but vowed to come back someday to win. His ambitions were limitless, but he quickly realized the pro ranks were unforgiving.

In 2000, he moved to the Amica Chips–Tacconi Sport team, racing alongside Russian legends Evegni Berzin and Viatcheslav Ekimov. He snagged his first wins as a professional during the Regio Tour, taking the first stage and a short time trial two days later—results that were good enough to help him finish second overall. He also completed his first Giro, coming home in 52nd place. Basso's stock was on the rise.

MAN OF IRON

In 2001, Giancarlo Ferretti came calling. Ferretti was the team director for the power-packed Fasso Bortolo squad and a tireless recruiter of new talent. He had been impressed by Basso's aggression in the amateur ranks, and Basso's all-round riding abilities seemed to tip him as Italy's newest breakout star.

And sure enough, Basso quickly got to work by winning the difficult Mont Faron stage of the Mediterranean Tour in February. But a crash in stage 4 left him with a broken collarbone that forced his early exit, denying him what would have been his first stage race title. (That honor wouldn't come until the 2005 Tour of Denmark, when he won an incredible four of six stages en route to the overall victory.)

Basso bounced back from the early-2001 injury to win the toughest stage of the Bicicleta Vasca ahead of Spain's Tour de France podium star Joseba Beloki. He also won a hard mountain stage at the Tour of Austria, and earned his ticket for Fassa Bortolo's Tour team. Basso's Tour de France debut started well enough, and his style of riding was indicative of the glory that awaited him in the French race. He attacked in the first mountain stage across the Vosges and sparked the day's five-man winning break, from which Laurent Jalabert won the stage and Jens Voigt snagged the yellow jersey. However, Basso faced a far less desirable finish, crashing on the descent to the finish in Colmar and breaking his collarbone for the second time that season. He gamely finished the stage, but his first Tour was over.

Basso's 2002 season started well. He placed second in the Tour of Valencia and took third at Liège-Bastogne-Liège. At the Tour, he rode with incredible depth in the mountains, often staying with the big guns, including a strong ride up Mont Ventoux, to seal 11th place overall and the white jersey for the best young rider.

Ferretti, however, had lost patience with Basso's steady development and instead organized his team entirely around the impressive sprinting legs of Alessandro Petacchi for the 2003 Tour. Basso went along for the ride, but the team was clearly working for Petacchi, who won four of the first six road stages. What happened next, though, was entirely unexpected: Food poisoning gutted the team at the end of that first week, leaving just three Fassas in the race by the time the Tour turned into the Alps. Basso, who had worked over the winter to change his ponderous pedaling style to emulate the faster cadence of Lance Armstrong, was one of the few riders to stay close to Armstrong in that nail-biting Tour. Basso finished in seventh place, the best placing by an Italian for the second year running.

How was it, though, that Basso was racing and doing well in the Tour, but didn't ride the Giro like most Italians? "At Fassa, no one ever wanted to race the Tour," Basso explained with a shy smile. "We had GC riders like Frigo and González for the Giro. So I went [to the Tour] instead."

Basso's willingness to ride the Tour and his top ten finish in spite of minimum team support wasn't enough for Ferretti. "Basso is a classy rider, he has a lot of skill and he's very dedicated, but he never wins any races," said the man of iron. Only victories could satiate Ferretti's appetite. So after Basso's second winless season, it was clear that a Tour top ten wasn't going to cut it with Ferretti.

Basso went looking for a new boss.

> **For the 1996 Tour champion, building Team CSC in his own iconoclastic vision has become an obsession. And make no mistake: In Bjarne's army, there is room for only one general.**

BJARNE'S ARMY

Bjarne Riis doesn't just sign racers; he looks for personalities who can fit into his unique team structure. For the 1996 Tour champion, building Team CSC in his own iconoclastic vision has become an obsession. And make no mistake: In Bjarne's army, there is room for only one general.

"I study riders before I offer them a contract. I look for individuals who can work as a team," Riis said. "In Ivan, I saw those qualities. I also believed he could become a big leader. He needed someone to work with him."

Basso quickly learned that Riis was not your typical director and Team CSC wasn't your typical team. The Dane speaks fluent Italian, but he insisted that Basso learn English to communicate with his international lineup. Another surprise for Basso was the team's annual boot camp during its December get-together, when riders, staff, directors, and even mechanics undergo a series of grueling, Outward Bound–style exercises for thirty-six straight hours.

During one such challenge off the coast of the Spanish island of Lanzarote, riders had to jump into the ocean 2km offshore. There was only one problem: Basso didn't know how to swim. The team pulled together, towing Basso back to shore on a surfboard. The bonds created there would last all season.

What was most important for Basso was that in Riis he had found the sport director he was aching for. They seemed an unlikely pair: a balding, middle-aged Dane hovering over an elegant Italian with mama-boy good looks. But they spoke every day on the phone, building a relationship that went deeper than just a contract. "Riis is like a father to me," Basso said. "When I need advice on something in my life, something that has nothing to do with cycling, Bjarne is the first person I call. He's more than just a director."

With Riis's endless support, Basso began to flourish as a leader both on and off the bike. Basso also reclaimed the aggressiveness that had gone missing under Ferretti.

For 2004, Riis narrowed Basso's focus to the Tour de France. Team CSC ripped through the spring, with Jörg Jaksche winning the Mediterranean Tour and Paris-Nice, while Basso rode quietly in the shadows.

In May, Basso, his teammate Carlos Sastre, and Riis traveled to Boston for wind-tunnel testing at the Massachusetts Institute of Technology to hone the riders' time trial positions. Basso's form, never a thing of beauty, improved markedly, and the next month he recorded a second place in the Italian national time trial championships. Other important tests came at the Tour de Romandie and the Dauphiné Libéré, where Basso's strong results confirmed he was on target for July.

Armstrong was gunning for a record sixth Tour title in 2004, and it soon became clear that Basso was the only rider who could even stay close to the American's ferocious charge through the French countryside. And then, on a decisive mountain stage finish at La Mongie, Basso led Armstrong across the line to take the win while Jan Ullrich, Tyler Hamilton, and Iban Mayo floundered in their wake. It was an impressive confirmation for Basso, who was immediately crowned Armstrong's heir apparent.

Basso didn't finish the '04 Tour with quite the same strength, slipping from second to third overall in the final time trial. Nevertheless, Basso's podium finish was Italy's best result since Marco Pantani won the race in 1998, and Basso had suddenly become one of cycling's hottest commodities.

NICE GUY

At Armstrong's insistence, Discovery Channel put a full-court press on Basso during the off-season, offering him a multiyear contract that would make him a millionaire overnight. But Basso's loyalty to Riis proved stronger than money in the bank. In fact, Riis was struggling with his team's budget, even using his own cash to help cover some expenses late in the 2004 season. By 2005, Riis was asking his riders to take pay cuts while he looked for cosponsors.

Riis told riders they were free to leave their contracts if they got better offers from other teams, and several of the star riders did receive offers, including Basso, Bobby Julich, and Jens Voigt. But nearly everyone decided to stick with Riis. Italian sprinter Fabrizio Guidi was the only rider to depart, taking an offer to become the 25th rider at Phonak to give the Swiss team its necessary minimum to race in the ProTour.

Eventually, software giant CSC came to the rescue, nearly doubling the team's budget for 2005 to $8 million. It was the infusion that the team needed to stabilize and focus on the upcoming season. However, just as things were settling in, Basso announced that he was determined to race the Giro d'Italia. When he told Riis, the great Dane was speechless. "He didn't speak for 20 seconds," Basso recounted with a laugh. "Then he said, 'Let me think about it for a few days and call you back.' When he called me back, he said he was supporting the idea."

And there was another thing: After racing the Giro, Basso wanted to return to the Tour and make another run for the podium. All of this, of course, was completely at odds with conventional wisdom, which says the modern Giro is too hard for a rider who hopes to seriously contend for the Tour. It was, however, exactly the kind of strategy that appeals to Riis's appreciation for the unexpected.

"I was not 100-percent keen at the beginning," Riis admitted after Basso's 2005 schedule was confirmed, "but after I thought about it, when I remembered his level last February, through the [2004] Tour and good again until October, he's proven he can do that." He paused for a moment, then added, "I think he can do it. He'll prove it."

Basso's audacious Giro dream fell short because of the stomach virus that zapped his strength. He had to stop three times on the climb up the Stelvio for calls of nature. But true to form, he was quick to get over his disappointment. It's always sunny in Basso's world, and by the time the Tour hit its first rest day, he couldn't wait to get to the hills. That's where the real fun would begin.

Basso also was not afraid to attack Armstrong in the mountains. The charismatic Italian's leg-bending accelerations in stage 14's Port de Pailhères climb, stage 15's summit finish at Pla d'Adet and stage 18's ultrasteep Côte de la Croix-Neuve at Mende were particularly effective. They were the moves that had earned him the second rung on the podium after his mediocre showing at Courchevel, though he salvaged his Tour there by pacing himself to just a one-minute loss. The rest of his final deficit would come from the two time trials.

During the Tour, CSC announced an even bigger budget for the team, extending Basso's contract for three years at a rumored annual salary of $1.8 million. Also benefiting from a contract extension was Dave Zabriskie, the understated American who grew effusive when asked about his teammate. "He's an extremely genuine person," said Zabriskie. "He has a good heart. And he really cares about the team, and doing well. Really a nice guy. He's very competitive. And he takes it very seriously."

At age 27, Ivan *il Terrible* had finally come of age.

CHAPTER 32 | STAGE 19
Climbers Become Sprinters

With the upcoming weekend's spotlight reserved for the top time trialists and sprinters, stage 19 represented the last hurrah for an unexpected stage winner. It was a relatively short race with five categorized climbs that weren't particularly difficult, but the blurring speed at which this Tour was being conducted made every climb harder than usual. It was a stage that promised to feature yet another breakaway.

Only two Tour stages have finished at Le Puy, a remote location in the heart of the Massif Central. This is a small town of cobbled medieval streets sits in the shadows of two massive volcanic hills, atop which one can find a pilgrim's chapel and a 50-foot statue of Notre Dame de France cast from cannons used in the Napoleonic Wars. In both of the Tour stages finishing in Le Puy, small breakaways have fought out the win. Most recently, in 1996, the stage went to Swiss racer Pascal Richard, who went on to take the Olympic road race title in Atlanta in the months that followed. Richard thrived in the heat, and with temperatures again in the 80s for this stage in the rolling hills to the northwest of town, only the more resilient racers stood a chance of coming out on top. The French were particularly anxious to do well as they had just David Moncoutlé's stage win at Digne-les-Bains to celebrate over three weeks of racing

After a short initial descent from the start in Issoire, the course soon headed up through thickly wooded country toward the day's first climbs, a Cat. 4 and Cat. 3. One of the initial breaks saw Ullrich attempt to get clear in a move with seventeen others, but Armstrong's men soon put a stop to that. Shortly after, on the early slopes of the 11km climb to St. Eloy-la-Glacière, Ullrich's veteran Italian teammate Giuseppe Guerini went up

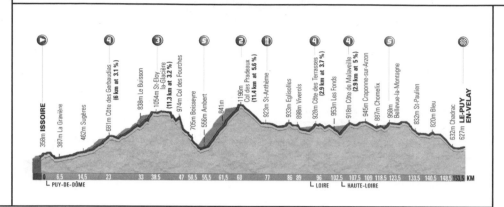

the road with one of France's more accomplished and eager riders, Sandy Casar of Française des Jeux. Within a kilometer, the tireless Pereiro made it three in front.

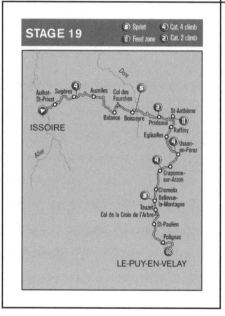

It seemed that half the peloton wanted to join the move, as rider after rider lit out on the fast, winding Cat. 3 climb (nearly 41km were raced in the first hour, nearly all uphill) to the crest of the Monts du Livradois. A second Italian, the blond Franco Pellizotti of Liquigas-Bianchi, was the strongest chaser, romping up the hill to close to within 12 seconds by the summit with the other chasers just 3 seconds behind him, and the peloton trailed by 40 seconds.

Pellizotti bridged to the other three on the plateau just before starting a long, fast, swishing descent into the town of Ambert, which sits in the deep, narrow valley of the Dore. Behind the four leaders were waves of chasers, who formed a ten-strong group that split on the sweeping 11.4km Col des Pradeaux, the final Cat. 2 climb of the Tour. At the 3,924-foot summit, Guerini's group had respectively leads of 1:20 and 1:55 on the two groups in pursuit, and 3:35 on the peloton.

The chasers, who were constantly attacking one another, were unable to close the gap further over the remaining 85km. But the work of the four riders in the break was commendable nonetheless. Knowing that they were always within striking distance, they shared their pulls at the front all the way into Le Puy, with Pereiro pushing particularly hard in a bid to move into the top ten overall.

SURPRISE FINISH

With just twenty-four hours before the vital St. Étienne time trial, Armstrong and the other main contenders simply told their troops to keep the tempo high once the break was established. That was the best tactic, both to keep Pereiro from gaining too much time and to enjoy a perfect warm-up ride through the beautiful countryside.

The four leaders ended up conducting a rapid 122km escape on the roller-coaster course. They were still together 1.5km out, apparently headed toward a sprint finish on a slightly uphill street in the center of ancient Le Puy. But who could pull ahead for the win? Casar was inherently the fastest finisher of the four men, but to win he would have to correctly interpret the intentions of the group's other three riders: the ever-ambitious Pereiro and the two Italians, Guerini and Pellizotti—all of whom were climbers, not sprinters.

Casar, who was probably overconfident, later recounted to reporters what happened next: "I was trying to be smart by letting Pellizotti come past me and, just at that moment, Guerini attacked. The barriers boxed me in a little, and I didn't see him go. I thought Pereiro would react, but he didn't move."

Casar didn't seem to realize that Pereiro was cooked. The Spaniard had done nearly all of the hard pulls in the latter part of the hilly stage

> Casar didn't seem to realize that Pereiro was cooked. The Spaniard had done nearly all of the hard pulls in the latter part of the hilly stage because he wanted to leapfrog Christophe Moreau and move into tenth place overall—which he did.

because he wanted to leapfrog Christophe Moreau and move into tenth place overall—which he did. Also, Casar didn't see Guerini make his darting, all-out acceleration along the barriers on the opposite side of the road because at that very second Pereiro slowed down and moved to his left, which momentarily blocked Casar's and Pellizotti's view of the Italian's pink team jersey dashing clear.

As for Guerini, who has ridden as a highly paid *domestique* for Ullrich since he won the Alpe d'Huez stage of the 1999 Tour, he didn't look back until he was halfway along the 200-meter-long finishing straight. He turned to see whether his move had worked. Then, after jubilantly crossing the line ten seconds ahead of the other three, he showed his complete appreciation of the group's dynamics in saying, "Pereiro was working for the GC, so I attacked when he was at the front." It was as simple as that.

Once again, the French received the consolation prizes. There was no stage win for Casar—only second place and the French panel's award for the day's most combative rider. And Moreau, once ranked as high as second in the overall standings, dropped to 11th behind the remarkable Pereiro.

STAGE 19: ISSOIRE—LE PUY-EN-VELAY

1. Giuseppe Guerini (I), T-Mobile, 153.5km in 3:33:04 (43.226kph); **2.** Sandy Casar (F), Française des Jeux, at 0:10; **3.** Franco Pellizotti (I), Liquigas-Bianchi, s.t.; **4.** Oscar Pereiro (Sp), Phonak, at 0:12; **5.** Salvatore Commesso (I), Lampre-Caffita, at 2:43.

GENERAL CLASSIFICATION

1. Lance Armstrong (USA), Discovery Channel, 81:22:19

2. Ivan Basso (I), CSC, 02:46

3. Michael Rasmussen (Dk), Rabobank, 03:46

4. Jan Ullrich (G), T-Mobile, 05:58

5. Francisco Mancebo (Sp), Illes Balears, 07:08

CHAPTER 33

Pushing the Pace:
Oscar Pereiro

When Oscar Pereiro slipped across the finish line in Le Puy-en-Velay in fourth place, it marked the third time in five stages that he drove the day's winning breakaway group. Indeed, when Giuseppe Guerini of T-Mobile attacked the leading quartet with 1.5km to go, the others looked to Pereiro to give chase. They realized too late that the Spanish rider had again raced to the point of exhaustion and, by then, Guerini was streaking across the line as the winner.

For Pereiro, a 27-year-old Spanish rider on the Phonak team, sparking the day's action was simply mission accomplished. It nudged him into the Tour's top ten and delivered on his promise to "make a show" at the 2005 Tour de France. "I came to this Tour intent on not following the wheels," he said. "The Spanish fans are hungry for a rider who attacks."

The quick-smiling fifth-year pro more than held up his end of the deal, infusing the final half of the Tour with exhilarating attacks, Spanish-style bravado, and a fearless will to go on the offensive. "I came to the Tour to do something in the overall, but from the beginning I saw there were a lot of riders fighting for the top ten," he said. "Instead, I dedicated myself to make a spectacle and try to win a stage."

Pereiro succeeded on both counts. He already had his dramatic stage victory in Pau in the bag, and to claim tenth place overall he only had to hold off Christophe Moreau in the final time trial at St. Étienne.

Pereiro was one of the few riders willing to risk losing in order to gain something in this Tour, and his eagerness to animate the race was gaining him new admirers daily. "Last year I finished tenth and no one even took notice of me," he said. "This year I've been on the attack and I have people yelling my name from the side of the road. This motivates me even more to give something back to the fans."

It was easier for Pereiro to take this philosophical approach when his hopes for a top-five finish took an early blow in the high-speed charge up Courchevel in stage 10. After attacking on an earlier climb, he couldn't stay with the pace set by Armstrong's Discovery Channel team, and he limped across the line in 37th place, 7:29 back, essentially eliminating him as a GC threat.

Sniffing an opportunity the next day on the stage to Briançon, Pereiro initiated the action with an attack on the *hors-catégorie* Col de la Madeleine. Teammate Santiago Botero and Alexander Vinokourov were among seven riders who chased Pereiro's wheel. On the treacherous descent, Pereiro overcooked one of the turns, narrowly avoided a serious crash, and took an unplanned detour across the grass. He chased back, and on reaching the next climb, the Col du Télégraphe, only Pereiro, Vinokourov, and Botero were still together. But Pereiro couldn't hold the pace set by the Kazakh on the following Col du Galibier, leaving Botero to make it a race.

> **On the treacherous descent, Pereiro overcooked one of the turns, narrowly avoided a serious crash, and took an unplanned detour across the grass.**

Once into the Pyrénées, Pereiro was told to help Phonak teammate Floyd Landis in the 220.5km stage 14 to Ax-3 Domaines, but the Spaniard couldn't stay with the strongest climbers over the punishing Port de Pailhères. Pereiro finished 30th that day, 8:34 back, and he slipped to 24th place overall, 24:40 behind Armstrong.

Without having come close to a stage win and looking unlikely to match his tenth-place Tour debut the previous year, Pereiro should have been in the dumps. So why was he smiling at the start of the next morning's stage in Lézat-sur-Lèze? "There's still hope," Pereiro told Spanish journalists. "I've talked with the team, and they're going to give me some more freedom to try some things in the final week. The Tour is three weeks, no?"

PEREIRO'S PROGRESS

Smiling in the face of adversity is a trait that serves Pereiro well. He's one of the biggest jokers in the sport, always quick with a quip, always ready for a laugh. "Oscar is one of the positive influences on this team," said Phonak team manager John Lelangue. "He is always laughing, always joking. I have never seen him in a bad mood."

Pereiro's sunny disposition is a refreshing contrast to the rainy Spanish province of Galicia that he calls home. Tucked in the northwest corner of the Iberian Peninsula, Galicia has more in common with Ireland and Wales than it does with the Costa del Sol or sunbaked Andalusia. Its inhabitants speak Gallego, a linguistic stew of Portuguese and Spanish. Galicia is a land of deep forests and rugged hills that held the last holdouts of the Celtic tribes against the Roman invasion two thousand years ago. Today, its tough fishermen ply the treacherous waters near the aptly named Costa de la Muerte, a deep-sea cemetery for more than two hundred unlucky ships.

Pereiro was born on August 3, 1977, in Pontevedra, a thriving historic town packed with dozens of Romanic churches, which are outnumbered only by the raucous pubs on every street that overflow with evening strollers snacking on sumptuous octopus, tangy cheese, and crisp white wine from the Rio Miño.

"I never liked studying and I really like going out with my friends, so it's always been hard for me to watch my weight," Pereiro said. "The food in Galicia is too good to sacrifice."

Pereiro's nickname is *Cascarilla*, which literally means "little shell." He said he earned it at age 14, when he was much smaller than his friends, weighing a paltry 84 pounds. His slight weight prompted him to start riding BMX and trials, but by 17, he enjoyed an *estirón* and shot to his present height of 5' 10". He loved speed and dabbled in mountain biking and then cyclo-cross, in which he won the Spanish national title four times.

Now he's addicted to fast cars. When asked what he was going to do with the prize money from his stage win in Pau, Pereiro was quick with his answer: "Make my first payment on the BMW Z5 I want to buy."

In the late 1990s, he went to live with grandparents to study and soon fell in love with the road racing scene. He happily spent hours training on his bike when he should have been hitting the books.

Spain's cycling hotbeds were in the faraway Basque Country and Catalonia, so Pereiro turned to nearby Portugal to cut his teeth as a pro. He won the Volta do Futuro as an amateur in 1999, which earned him a modest contract on the Portuguese Porta de Ravessa team. That year, fate would bring him to meet Alvaro Pino, the legendary Gallego ex-pro who had recently quit as the sport director of the Kelme team. "I asked him to keep an eye on me," Pereiro said. "I asked him to follow my progress."

Pereiro won only one race in two years with the Portuguese team and he soon found himself flat broke, living with his parents again, and seriously considering the unsavory prospect of returning to his studies. For what purpose he didn't know, but his cycling career was going nowhere. Then, in the fall of 2001, the phone rang while he was driving with his girlfriend, Maria. It was Pino, who had just taken over as sport director at Phonak. "Alvaro told me he had space for me on the team with him at Phonak," he said. "I stopped the car at a pull-off and started to cry."

Pereiro quickly made the most of the opportunity. Within six months, he went from nearly joining the countless thousands of wannabe professionals in Europe whose careers stalled out to riding in the 2002 Giro d'Italia. He promptly finished 11th overall in this, his grand tour debut. He paid back Pino for his loyalty with a stage win at the Setmana Catalana, and then finished 30th in the Vuelta a España. Pereiro couldn't believe his luck.

Despite winning a stage of the 2003 Tour of Switzerland and finishing in the top twenty at that year's Vuelta, however, Pereiro was garnering little attention in the Spanish press. Spain had plenty of big-time riders, and the meteoric rise of Iban Mayo, Alejandro Valverde, and Aïtor González outshone the easygoing Galician, especially as he raced for a foreign team.

By 2004, Pereiro was ready for his first Tour de France. The team was coming with an ambitious leader in Tyler Hamilton, who had his sights set on the podium. It was Pereiro's job to help the American as best he could.

As preparation for the Tour, Pereiro proved he was up to the task by winning what would turn out to be the final edition of the Classique des Alpes, held a few days ahead of the Dauphiné Libéré. Phonak would do well at the Dauphiné, in which Hamilton, Oscar Sevilla, and Pereiro all finished in the top ten.

At the Tour, Hamilton's hopes took a tumble in a first-week crash, leaving his back scarred and mangled, and the hard-luck New Englander dropped out of the race in the Pyrénées. Pereiro then showed remarkable resilience by finishing ninth in stage 8 and sixth in stage 12, results that were good enough to slip him into tenth overall. Earlier, a flat tire in Phonak's team time trial cost him 3:44 when he was forced to ride in alone. "Without losing that time, I would have finished seventh," he said.

FIRST SECOND, THEN FIRST

Pereiro's grin at the start village in Lézat-sur-Lèze quickly turned into a grimace. It was going to be a long day in the saddle. He followed an attack by Michael Boogerd about 30km into the stage before others, including George Hincapie, shot out to cover the move. Soon, a baker's dozen was ripping up the road to build a 17-minute lead by the first of the day's six climbs. Riding hard in the break were Rabobank's Erik Dekker and Karsten Kroon, hoping to spring Boogerd to victory.

The conditions were horrendous. Intense heat beat down on the riders as they trudged through the Pyrénées. The tough climbing would trim the lead group to four riders—Pereiro, Hincapie, Boogerd, and Pietro Caucchioli of Crédit Agricole—by the final punishing stretch of the *hors-catégorie* climb to Pla d'Adet.

Pereiro thought his moment had come. He attacked with 5km to go to spit out Boogerd and Caucchioli, and he envisioned soloing to victory in front of the highly charged crowd, packed with thousands of cheering Basque fans. After seven years of complaints that the Tour had become nothing more than a ragged parade of riders trying to stay on Armstrong's wheel in the mountains, now it was time for a Discovery Channel rider, Hincapie, to play wheel-sucker.

Pereiro attacked again, but couldn't shake the surprisingly stubborn Hincapie. The Spaniard dug deeper, again accelerating, but the American was riding like he had magnets in his tires. With 250 meters to go, Hincapie shot past the demoralized Pereiro to win the hardest stage of the Tour.

The normally smiling Pereiro couldn't hide his exasperation.

"I told him, 'congratulations,' but I also told him what I thought. He stayed on my wheel the whole climb. When he sprinted, I felt blocked. Then the whole world fell down on top of me."

"I told him, 'congratulations,' but I also told him what I thought," Pereiro said. "He stayed on my wheel the whole climb. When he sprinted, I felt blocked. Then the whole world fell down on top of me."

What Pereiro did on the following stage to Pau was even more impressive. After an early break went up the road, Pereiro began a strong chase on the day's second climb, the ultrasteep Marie-Blanque. After getting closer to the leaders in the valley, he bridged to the break on the *hors-catégorie* Aubisque, and then caught solo leader Cadel Evans on the descent. Two others joined them and they combined forces to ride for the last hour into Pau. Coming into the four-up sprint, there was no stopping Pereiro.

Pereiro said, "I knew if I could get to the leaders on the Aubisque, it would be a great day for me. This win erases all the bad taste from Pla d'Adet." The smile was back on Pereiro's face. It hadn't been gone for long.

With his repeated attacks and hard work in his many breakaways, Pereiro eventually earned the race jury's nod as the most combative rider of the 2005 Tour. Perhaps, after his confidence-boosting stage win and another top ten finish, the modest rider from Galicia had the makings of a true overall contender.

CHAPTER 34 | STAGE 20
One Last
Victory

There would be something missing if Lance Armstrong's final Tour triumph didn't include an individual stage win. He said that winning the team time trial was more important, and that coming in second at St. Étienne would have been just fine, but with a win in this, the final time trial of his career, Armstrong could truly seal a magnificent seventh victory. But it wouldn't be easy.

If you ignore the final time trial at Nantes in 2003, when Armstrong eased up after his only remaining opponent, Ullrich, crashed on a slick turn, the Texan had won all of these ultimate races against the clock. The closest anyone came to beating him was that first victory year, 1999, when his margin over runner-up Alex Zülle on a flat 57km course at Futuroscope was just nine seconds. Six years later, his nearest challenger was expected to be Ullrich on a very difficult 55.5km course in the hills above St. Étienne.

With 2,242 feet of climbing (and descending!) on a course that would constantly challenge a rider's bike-handling skills, this was by far the most demanding time trial at the Tour since Armstrong made his debut at the race twelve years earlier. To win it would take patience, power, and meticulous preparation. Those are all qualities that set Armstrong apart from the rest of his generation, particularly on a course such as this.

Just take the preparation part of the equation. The defending champion was beaten in all of his previous 2005 time trials, but he and coach Chris Carmichael knew how to get Armstrong's body ready for the Tour in the three weeks between an "adequate" performance at the Dauphiné Libéré and the Tour de France. On his way to the Tour start,

Armstrong stopped off in St. Étienne to ride the complete time trial course, not once, but twice.

There was another reconnaissance the morning of the stage to check on any changes. One major decision was to ride with tri-spoke wheels in front and back, unlike the other teams that all chose to ride with a traditional rear disc. "We went with the lighter wheel because there was so much climbing," explained Discovery Channel's Hincapie who was also trying for a good result.

Then there was the warm-up. The layout of the Discovery team's compound at the start kept Armstrong in the shade and well clear of the rubberneckers standing behind the barriers, which were placed between the ends of the team bus and equipment truck. Other contenders were in closer view of the public, and not shaded from the late-afternoon sunshine.

Finally, while immediate GC rivals Basso, Rasmussen, and Ullrich spent the final three or four minutes before their starts by sitting on their bikes in the start house, Armstrong kept pedaling, slowly circling the street behind the start zone to keep his muscles warm until it was time to roll up the ramp, sign on, shake hands with the race officials, and be on the start line for less than a minute. As Armstrong often says, it's the little things that count.

THE CHALLENGERS

Once on their bikes, the contenders continued to display different approaches to this ultimate challenge. Not surprisingly, one of Armstrong's former teammates, CSC's Julich, set the standard. Showing the time trial confidence he displayed in his efforts at the 2004 Tour's final time trial, the Athens Olympics, and his early-season victories at Paris-Nice and the Critérium International, Julich posted new fastest times at all four intermediate checkpoints and the finish: 26:22 at 17km (after a flat 4km followed by 13km of mostly uphill work to the course's high point 1,000 feet above St. Étienne); 47:38 at 35km in the village of St. Romain-en-Jarez (a section starting with more false flats over a ridge exposed to crosswinds before a technical, twisting descent on a narrow back road); 58:01 at 40.2km atop the Col de la Gachet (a 5km climb averaging 5-percent grades); 1:07:30 at 49.6km (after a descent less technical and faster than the first one); and 1:13:19 at the 55.5km finish (after a flat 6km run-in to the city that included three roundabouts).

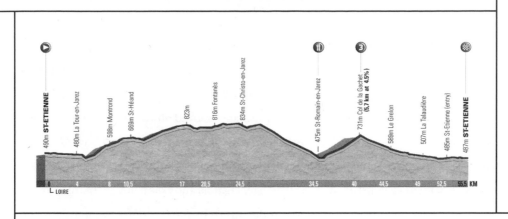

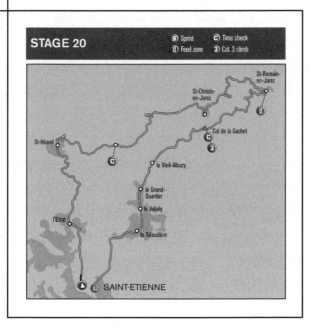

The first rider to challenge Julich's excellent ride was Vinokourov, the man who had been closest to Armstrong (and stage winner Dave Zabriskie) in the flat opening time trial three weeks earlier. At St. Étienne, Vino was ready to not only prove that that result wasn't a fluke but also to confirm his right to be in the Tour's top ten—or even top five.

The blond Kazakh star had great incentive. Just beyond the summit of the Col de la Gachet, overlooking the whole city of St. Étienne, stands a memorial to Vino's late friend Andreï Kivilev. His beloved "Kivi" lived near here and died in a race crash on a stage of the 2002 Paris-Nice that finished in St. Étienne. Inspired by his friend's memory, Vinokourov started like a rocket, thumping his pedals on the opening climb just as he had in his winning break over the Madeleine and Galibier in the Alps.

In contrast to Julich's precisely aligned torso and low, aerodynamic tuck, Vino rocks his squat body from side to side, getting the most speed he can from a big gear. His style was particularly effective on the long false flats, and he went through the 17km mark 12 seconds faster than Julich. But Julich's great cornering skills made a big difference on the technical downhill because he had drawn dead level with Vino by the foot of the Gachet climb. The Kazakh said he was thinking of Kivilev on the long uphill and, cheered on by a tunnel of fans, he reached the open summit 17 seconds faster than Julich. He had the same margin 15km later, earning a final time of 1:13:02.

In the overall standings, Vino's fine performance moved him above Evans, despite the Aussie also completing one of the best time trials of his career, only 40 seconds slower than Vino. In future Tours, besides having Vinokourov as a rival, Evans will no doubt be constantly racing against American challengers Landis and Leipheimer. On this particular day, Landis came from behind to nip the Aussie by four seconds, while Leipheimer admitted he started too slowly and never got into the rhythm that enabled him to beat Armstrong at the Dauphiné time trials. As for Spain's most solid performer, Mancebo, he did one of his best time trials, 1:03 behind Evans, to stay in the top five.

RASMUSSEN'S WOES

Then it was Ullrich's turn, who was starting the stage 2:12 out of third place. The German, riding at his strongest, was impressive up the first long climb, crossing the 17km point 12 seconds faster than teammate Vinokourov. The podium was already much closer, and it suddenly looked like becoming a lock for Ullrich when Rasmussen, three minutes back down the road, started having terrible problems.

His anxiety turned to panic just 3km into the race when instead of taking a roundabout to the right like everyone else, and as he did in training, Rasmussen "blindly" followed his lead motorcycle police outrider the long way around, to the left.

The unfancied Dane had been having a wonderful Tour, albeit a stressful one. He never expected to be a podium candidate, and since the Alps the tension was such that he cocooned himself within the Rabobank team and even stopped talking to the media. On arriving to the start of this time trial, Rasmussen was desperate to defend his third place—he looked very nervous and his pallor was more ghostlike than ever.

His anxiety turned to panic just 3km into the race when instead of taking a roundabout to the right like everyone else, and as he did in training, Rasmussen "blindly" followed his lead motorcycle police outrider the long way around, to the left. As a result, he took the tight turn too fast and skidded out. That was just the start of his troubles. He was forced to change bikes, but he wanted his original bike back, which he finally got, but then he needed a wheel change.

If that weren't enough, coming down the first descent at half-distance, Rasmussen misjudged a turn, wobbled toward the edge of the narrow road, and slowly tumbled onto the grass. "You can try for three weeks to try to win the Tour and it only takes half an hour to lose it," Rasmussen said the next day, having been too distraught to say a word after finishing his time trial in 77th place and dropping to seventh overall.

With Ullrich assured of a place on the podium, the remaining question of the day was: Who will win the stage? The answer was a long time coming.

BATTLE FOR THE WIN

The big surprise was Basso. Following his disastrous ride at Noirmoutier in the opening time trial, and with his second-place overall on the line, he needed to make some sort of statement about his form racing against the clock. He started his effort at full throttle, blasting up the opening climb to reach the summit in 25:41, which was 17 seconds faster than Ullrich and 29 seconds ahead of Vinokourov. And when Armstrong came through seven seconds slower than Basso, it seemed that the Italian might be on his way to scoring a huge upset.

"I went as hard as I could," said Basso. "I started fast because it's important to be aggressive in the time trial. You cannot race defensively. I was careful on the descents because it was very dangerous. I didn't want to crash and lose everything."

The elegant CSC rider's hesitancy on the downhill dropped him from first to third place by the St. Romain checkpoint, while a fearless Armstrong zoomed down the descent and moved into the lead, 19 seconds up on Ullrich, and 53 seconds ahead of Basso.

To clinch the stage win, Armstrong still needed to put in a strong effort on the Gachet climb. He did. The yellow jersey went up the hill in just 9:45, an amazing 32kph (20mph) average, 13 seconds faster than Ullrich on the 5km uphill.

With a 32-second lead that was the same after the long downhill to the city, Armstrong knew he could go on cruise control over the flat 6km to the finish, where his three young children were waiting to greet him. "I wanted the last image of their father as a sportsman to be that of a champion, and that means being in the yellow jersey," Armstrong said. "To have three precious little people maybe remembering one last yellow jersey was one big incentive for me."

Even though the American champion did average a remarkable 60kph on this final stretch, Ullrich went even faster, riding as hard as he has ever gone. He went two seconds per kilometer faster than the Texan, to get within 23 seconds of Armstrong's stage-winning time of 1:11:46, with Vinokourov another 53 seconds back in third, Julich fourth, and Basso fifth.

"Hats off to Lance. He's a superman," said Ullrich, who leapfrogged Rasmussen into third place on the podium. "It was hell [for me] today. I was still hurting from my crash in the Vosges." Without his two accidents, perhaps Ullrich would have gotten closer to Armstrong. But not close enough to win. The six-time champion was only a day away from his seventh consecutive title after taking the 22nd individual stage win of his incomparable Tour career.

STAGE 20: ST. ÉTIENNE TT
1. Lance Armstrong (USA), Discovery Channel, 55.5km in 1:11:46 (46.400kph); 2. Jan Ullrich (G), T-Mobile, 1:12:09; **3.** Alexander Vinokourov (Kaz), T-Mobile 1:13:02; **4. Bobby Julich (USA), CSC, 1:13:19; 5.** Ivan Basso (I), CSC, 1:13:40; **6. Floyd Landis (USA), 1:13:48; 7.** Cadel Evans (Aus), Davitamon-Lotto, 1:13:52; **8. George Hincapie (USA), Discovery Channel, 1:14:11; 9.** Francisco Mancebo (I), Illes Balears, 1:14:37; **10.** Vladimir Karpets (Rus), Illes Balears, 1:14:55.

GENERAL CLASSIFICATION
1. Lance Armstrong (USA), Discovery Channel, 82:34:05
2. Ivan Basso (I), CSC, 04:40
3. Jan Ullrich (G), T-Mobile, 06:21
4. Francisco Mancebo (Sp), Illes Balears, 09:59
5. Levi Leipheimer (USA), Gerolsteiner, 11:25

CHAPTER 35
Jan Ullrich:
The German Enigma

While Lance Armstrong was building an empire with his successive victories at the Tour de France, his chief rival over the years, Jan Ullrich, never moved beyond the fiefdom he created by winning the Tour at age 23. Ullrich has been the Sonny Liston to Armstrong's Muhammad Ali, full of dazzling ability but always out-trained, out-thought, and out-maneuvered by his illustrious opponent. But it needn't have been that way.

In the euphoria that followed Ullrich's break-through victory at the 1997 Tour—two years before Armstrong returned to the scene to start his winning streak—seasoned journalists and informed race followers gushed with praise, saying things like, "A new champion has been born. Ullrich can win six Tours in a row. The young German is unbeatable." Just eight months later, in March 1998, some of those same people were saying, "He's a disgrace to cycling. How could he let himself get so fat? He may not even *start* the Tour this year."

Ullrich's ballooning weight was his biggest problem. He quit that spring's Tirreno-Adriatico race after showing up 13 kilograms (almost 29 pounds!) heavier than his Tour de France weight. Closer to the Tour, Ullrich was telling his confidants that he had trimmed down to the same weight he had hit before winning the 1997 Tour, only 5 kilograms (11 pounds) over his ideal weight. He planned to shed the excess baggage during the first week of the Tour to hit his fighting weight when the race reached the mountains. "What's all the fuss about?" Ullrich said.

As in other years, including 2005, the freckle-faced six-footer, a product of the old East German sports machine, would then go to a pre-Tour training camp, either in the hills of the Black Forest or in Tuscany. His final preparations have nearly always included the ten-day Tour of Switzerland—where, in 2005, he won the time trial stage but struggled on some of the long alpine climbs.

Most years, Ullrich's preparation has delivered him to the Tour with form that is just shy of realizing his optimum performance. But winning the Tour is not only about form and fitness. Respected Swiss cycling coach Paul Köchli, who directed both Greg LeMond and Bernard Hinault to Tour de France victories in the 1980s, remains a keen observer of the sport. He has strong opinions about Ullrich. Köchli said, "Ullrich won the Tour because he had Bjarne Riis on his team," referring to the Dane who won the 1996 Tour. "If not, he would not win the Tour!"

Even more important than the Riis factor, Köchli said, was Ullrich's mental shape. "It will never be the same for Ullrich as last year," he said in 1998, "because it's not the same if you are *obliged* to win the Tour. That affects the way your competitors treat you. If everybody is against you, you can't win. But if you are smart, you can get the other teams working for you without them knowing it. Riis [in 1996] and Ullrich [in 1997] didn't win the Tour because they were very, very strong, but because the other teams didn't do everything they could to win."

TACTICAL MISTAKES

Ullrich's reliance on Riis was obvious in 1997, both on and off the bike. The day after the *wunderkind* took over the yellow jersey for the first time, journalists crowded into a Team Telekom news conference eager to talk to this young champion who had ridden all the top climbers off his wheel in the Pyrénées and gone on to win the stage at the Arcalis summit in Andorra. But Ullrich said barely a word. All the questions were fielded by Riis.

Ullrich depended on Riis the same way when they were racing. Pacing him on climbs, sheltering him from crosswinds, chasing down breaks, Riis rode side by side with Ullrich and coaxed him to his greatest performances.

The day after the press conference, Ullrich scored what was perhaps the most impressive stage win of his career, in a 55.5km time trial at St. Étienne. He caught the runner-up, Frenchman Richard Virenque, and won the stage by three minutes. But in the Alps two days later, Ullrich panicked when Virenque's Festina team attacked *en masse* on the first of three giant climbs in a stage that ended at Courchevel. The young race leader stayed with the attackers on the uphill, but lost a minute on the long descent; eventually, he had to wait for Riis, who then paced Ullrich up and over the Col de la Madeleine before Virenque was caught and the yellow jersey was saved. That day ended well, but Ullrich needed rescuing again by his team a few days later, on a climbing stage through the Vosges. Over the years, he would make other strategic errors, particularly those made without Riis by his side in 1998.

Asked in 2004 whether he regretted any of his apparent tactical mistakes, Ullrich replied, "It's clear that people will look for mistakes from the guy who was second. The winner never makes mistakes. So I don't really regret things, especially the times that I've made mistakes [because they] didn't make me lose the Tour de France.

"The only mistake throughout the years that I regretted was in 1998 [on the stage over the Galibier to Les Deux-Alpes], when I was in difficulty through hunger, through the cold, and I didn't eat enough. Also, I didn't carry enough warm clothing, and I lost the Tour de France [to Marco Pantani]. That's the thing that I regret the most."

There was a photo taken on that stormy day in the Alps in 1998 that captured Ullrich's problems: He is stopped by the roadside in a downpour, straddling his bike and putting on a plastic rain jacket as a mechanic is rushing to replace a flat rear tire before team manager Walter Godefroot grabs hold of the saddle and pushes Ullrich back into the race. It all went down just before the climb to the finish at Les Deux-Alpes, where Ullrich arrived in 25th place, almost nine minutes behind Pantani.

It was the turning point in Ullrich's Tour career. He never wore the yellow jersey again.

ALWAYS AN ATHLETE

Jan Ullrich was born December 2, 1973, in Rostock, a northern industrial city and port in what was then the German Democratic Republic. Not unlike Armstrong, Ullrich barely knew his father, an alcoholic, who abandoned his family when Jan was very young. Sports soon became Ullrich's whole life. After toying with middle-distance running, he won his first bike race at age 9, moved with his mother's permission to a sports school in East Berlin at age 13, and eventually became a star rider on communist East Germany's world-class athlete program, counseled by a disciplinarian coach, Peter Becker.

After the Berlin Wall fell in 1989, Ullrich and some teammates moved with Becker to Hamburg in the former West Germany. Now racing for the German national team, Ullrich became a symbol of the reunified country when he won the world amateur road championship in 1993 at age 19, the youngest rider to win that title since Eddy Merckx did so thirty years earlier. That same weekend on the same course in Oslo, Norway, a 21-year-old named Lance Armstrong was the youngest winner of the professional road race in more than fifty years.

It seemed inevitable that the paths of the two men would cross. But the year that Ullrich made his debut at the Tour in 1996, Armstrong quit at the end of the first week, and a few months later he was diagnosed with cancer. The two didn't really face off until four years later, when Armstrong destroyed Ullrich on the Tour's mountaintop finishes, but Ullrich bounced back to win the 2000 Olympic road race in Sydney after the American missed the winning break.

Armstrong again defeated Ullrich, in a good-natured contest, at the following year's Tour. And then came 2002—a year of crisis for the German. Unsuccessful surgery on a damaged knee was followed by a drunk driving arrest in May, and a positive test for amphetamines in an out-of-competition drug test in June. His team suspended him without pay, and after he confessed that he'd popped ecstasy at a party, he was suspended from the sport for six months. At a news conference, Ullrich said, "I can't leave the sport like this. I want to race again. Now I'm completely down, but I'll get right back up."

> **"I can't leave the sport like this. I want to race again. Now I'm completely down, but I'll get right back up."**

At the same time, there was an acrimonious split between Team Telekom manager Godefroot and Rudy Pevenage, both Belgians, who had worked together since their racing days. Pevenage became Ullrich's personal trainer, taking over from the aging Becker. Because of the split, Pevenage moved with Ullrich to a new team. Ullrich returned to racing in April 2003, and went on to nearly beat Armstrong at the Tour. But sponsorship woes forced Ullrich's team to disband, and he returned to the T-Mobile squad managed by Godefroot. Pevenage was not allowed back, though, except as a consultant.

Ullrich might well have done better by accepting an offer to join the CSC team and ride for Riis, who had become a very savvy team director after retiring from racing. But he decided to go for a fat contract, abandoning the chance to absorb the tactical benefits he might have gained from his old teammate.

ANOTHER PODIUM

Going into this Tour, Ullrich sputtered through the same problems he seemed to face every year: a springtime cold, excess weight (though not to the same extreme), a late start to the season, and an absence of good form. The official spin from his team was also the same: his preparation was on target, his training was going well, and everything would be fine by Tour time. So who was right? The skeptical press who still poked fun at "Humpty Dumpty" Ullrich? Or all the king's men, who did everything to put Jan's reputation together again?

Reports of Ullrich's poor form never changed Armstrong's focus. Whenever he was asked whom he thought his main opponents would be at the Tour, Armstrong would say, "Only Ullrich. Ullrich's far and away the biggest rival. We follow him closely. That's who we spend most of our time analyzing . . . the only one we really pay attention to . . . what he's racing, what are his race results, what he's saying, how big he is."

Ullrich's size remained a reference point for everyone, except the rider himself. "The thing about my weight is rubbish," Ullrich said. "I could be 2 or 3 kilos [5 or 6 pounds] lighter, but I trained a lot in the winter and built up muscle mass. This additional strength will help me cope with the demands of the Tour and overcome them. Armstrong is different from me, and it is not the first time I've been in this situation."

And it's true that the German has nearly always turned things around by the start of the Tour. He was more confident going into the 2005 race than usual following his time trial victory in Switzerland. But Ullrich was coping with some personal problems. His longtime partner Gaby Weis left him and took their two-year-old daughter Sarah with her to live with her parents back in Germany. Ullrich remained in Switzerland at his mansion overlooking Lake Constance, revealing just before the Tour that he had fallen in love with Sara Steinhauser, the sister of his training partner and teammate Tobias Steinhauser.

Then, the afternoon before the Tour started in Fromentine, came Ullrich's high speed, headfirst collision with his team car. Perhaps he would have better matched Armstrong without that crash. Instead, he was humiliated by the Texan's catch-and-pass on the opening time trial.

Despite the setbacks, Ullrich's morale was slowly restored: first, his T-Mobile squad managed a strong third place in the team time trial; next, he had the opportunity to stop and kiss his daughter, whose mother had come to watch the Tour on the German part of stage 8; and later the same day, T-Mobile rode aggressively to isolate Armstrong on the Col de la Schlucht in the Vosges.

The very next morning, though, a momentary distraction caused Ullrich to go off the road on the steep descent of the Cat. 3 Col de Grosse Pierre. He somersaulted over the handlebars and landed on his back. Nothing was broken, but his injuries certainly affected his performance forty-eight hours later when he was dropped on the finishing climb to Courchevel and lost another two minutes.

Ullrich was still hurting in the final time trial eleven days later. "It was hell. I still have a lot of pain in my back," he said after losing to Armstrong by only 23 seconds at St. Étienne. That performance clinched Ullrich's seventh podium finish in eight Tour starts. He had kept his promise to keep on attacking whatever the situation.

Ullrich's determination was at its strongest in the 2003 Tour, when he was close to quitting in the first week because of a debilitating virus that was kept under cover by his team. "I had a fever, I was sick, and I was at the limit of my abilities," he revealed later. "But if you train a whole year for it, and if you prepare yourself a whole year, then you want to fight, to continue in the race. And that's what made me go on." In riding out the 2003 Tour, Ullrich may have lost time at L'Alpe d'Huez, but then he thrashed a dehydrated Armstrong in the first long time trial, and finally lost the Tour by only 1:01. It was the closest he would ever come to defeating the Texan.

It's not likely that Ullrich will have to worry about Armstrong in 2006, nor will there be the same turmoil in his own team. The German, at 32, should rediscover the stability he enjoyed in the 1997 Tour. T-Mobile's manager Godefroot is retiring, Pevenage will be back in favor, and perhaps Ullrich will finally get a chance to create an empire of his own.

CHAPTER 36 | STAGE 21
Fireworks
on the Champs

There's no more glorious setting for a major sports event than the Champs-Élysées. On this final day of the 92nd Tour de France, spectators were packed five- to ten-deep along both sides of the tree-lined avenue, and around the bottom end of the circuit on the right bank of the Seine, past the Louvre, along the Rue de Rivoli and across the Place de la Concorde. At the foot of the Arc de Triomphe and within sight of the Eiffel Tower, the Tour was finishing on the world's grandest stage.

The final pedal strokes of the race are always a mad dash, with a fury that belies the more sedate promenade into the city via the suburbs of the French capital. On the lazy ride into town the press photographers began their ritual photos of the yellow, green, and polka-dot jerseys, lining up Lance Armstrong, Thor Hushovd, and Michael Rasmussen with the ceremonious formality one would expect at a wedding. Armstrong clinked champagne glasses with team manger Johan Bruyneel and race director Jean-Marie Leblanc, and the hum of the race hit a new lull where friendly chats ensued between athletes who had been closeted together for the previous three weeks. It was a lovely party that was nearly rained out.

Because of the slippery streets, the green jersey contenders, Hushovd, Stuart O'Grady, and Robbie McEwen, decided not to contest the first of two intermediate sprints, one at 75km into the 144.5km stage, and the second just 15km before reaching the final circuit. This opened a door of opportunity for 5th-place Levi Leipheimer and 6th-place Alexander Vinokourov—separated by only 2 seconds—to race for the sprint bonuses of 6, 4, and 2 seconds.

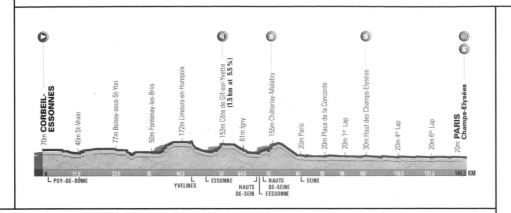

"It was a very difficult sprint," said Leipheimer. "It was 2km uphill. [Vino] went big. [My team] had to accelerate to get on his wheel. He let off a little bit, went again. He basically dropped my teammates, and I was the only one left on the wheel. He was smart enough to go 90 percent and then he gave it everything, and I tried to come around but there was just no way. He was too powerful for me."

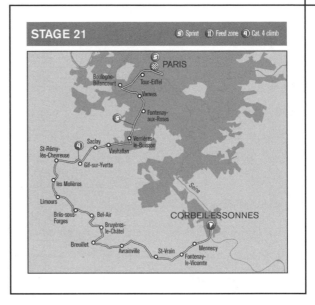

The extra two seconds Vino earned there brought him even with the American on overall time, although Leipheimer was still hanging on to fifth place as his times in the two individual time trials were a few hundredths of a second faster. The Gerolsteiner leader could still achieve his top five goal if he could prevent Vinokourov claiming more bonus seconds at the second sprint (on the Champs-Élysées), or at the stage finish itself.

"I still had the same strategy, to defend," said Leipheimer. "But we were coming into Paris and there were many crashes and it was very dangerous. I heard on the radio that the jury had made the decision to take the stage time at the first line [on the Champs-Élysées], and there were no more bonuses. It was a little bit confusing, so I tried to stay near [Vinokourov] as much as possible."

UP FOR GRABS

For only the third time in a quarter century, the Tour's final road race didn't end in a field sprint. The other times were in 1994, when a small breakaway group was led home by Frenchman Eddy Seigneur and American Frankie Andreu, and 1987, when Californian Jeff Pierce and Canadian Steve Bauer finished the stage first and second.

At this 2005 Tour, it looked as though another American might be involved in the showdown when the irrepressible Chris Horner escaped with Quick Step's big Dutchman Bram Tankink inside four laps to go of the 6.5km finishing circuit.

"I was thinking, 'Why not go for the win on the Champs-Élysées?'" said Horner, who was pleased that the sun had eventually came out to dry the cobbles of the Champs for the final few laps. "We were still a ways out, but we were out there for two laps. I mean, it was still an impressive show for two guys, and I had a good time. It was a good way for me to finish off my first Tour de France."

Horner and Tankink, who averaged 53kph for their two laps off the front, were brought back into the fold only a lap and a half from the finish. Exactly one lap later, with 3km of the stage remaining, Horner was again in a great position. "I was on Vinokourov's wheel with half a lap to go," the Saunier Duval rider continued, "and I was like, 'Okay, I've recovered from the attack, Vinokourov is right there, stay with him, he's going to go.' You just know it. The guy never quits working, never gives up."

Despite being on alert, Horner was passed on the next corner by the Davitamon-Lotto riders trying to set up McEwen for the win, while Vino came out of the turn chasing an attack by French veteran Laurent Brochard of Bouygues Télécom. And then came Leipheimer still pushing to stay with Vinokourov. "With half a lap to go it was all together, all the sprinters' teams were there, it was crazy. Chaos," said the American. "I lost the wheel. And I thought, if he gets top three now, and gets the bonus, it's pretty amazing."

Vino managed to stay within a few meters of Brochard, whose effort lasted for a kilometer. But just as the Frenchman drifted back on turning the corner into the cobbled Rue de Rivoli—where a Texas flag was hanging for the final time at Armstrong's preferred Paris accommodations, the Hôtel de Crillon—Vino jumped again.

McEwen, whose team was still trying to close the gap, analyzed the situation. "I just ran out of riders to work at the end," he said. "Hushovd didn't really want to be sprinting for the win and risk his [green] jersey at all, so he told his guy not to go. And that sort of made everybody balk, and the gap was there. Brad then jumped away and tried to win the stage."

Brad McGee, the Australian Olympic track gold medalist and Française des Jeux team leader, quickly bridged to Vinokourov. They were 100 meters clear under the 1km-to-go kite. Then, 800 meters from the line, McGee jumped hard in a last-ditch effort to save his Tour. He sprinted out of the saddle, hoping to drop Vinokourov. But the Kazakh stuck to his wheel. "The f——r, he must have known I was so desperate [to win]," a frustrated McGee said right after the finish. "He knew I had to go. And I was feeling strong . . . for the first time in three weeks."

McGee tried again after turning the corner into the Champs-Élysées for the final time, but this time Vino jumped too, and sped away for what he called his most memorable moment of a memorable Tour: victory in Paris, the 20-second win bonus, and fifth place overall. Horner, who knew how close he had come to being the stage winner, stated in his typical frank style, "It just killed me to see him win."

Crossing the line in 118th place, 22 seconds after Vinokourov, Armstrong was smiling as he completed what he said was the final professional bike race of his career. The first to tap him on the shoulder with his congratulations was Spanish teammate Rubiera, the faithful Chechu, who placed 119th. The other Discovery Channel riders were waiting with their own hugs and words of reverence for a leader who never doubted he would win again.

As for the one colleague who had helped Armstrong through all seven Tour victories, he was just relieved it was all over. George Hincapie crashed on wet pavement at one of the traffic circles coming into Paris, but said he was unhurt. "Somebody attacked for no reason, and I went after him," said Hincapie, his French wife by his side that evening at the Hôtel de Crillon before heading to post-race parties. "I think I hit some oil and went down. Didn't hurt too bad. It was a tough Tour, and I'm glad to have it over with."

Maybe in a year's time, it would be Hincapie's turn to lead the team. But to victory? It was too soon to say.

STAGE 21: CORBEILLE-ESSONNES–PARIS (CHAMPS-ÉLYSÉES)

1. Alexander Vinokourov (Kaz), T-Mobile, 144.5km in 3:40:57 (39.239kph); **2.** Brad McGee (Aus), Française des Jeux; **3.** Fabian Cancellara (Swi), Fassa Bortolo; **4.** Robbie McEwen (Aus), Davitamon-Lotto; **5.** Stuart O'Grady (Aus), Cofidis, all s.t.

CHAPTER 37
Armstrong's
Yellow Brick Road

Perhaps the most remarkable thing about Lance Armstrong's victory in the 92nd Tour de France, by 4:40 over Ivan Basso and 6:21 over Jan Ullrich, was the manner in which he manipulated the competition. His asserted his control from the very first day when he caught and passed Ullrich, gaining one full minute over his rival after just 15.8km of the flat time trial across the marshlands of Noirmoutier Island. Armstrong's dominance ended twenty-two days later as the sunlight sparkled on the Champs-Élysées. He leaned over to give Ullrich an awkward hug from the podium and called the rider who tested him the most over the years "a special rider and a special person."

"What about Basso?" yelled some American race fans on the far side of the world's most beautiful avenue. Armstrong, giving the first-ever public address by a Tour champion, turned, reassuring them, "I'll get to Basso in a moment." When he did, the once-raw Texan was honey-smooth in his praise: "Ivan is a good friend . . . he's the future of the sport." Armstrong quickly caught himself again and turned back to Ullrich to say that, yes, the T-Mobile leader still had a Tour win or two in his legs. "I'm out of it," the champ concluded, "so it's up to you guys now."

After praising his opponents, Armstrong showered compliments on his teammates, coaches, directors, and support staff, just as he had at a news conference the evening before when he said that without his "close friend" Johan Bruyneel he wouldn't have taken one Tour de France, let alone seven. But unlike the previous six victories, it seemed that Armstrong could have won this Tour even without a team. He was so self-assured, so confident of his own strengths, that not Ullrich, not Basso, nor any of the other top finishers kept him awake at night.

In the crucial moments of stage 8, on the phenomenally fast ascent of the Col de la Schlucht in the Vosges mountains of Alsace, all of Armstrong's teammates were dropped from a front group of thirty-two riders. "What's going on?!" gasped race followers. But the defending champion was not in the least fazed by his colleagues' collective ineffectiveness. An hour after the stage finish while relaxing on the patio of his team's Hôtel de la Route Verte at Gérardmer, the Texan joked and smiled his way through a lengthy interview with French TV's Jean-René Goddart. It was as if losing his entire bodyguard on the Schlucht was no big deal.

In critique of his team's apparent meltdown Armstrong only went so far as to say: "Under situations like that, it would be hard to win the Tour. We have to evaluate where we are and make some adjustments."

The Discovery riders readjusted the following day on a hilly trek over and around the Grand Ballon and Ballon d'Alsace peaks, and then they destroyed Basso, Ullrich, and Alexander Vinokourov on the brutal alpine climb to Courchevel. The French press questioned the Discovery team's rapid turnaround. There were even rumblings that Armstrong's men must have doped to enable them to switch from "losers" to "winners" within twenty-four hours.

Partly in response to this and many other insinuations over the years that he and his riders have resorted to illicit substances or methods, Armstrong used the Paris podium as his bully pulpit. Mocking the "cynics and skeptics," he said, "I'm sorry for you. I'm sorry you can't dream. . . . I'm sorry you don't believe in miracles. But this is one helluva race. And there are no secrets. This is a hard sport, and it is hard work [that] wins it."

Among the skeptics was the French government's antidrug agency that singled out Armstrong for two surprise blood tests, one the evening before the first time trial and the other right after the finish of the final time trial. Both tests proved negative, like all of the hundreds of others that the seven-time Tour champion had taken in his pro cycling career.

THE EPO ACCUSATION

The degree of skepticism over Armstrong's string of seven championships was emphasized a month after the 2005 Tour finished when the August 23 edition of the French sports daily, *L'Équipe*, published a front-page story claiming that Armstrong had doped at the 1999 Tour de France. The newspaper editorial introducing the piece, titled "The Armstrong Lie," contained a definitive accusation just weeks after the celebration of Armstrong on the Champs-Élysées: "*L'Équipe* has received the results of scientific analyses that took place at the national anti-doping laboratory at Châtenay-Malabry, backed up by official documentation. Our investigation shows Lance Armstrong used EPO in winning his first Tour de France in 1999, contrary to everything he has said."

The author of the report, Damien Ressiot, discovered back in April that, starting in December 2004, the Châtenay-Malabry lab had been testing B-samples of urine given by competitors at the 1998 and 1999 Tours. The testing was part of the lab's ongoing research to improve the international testing methods for identifying synthetic erythropoietin (EPO), which helps generate red blood cells and consequently boosts the oxygen-carrying capacity of blood. Permission for testing these B-samples was approved by the World Anti-Doping Agency (WADA) as experimental research. WADA believed there was a strong chance that many of the preserved samples would prove positive because an EPO test did not exist in 1999, when the A-samples were originally tested. The frozen samples had been stored at the French lab for more than five years.

According to established protocol, the lab did not have the ability to link the numbers on the twelve positive 1999 samples to the names of the riders who supplied the urine. That information came from another source, and *L'Équipe* did not reveal the origin of the supporting documents.

On an inside page, the newspaper provided images of the documentation showing the code numbers circled in red, with lines connecting them to the code-number blanks on the accompanying paperwork, which was printed on the letterhead of the sport's governing body, the UCI. In the case of Armstrong's 17 samples, 6 of which the paper claimed to show signs of EPO use, each form was countersigned by U.S. Postal Service team director Johan Bruyneel. The names of the riders who supplied the other six "positive" samples were withheld because, said Ressiot, he did not have the same back-up documentation he had in the case of Armstrong's samples. The UCI later said the document that was reproduced in the newspaper was obtained under "a false pretext." Armstrong then revealed that Ressiot told him he was researching a story on the medical exemptions given to riders by the UCI to treat normal complaints (such as saddle sores or asthma) with controlled substances such as corticosteroids. The French journalist subsequently visited the UCI head-quarters in Aigle, Switzerland, where he was allowed to examine the 1999 documents and came away with a copy.

Although the French lab established the EPO urine test in time for the 2000 Olympic Games in Sydney, the methodology has often been criticized as not being foolproof, and a number of athletes have produced false positives. That's why WADA had funded different projects to improve the test or find an alternative. A spokeswoman for an Australian company, Proteome Systems, which received one of the research grants, told the *International Herald Tribune*, "This is not a pregnancy test, where you are either pregnant or you're not. It has to be prepared carefully and interpreted by an expert, who can mostly call it, I believe. But it is definitely skill based, and that is why WADA is looking for a more clear-cut test. There is a lot of argument, and a lot of politics, about whether the test is good . . . there are certainly false positives."

Further questions have been raised regarding the long period of storage of the samples. Dr. Christiane Ayotte, director of the Doping Control Laboratory at Montreal's Institut National de la Recherche Scientifique, told *VeloNews* that she was "surprised" that scientists at Châtenay-Malabry had actually been able to detect EPO in a sample of that age. "We are extremely surprised that urine samples could have been tested in 2004 and have revealed the presence of EPO," Ayotte said. "EPO, in its natural state or synthesized version, is not stable in urine, even if stored at minus 20 degrees."

However, Dr. Jacques de Ceaurriz, director of the Châtenay-Malabry lab, said he was confident the samples had been stored correctly and there was no degradation of the EPO in the samples. "One of two things happens," he stated. "Either EPO, which is a protein, degrades as time passes and becomes undetectable . . . or, as in this case, the EPO persists as it is. We therefore have no doubt about the validity of our results."

Even if the accusations made by *L'Équipe* were accurate, though, the absence of corroborating A-samples meant that neither WADA nor the UCI could seek disciplinary action against Armstrong under present legislation. If any action were taken, it would have to go through USA Cycling, whose chief executive publicly supported Armstrong in his immediate condemnation of the doping accusations.

In the face of the investigation, Armstrong adamantly denied ever using performance-enhancing substances. He was particularly angry with some comments the EPO story made by Tour de France race director Jean-Marie Leblanc. The day after the report was published Armstrong said in a conference call, "[For Jean-Marie] to say that I've fooled the fans is preposterous. . . . You know my history with the French media, the French Ministry of Sport, the organizers, the labs, the prosecutors, the police, et cetera. It has been a witch hunt. That was not just a catchphrase to put in the press release."

Ironically, Armstrong made that conference call after a hero's welcome at the headquarters of his team sponsor Discovery Channel in Silver Spring, Maryland. Referring to the many corporations that pay him handsomely for his commercial services, the all-time Tour champion said, "We haven't seen any damage. The partners and sponsors that I've been involved with for a long time immediately wrote back letters of support."

In a Web poll carried out by American sports media giant ESPN the day the article appeared in *L'Équipe*, 72 percent of the more than 50,000 respondents said they did not believe the doping allegations against Armstrong. In contrast, a similar survey conducted the following day by *L'Équipe* showed that 81 percent of French respondents agreed that the EPO revelations put into question the entirety of Armstrong's cycling career.

Undercurrents of the dichotomy in public opinion, demonstrated by the American and French polls, were felt long before the *L'Équipe* article was published, and they served as the trigger for Armstrong's "cynics and skeptics" speech on the Champs-Élysées.

OUT ON TOP

Aside from addressing the doubting Thomases when speaking to the half-million fans in Paris, Armstrong also alluded to the good luck he had enjoyed during his seven-year reign. Many observers made reference to how the gods seemed to have smiled on the man some call Saint Lance. Typical was a comment from Chris Horner, the fearless Tour rookie from San Diego, California. "It's amazing the power he's put out every year, the luck that he's had every year," said Horner, who then cited Armstrong's near-crash in stage 21 as an example. "Just look at today and how slippery it was. [Three] of his teammates go down right in front of him, and the guy still stays up."

While Armstrong came through the Tour unscathed—and even escaped with only a black eye and superficial cuts when he crashed in training a week before the race—his opponents seemed to be hexed. Perhaps only a Harry Potter spell could provide an explanation for the freaky crashes that befell podium contenders Ullrich and Michael Rasmussen, and early race leader Dave Zabriskie.

Had the "blessed" Armstrong lived in Greece three millennia ago, his middle name would likely have been Hercules, a man who was so strong and courageous, and his deeds so mighty, that when he died he was chosen to live with the gods on Mount Olympus. Modern theology generally takes a different view, however, and Armstrong agreed that his seventh-consecutive victory at the Tour de France was no guarantee of ascendancy to a higher place. After wrapping up what was probably his least stressful overall win, he simply said, "I don't think [my] sport accomplishments are going to make my trip to heaven any easier."

He need not worry. He's already claimed his place in the cycling firmament as the only Tour champion to go out on top—if, indeed, he held to his decision to stop racing after the 2005 Tour. The four riders who won five Tours had much different endings to their careers.

Jacques Anquetil rode one Tour too many, dropping out with bronchitis a few days before the finish of the 1966 Tour, and ended his career in Charleroi, Belgium, at an indoor track meet in November 1969. Eddy Merckx also raced his last Tour when he was on the decline, taking sixth place, 12:38 behind Bernard Thévenet, in 1977, and he quit the sport by the back door after placing 12th in a Belgian kermesse race at Kemzeke in March 1978.

The third five-time Tour winner Bernard Hinault enjoyed a better ending. He was second at his last Tour, 3:10 behind teammate Greg LeMond, in July 1986, and in his last road race the following month, he placed 59th at the world championship, held in Colorado Springs that year. As for Miguel Induráin, after finishing 11th at his final Tour, 14:14 down on Bjarne Riis, his career ended two months later when he abandoned the Vuelta a España midway through its 13th stage in September 1996.

So how is it that Armstrong, who could have been satisfied with trumping his illustrious predecessors with a record sixth win, was able to continue so strongly and pull off a near-perfect No. 7? The simple answer would be that he *had* to win because his contract with the Discovery Channel team dictated that he race one last Tour, and in the Tour de France Armstrong can do no less than win. But Armstrong said after clinching his seventh title in the stage-20 time trial at St. Étienne on July 23, "For me there was no pressure for this victory. It was just something that I had within myself. As a sportsman, I wanted to go out on top. And so that was the only incentive and the only pressure."

Aside from the ever-aggressive Basso, the only rider who even hinted at disturbing Armstrong's smooth passage through the 2005 Tour was the young Spanish rider Alejandro Valverde. The Illes Balears coleader was riding a distinguished first Tour before a knee injury forced him to quit on the transitional stage between the Alps and Pyrénées. At that point, Valverde was in fifth place overall, only 36 seconds behind Basso, and was wearing the young riders' white jersey that he took after his superb and shocking stage win over Armstrong at Courchevel. That defeat was the biggest surprise of Armstrong's Tour and perhaps an indication that his Herculean strength was beginning to fade, if ever so slightly.

SEVEN OF ELEVEN

If this Tour really was Armstrong's final race, it was the end of a remarkable pro cycling career that included 91 race wins. He turned pro at age 20 with the Motorola team, after finishing 14th in the final all-amateur 1992 Olympic Road Race at Barcelona, which was won by his future teammate Fabio Casartelli of Italy. Six days later, Armstrong lined up with 206 others for his first pro race, the San Sebastian World Cup classic. The hilly 234km race was the longest the young Texan had tackled. He was dropped in the hills, but while 95 riders abandoned the event, he carried on. Urged on by his team director Hennie Kuiper, a former world and Olympic champion, Armstrong struggled to the finish alone, in 111th place, 26:56 behind the winner, Raúl Alcalá of Mexico.

Armstrong soon turned things around. Two days after the San Sebastian race, he started Spain's Tour of Galicia. He won the 99km fourth stage in a sprint past Britain's Malcolm Elliott, placed second in the next day's stage, and was beaten in another sprint by Belgian Peter De Clercq. In the end, Armstrong finished 14th overall, three seconds behind 13th-place finisher Johan Bruyneel, his future friend and team manager.

With a first victory in the bag, the very ambitious Armstrong traveled to Switzerland's World Cup race at Zürich the following week, and duly made it into the winning break-away. This time he was prepared for the 240km distance, but his inexperience cost him the race. Russia's Viatcheslav Ekimov, a future teammate, outsmarted him by slipping away on the run-in, to finish 15 seconds ahead of the second-place Armstrong.

That performance helped establish the talented young American as one of the world's best single-day racers. Confirmation of his new status came with two big wins in

Italy: a pre-world's race at Marostica where he beat out Italian Davide Rebellin on September 1, followed in February 1993 by the Laigueglia Trophy, in which he outsprinted a four-man group containing former world champion Moreno Argentin. In this breakout year, Armstrong went on to win the USPRO Championship at Philadelphia in an unprecedented solo ride, and then took the world title in Oslo in another solo move, 19 seconds ahead of the reigning Tour de France champion, Miguel Induráin.

Armstrong went on to win the San Sebastian World Cup race in 1995 and the Belgian classic, Flèche Wallonne, in 1996. But his greatest successes would come not in one-day classics, but in stage races. He showed signs of his later dominance with victories in America's ten-day Tour DuPont in 1995 and 1996, but the Tour de France was where his true destiny lay.

Highlighting his precancer years, there was his ecstatic first Tour stage win at Verdun in 1993, when he outkicked Mexican nemesis Alcalá. The 1995 Tour saw Armstrong's overconfident sprint defeat against breakaway companion Sergei Uchakov at Revel, which ended in defeat. Just two days later Armstrong suffered the terrible death of teammate Casartelli, whose memory he immortalized by winning the stage into Limoges "with the strength of two men."

Then came 1996. After an opening week of cold rain, Armstrong pulled out of the Tour in stage 6 to Aix-les-Bains. "I couldn't breathe," he said in his hotel room after the stage. Ten weeks later, he was having a cancerous testicle surgically removed in an Austin, Texas, hospital. More surgery and nauseating chemotherapy followed before the cancer in his testicle, lungs, and brain was halted.

Armstrong made his return to the Tour in 1999. When he won the prologue at Le Puy du Fou and slipped on the first yellow jersey of his life, his tears of emotion reflected not only the illness he had survived but also the shock of winning a time trial in Europe for the first time. The surprise wasn't as great when he blitzed the Metz time trial a week later, to again take the race lead.

The real shocker came on the first stage in the Alps. After Armstrong dropped the Tour's best climbers one by one to win at Sestriere, the skepticism could no longer be contained. The European media, poisoned by the previous year's Festina scandal, said a cancer survivor and former classics specialist couldn't possibly win the Tour's toughest mountain stage without some artificial aid.

Those who knew Armstrong, then 27, told the disbelieving French reporters that he was always an explosive climber on shorter hills, and he was now better adapted to long alpine climbs because of a dramatically improved power-to-weight ratio thanks to his shedding upper-body muscle during chemotherapy. Also, he had developed a fast-cadence climbing style with coach Chris Carmichael and consultant Michele Ferrari, had trained more intensely in the mountains than ever before, and had phenomenal support on the climbs from teammates like Kevin Livingston and Tyler Hamilton.

After winning that 1999 Tour, the skeptics said Armstrong's victory was a result of a lack of real opposition. Just wait until 2000, they said, when he would face former Tour winners Ullrich and Marco Pantani. Armstrong couldn't wait to show everyone what he could do, and when Pantani was the first to attack in the Tour's tenth stage during a rainstorm on the finishing climb to Lourdes-Hautacam, Armstrong bided his time, then rode away on his own, leaving Ullrich and Pantani respectively 3:19 and 5:10 behind him. It had taken just 10km of one mountain climb to put Tour win No. 2 in the bag. And even when Armstrong bonked on that year's last alpine climb, the Joux-Plane, there was no real panic.

But the Euro media still didn't believe, and a shadow hung over the Tour's *grand départ* in 2001. An article in the *Sunday Times* of London, written by the paper's chief sportswriter David Walsh, cast suspicion on Armstrong's preparations for the July race. Walsh detailed a number of "secret" visits to Italy to see Dr. Ferrari, the sports doctor who was being investigated for "sporting fraud" after Italian rider Filippo Simeoni accused him of supplying EPO to top athletes. A few journalists were invited to a press conference at the Postal team's hotel, a walled chateau in the leafy countryside of northern France. But Armstrong didn't appear. The only things the reporters received were a hastily composed letter that explained the Ferrari visits and a couple of beers with Armstrong's attorney-agent Bill Stapleton and the Postal team's head of public relations Dan Osipow.

The promised press conference never happened. Instead, a strange Tour saw Postal make a mistake in not chasing down a break that finished a half hour ahead of the pack in Pontarlier, forcing Armstrong to make some big time gains with three mountain stage wins. He took two minutes out of Ullrich on the stage to L'Alpe d'Huez after bluffing the German that he was suffering on earlier climbs that day, and he took yet another minute on both the uphill time trial to Chamrousse and the climbing stage to Pla d'Adet before claiming the yellow jersey.

Tour win No. 4 in 2002 was the easiest of the lot. There was no Ullrich to face and Spain's Joseba Beloki was no match for an Armstrong who took a morale-boosting win in the prologue at Luxembourg City, and then wrapped things up with back-to-back stage wins at La Mongie and Plateau de Beille in the Pyrénées.

Perhaps it was the ease of that victory that prompted Armstrong's overconfidence in 2003. "The most confident I ever was, was in 2003," Armstrong confirmed, "and you saw where that got me. Every other year I've been nervous and insecure and full of doubt, and I think that's a good thing for a sportsman because there's always somebody that wants your place, there's always somebody coming up, somebody younger, stronger, hungrier."

"Every other year I've been nervous and insecure and full of doubt, and I think that's a good thing for a sportsman because there's always somebody that wants your place, there's always somebody coming up, somebody younger, stronger, hungrier."

After pushing himself unnecessarily a few weeks before the '03 Tour to win the week-long Dauphiné Libéré stage race, a series of small injuries and illnesses in the Tour's first week sent his morale the wrong way, despite a breakthrough team time trial victory at St. Dizier. There followed his poor climb at L'Alpe d'Huez and his flirting with disaster on the tar-melted descent before Gap that claimed a threatening Beloki and left Armstrong cyclo-crossing back into the race.

The Texan should have lost it all when he became dehydrated on the 47km time trial from Gaillac to Cap'Découverte in heat-wave temperatures, but he fought through extreme fatigue to still place second and concede just 96 seconds to Ullrich. Armstrong was still wearing yellow, and he managed to survive the first two Pyrenean stages to retain a 15-second overall lead on Ullrich, with Alex Vinokourov at 18 seconds. With only six stages remaining, it was proving to be one of the closest Tours in history.

With his back against the wall, Armstrong survived an attack by Ullrich on the next day's Col du Tourmalet, and then accelerated at the base of stage 15's final climb to Luz-Ardiden. That was when the yellow jersey was brought crashing to the pavement by the strap on a fan's race bag entangling his handlebars. Miraculously, Armstrong bounced up, straightened his bike, caught back to the Ullrich group, and then made another strong attack, going on to take a solo stage victory and put the Tour on ice.

There was no overconfidence in 2004. Instead he had high motivation from a contro-versial book by *Sunday Times* writer Walsh and former *L'Équipe* reporter Pierre Ballester, which was published only in France due to strict libel laws in Britain. Titled *L.A. Confidentiel: Les Secrets de Lance Armstrong*, the book used the testimony of former team-mates, team doctors, and personal *soigneurs* to intimate that Armstrong had been using performance-enhancing drugs since before his cancer diagnosis.

The negative publicity and accusations only served as further incentive for Armstrong to race even harder at the Tour de France. Combined with his more focused training, Armstrong reached new heights. He led U.S. Postal to a dominant team time trial victory in the first week. And then he won four of five mountain stages and took the race's only long time trial, all within the space of seven days. His angry tête-à-tête with Ferrari-accuser Filippo Simeoni in stage 18 was the only sour note of what proved to be a sweet sixth success.

When Armstrong put off a decision to ride the 2005 Tour until February, some doubted that he would have time to be ready for the July race. Events seemed to confirm that view. His season started in March with a dismal performance at Paris-Nice, when he pulled out halfway through the eight-day race. He then badly lost the time trials at May's Tour of Georgia and June's Dauphiné. His climbing, too, wasn't clicking, which set up more doubts about his form.

"I always doubted," Armstrong admitted during the Tour. "It works better for me to be nervous and hungry. Paris-Nice was not a pleasant experience, nor was Georgia, nor was the Dauphiné. All of those things led me to ask questions, to re-evaluate where I am and ask myself, 'How bad do you want it?' And so, hopefully, every time I've answered and stepped it up, and maybe a good three weeks is the end result."

The end result was even better than he expected. Armstrong's seventh consecutive victory was distinguished by its apparent straightforwardness, despite the stronger oppo sition from Basso in particular. "For me, there was no pressure for this victory," he con-firmed. "It was just something that I had within myself. As a sportsman, I wanted to go out on top. And so that was the only incentive and the only pressure."

But when the "Star Spangled Banner" boomed out over the Champs-Élysées for the tenth time in twenty years (three for LeMond, seven for Armstrong), it didn't seem impos-sible that Lance Armstrong did have another victory within his capabilities. And a few weeks later, after the EPO accusations and his engagement to pop singer Sheryl Crow, Armstrong said that un-retiring was a possibility. Sensibly, on September 15, he changed his mind again, and confirmed that he was not coming back. "There's no reason to continue," he said in Paris. "I don't need more. It's time for a new face. No regrets. I will live vicariously through the others."

So these were the parting words of a man who won seven Tours from eleven starts: "My children are here, thank goodness. Come Monday morning, we're going to wake up in Paris, and the kids and Sheryl and I and a group of close friends and family, we're going to fly to the South of France and enjoy ourselves for a week, and lay on the beach and drink wine and not ride a bike, and eat a lot of food and swim in the pool, splash around with my kids and not worry. . . . Thing is, this job is stressful, and this event is stressful, so it will be hopefully a week's preview of what my life will be like for the next fifty years, with no stress."

A safe haven from stress and competition might be the one elusive treasure for a champion as revered and controversial as Lance Armstrong.

Lance Armstrong's
Tour Career Stats

THE 5 FASTEST TOURS

The favorable west winds of the opening week and the constant attacks made the 2005 Tour the fastest on record. Lance Armstrong won the 5 fastest Tours with speeds averaging over 40kph.

2005 41.654kph (3,593km in 86:15:02)
2003 40.940kph (3,427km in 83:41:12)
2004 40.553kph (3,391km in 83:36:02)
1999 40.276kph (3,870km in 91:32:16)
2001 40.070kph (3,458km in 86:17:28)

ARMSTRONG'S WINNING MARGINS

7:37 over Alex Zülle in 1999
7:17 over Joseba Beloki in 2002
6:44 over Jan Ullrich in 2001
6:19 over Andreas Klöden in 2004
6:02 over Jan Ullrich in 2000
4:40 over Ivan Basso in 2005
1:01 over Jan Ullrich in 2003

ALL-TIME YELLOW JERSEYS

Lance Armstrong led the 2005 Tour for 17 days, moving him into second place on the all-time list of yellow jerseys worn during the race.

1. Eddy Merckx   96
2. Lance Armstrong   83
3. Bernard Hinault   78
4. Miguel Induráin   60
5. Jacques Anquetil   51

ALL-TIME STAGE WINS

With one stage victory at the St. Étienne time trial, Armstrong moved into a tie for fourth on the list of all-time stage winners:

1.	Eddy Merckx	34
2.	Bernard Hinault	28
3.	André Leducq	25
4.	Lance Armstrong	22
5.	André Darrigade	22

ARMSTRONG'S 22 STAGE WINS

Half of Armstrong's 22 stage wins have been in time trials (2 prologues, 7 regular TTs, and 2 hill climbs), and the other 11 in road races (7 mountaintop finishes, 2 regular mountain stages, and 2 flat stages):

1993	**stage 8**	Châlons-sur-Marne–Verdun
1995	**stage 18**	Montpon-Ménestérol–Limoges
1999	**prologue**	Le-Puy-du-Fou TT
1999	**stage 8**	Metz TT
1999	**stage 9**	Le Grand Bornand–Sestriere*
1999	**stage 19**	Futuroscope TT
2000	**stage 19**	Freiburg-Mulhouse TT
2001	**stage 10**	Aix-Les-Bains–L'Alpe d'Huez*
2001	**stage 11**	Grenoble-Chamrousse TT*
2001	**stage 13**	Foix–Pla d'Adet*
2001	**stage 18**	Montluçon–St. Amand-Montrond TT
2002	**prologue**	Luxembourg TT
2002	**stage 11**	Pau–La Mongie*
2002	**stage 12**	Lannemezan–Plateau de Beille*
2002	**stage 19**	Regnié-Duret–Mâcon TT
2003	**stage 15**	Bagnères-de-Bigorre–Luz-Ardiden*
2004	**stage 13**	Lannemezan–Plateau de Beille*
2004	**stage 15**	Valréas–Villard-de-Lans
2004	**stage 16**	Bourg d'Oisans–L'Alpe d'Huez TT*
2004	**stage 17**	Bourg d'Oisans–Le Grand Bornand
2004	**stage 19**	Besançon TT
2005	**stage 20**	St. Étienne TT

* Mountaintop finishes

ARMSTRONG'S TEAM TIME TRIAL WINS

In the final three years of his career, Armstrong led his team to victory in each of the Tour's three team time trials:

2003	**stage 4**	Joinville–St. Dizier TTT
2004	**stage 4**	Cambrai-Arras TTT
2005	**stage 4**	Tours-Blois TTT

Tour Jerseys
and What They Mean

YELLOW JERSEY

The yellow jersey, or *maillot jaune*, is worn by the overall race leader—the rider who has covered the overall distance in the least amount of cumulative time. Time bonuses (12 seconds for winning a road stage, 6 seconds for winning an intermediate sprint) are deducted, and time penalties (for infractions like dangerous riding or accepting pushes from spectators on the climbs) are added to riders' stage times before calculating their G.C. (general classification) times.

A major change in 2004 was the limit on time lost by any team (and consequently by each rider who arrives with the first man to finish in the team) in the team time trial. The riders on the winning team (except for those who are dropped by their team) have their actual finish time added to G.C., but there is a maximum loss of 20 seconds for the second team, 30 seconds for the third, then 10-second gaps to 13th place (a 2:20 maximum loss), and 5-second gaps down to 3:00 for the 21st (and last) team.

2005 WINNER: Lance Armstrong, Discovery Channel

KING OF THE MOUNTAINS

The polka-dot King of the Mountains (KOM) jersey is awarded to the rider who most consistently reaches designated summits at the front of the peloton. KOM points are given not only on major mountain passes, but also on the smaller climbs. There are fewer points available at the intermediate climbs and double points on the final climb of every stage—assuming that it has at least a Cat. 2 designation. The aim is to put more excitement into the competition by placing the emphasis on the critical climbs.

Tour climbs are classified in five, somewhat arbitrary categories:

CAT. 4: Usually less than 3km in length, an easy pitch that amounts to no more than a sustained rise in the road

CAT. 3: Slightly harder, up to 5km in length

CAT. 2: Between 5km and 10km and steeper than a 4-percent grade

CAT. 1: Long and steep—between 10km and 20km and steeper than a 5-percent grade

HORS CATEGORIE (HC) or ABOVE CATEGORY: Extremely difficult climbs, sometimes 15km to 20km, with grades often exceeding 10 percent

2005 WINNER: Michael Rasmussen, Rabobank

POINTS LEADER

The green points leader's jersey, or *maillot vert*, is awarded to the best all-around finisher on flat, rolling, and mountainous stages, as well as time trials and intermediate "hot spot" sprints. With the highest points being awarded on flat stage finishes, the points jersey is often thought of as the sprinters' jersey, but a consistent and strategic all-rounder can also be a contender.

2005 WINNER: Thor Hushovd, Crédit Agricole

How points are awarded

FLAT STAGES: 1st place 35pts

2nd 30pts; 3rd 26pts; 4th 24pts; 5th 22pts; 6th 20pts; and descending in 1-point increments to 25th place

ROLLING STAGES: 1st place 25pts

2nd 22pts; 3rd 20pts; 4th 18pts; 5th 16pts; 6th 15pts; and descending in 1-point increments to 20th place

MOUNTAIN STAGES: 1st place 20pts

2nd 17pts; 3rd 15pts; 4th 13pts; 5th 12pts; 6th 10pts; and descending in 1-point increments to 15th place

TIME TRIALS: 1st place 15pts

2nd 12pts; 3rd 10pts; 4th 8pts; 5th 6pts; 6th 5pts; and descending in 1-point increments to 10th place

INTERMEDIATE SPRINTS: 1st place 6pts

2nd 4pts; 3rd 2pts (three each day in stages 2–9, two each day in stages 10–21)

BEST YOUNG RIDER

The white jersey, or *maillot blanc*, is awarded to the best-placed G.C. rider aged 25 or under. In order to qualify for this competition at the 2005 Tour, riders had to be born after January 1, 1980.

2005 WINNER: Yaroslav Popovych, Discovery Channel

TEAM CLASSIFICATION

Established by the cumulative time of the top three individuals from each team on each stage.

2005 WINNER: T-Mobile

MOST COMBATIVE

Signified by a red race number, the most combative award is a somewhat subjective points total given by race judges each day to the riders who demonstrate the most consistent efforts in attacks and breakaways. Each rider's points are cumulative every stage to give an overall classification.

2005 WINNER: Oscar Pereiro, Phonak

2005 TOUR DE FRANCE
Final Results

GENERAL CLASSIFICATION

1. Lance Armstrong (USA), Discovery Channel, 3,593km in 86:15:02 (41.654kph); 2. Ivan Basso (I), CSC, 04:40; **3.** Jan Ullrich (G), T-Mobile, 06:21; **4.** Francisco Mancebo (Sp), Illes Balears, 09:59; **5.** Alexander Vinokourov (Kaz), T-Mobile, 11:01; **6. Levi Leipheimer (USA), Gerolsteiner, 11:21; 7.** Michael Rasmussen (Dk), Rabobank, 11:33; **8.** Cadel Evans (Aus), Davitamon-Lotto, 11:55; **9. Floyd Landis (USA), Phonak, 12:44; 10.** Oscar Pereiro (Sp), Phonak, 16:04

11. Christophe Moreau (F), Crédit Agricole, 16:26; **12.** Yaroslav Popovych (Ukr), Discovery Channel, 19:02; **13.** Eddy Mazzoleni (I), Lampre-Caffita, 21:06; **14. George Hincapie (USA), Discovery Channel, 23:40; 15.** Haimar Zubeldia (Sp), Euskaltel-Euskadi, 23:43; **16.** Jörg Jaksche (G), Liberty Seguros, 24:07; **17. Bobby Julich (USA), CSC, 24:08; 18.** Oscar Sevilla (Sp), T-Mobile, 27:45; **19.** Andrey Kashechkin (Kaz), Crédit Agricole, 28:04; **20.** Giuseppe Guerini (I), T-Mobile, 33:02

21. Carlos Sastre (Sp), CSC, 34:24; **22.** Xabier Zandio (Sp), Illes Balears, 36:20; **23.** Leonardo Piepoli (I), Saunier Duval, 36:20; **24.** Michael Boogerd (Nl), Rabobank, 38:29; **25.** Paolo Savoldelli (I), Discovery Channel, 44:30; **26.** Georg Totschnig (A), Gerolsteiner, 49:14; **27.** Mikel Astarloza (Sp), ag2r Prévoyance, 54:03; **28.** Laurent Brochard (F), Bouygues Télécom, 55:29; **29.** Sandy Casar (F), Française des Jeux, 56:47; **30.** José Azevedo (P), Discovery Channel, 59:48

31. Alberto Contador (Sp), Liberty Seguros, 1:03:25; **32.** Stefano Garzelli (I), Liquigas-Bianchi, 1:04:49; **33. Chris Horner (USA), Saunier Duval, 1:07:57; 34.** Stephane Goubert (F), ag2r Prévoyance, 1:10:53; **35.** José Luis Rubiera (Sp), Discovery Channel, 1:11:48; **36.** Pietro Caucchioli (I), Crédit Agricole, 1:16:21; **37.** Maxim Iglinskiy (Kaz), Domina Vacanze, 1:18:44; **38.** Jorg Ludewig (G), Domina Vacanze, 1:19:05; **39.** Axel Merckx (B), Davitamon-Lotto, 1:20:15; **40.** Marcos Serrano (Sp), Liberty Seguros, 1:21:31

41. Michael Rogers (Aus), Quick Step, 1:24:32; **42.** Alexandre Moos (Swi), Phonak, 1:25:35; **43.** Jérôme Pineau (F), Bouygues Télécom, 1:31:38; **44.** Cédric Vasseur (F), Cofidis, 1:33:17; **45.** Roberto Heras (Sp), Liberty Seguros, 1:38:33; **46.** Pierrick Fédrigo (F), Bouygues Télécom, 1:41:14; **47.** Franco Pellizotti (I), Liquigas-Bianchi, 1:41:38; **48.** Egoi Martinez (Sp), Euskaltel-Euskadi, 1:42:29; **49.** Gutierrez José Enrique (Sp), Phonak, 1:42:35; **50.** Vladimir Karpets (Rus), Illes Balears, 1:43:45

51. Santiago Botero (Col), Phonak, 1:49:22; **52.** Patrice Halgand (F), Crédit Agricole, 1:53:26; **53.** David Arroyo (Sp), Illes Balears, 1:54:12; **54.** Dario Cioni (I), Liquigas-Bianchi, 2:00:39; **55.** Daniele Nardello (I), T-Mobile, 2:02:23;

56. Christophe Brandt (B), Davitamon-Lotto, 2:03:10; **57.** Matthias Kessler (G), T-Mobile, 2:03:56; **58.** Sylvain Chavanel (F), Cofidis, 2:05:20; **59.** Patrik Sinkewitz (G), Quick Step, 2:07:48; **60.** Iban Mayo (Sp), Euskaltel-Euskadi, 2:07:48

61. Thomas Lövkvist (Swe), Française des Jeux, 2:07:48; **62.** Lorenzo Bernucci (I), Fassa Bortolo, 2:08:37; **63.** David Canada (Sp), Saunier Duval, 2:08:56; **64.** Angel Vicioso (Sp), Liberty Seguros, 2:09:37; **65.** Sebastian Lang (G), Gerolsteiner, 2:11:18; **66.** Juan Manuel Garate (Sp), Saunier Duval, 2:15:17; **67.** David Moncoutié (F), Cofidis, 2:15:23; **68.** Walter Beneteau (F), Bouygues Télécom, 2:17:06; **69.** Iker Camano (Sp), Euskaltel-Euskadi, 2:22:41; **70.** Philippe Gilbert (B), Française des Jeux, 2:24:00

71. Nicki Sörensen (Dk), CSC, 2:24:08; **72.** Pieter Weening (Nl), Rabobank, 2:24:16; **73.** Juan Antonio Flecha (Sp), Fassa Bortolo, 2:24:21; **74.** Jose Luis Arrieta (Sp), Illes Balears, 2:25:27; **75.** Joseba Beloki (Sp), Liberty Seguros, 2:26:26; **76.** Carlos Da Cruz (F), Française des Jeux, 2:26:49; **77.** Stuart O'Grady (Aus), Cofidis, 2:27:19; **78.** Andriy Grivko (Ukr), Domina Vacanze, 2:28:08; **79.** Fabian Wegmann (G), Gerolsteiner, 2:29:32; **80.** Massimo Giunti (I), Fassa Bortolo, 2:29:34

81. Tobias Steinhauser (G), T-Mobile, 2:31:02; **82.** Didier Rous (F), Bouygues Télécom, 2:33:10; **83.** Joost Posthuma (Nl), Rabobank, 2:33:59; **84.** Allan Davis (Aus), Liberty Seguros, 2:34:40; **85.** Denis Menchov (Rus), Rabobank, 2:35:00; **86.** Stephan Schreck (G), T-Mobile, 2:35:52; **87.** Gorazd Stangelj (SLO), Lampre-Caffita, 2:36:13; **88.** Nicolas Portal (F), ag2r Prévoyance, 2:38:01; **89.** Kurt-Asle Arvesen (Nor), CSC, 2:39:27; **90.** Yuriy Krivtsov (Ukr), ag2r Prévoyance, 2:39:51

91. Ronny Scholz (G), Gerolsteiner, 2:43:03; **92.** Rubens Bertogliati (Swi), Saunier Duval, 2:45:03; **93.** Beat Zberg (Swi), Gerolsteiner, 2:46:24; **94.** Francis Mourey (F), Française des Jeux, 2:47:14; **95.** Pavel Padrnos (Cz), Discovery Channel, 2:49:53; **96.** Ludovic Turpin (F), ag2r Prévoyance, 2:51:28; **97.** Anthony Geslin (F), Bouygues Télécom, 2:51:58; **98.** Alessandro Cortinovis (I), Domina Vacanze, 2:52:02; **99.** David Loosli (Swi), Lampre-Caffita, 2:52:41; **100.** Inigo Landaluze (Sp), Euskaltel-Euskadi, 2:52:41

101. Salvatore Commesso (I), Lampre-Caffita, 2:53:46; **102.** Luke Roberts (Aus), CSC, 2:54:12; **103.** Bert Grabsch (G), Phonak, 2:54:35; **104.** Volodymir Gustov (Ukr), Fassa Bortolo, 2:54:56; **105.** Bradley McGee (Aus), Française des Jeux, 2:55:59; **106.** Sébastian Joly (F), Crédit Agricole, 2:56:10; **107.** Benjamin Noval Gonzalez (Sp), Discovery Channel, 3:00:59; **108.** Luis Sanchez (Sp), Liberty Seguros, 3:03:19; **109.** Erik Dekker (Nl), Rabobank, 3:03:36; **110.** Daniele Righi (I), Lampre-Caffita, 3:04:17

111. Bram Tankink (Nl), Quick Step, 3:05:12; **112.** Mario Aerts (B), Davitamon-Lotto, 3:07:30; **113.** Alessandro Bertolini (I), Domina Vacanze, 3:09:13; **114.** Samuel Dumoulin (F), ag2r Prévoyance, 3:11:02; **115.** Sebastian Hinault (F), Crédit Agricole, 3:14:33; **116.** Thor Hushovd (Nor), Crédit Agricole, 3:15:40; **117.** Laurent Lèfevre (F), Bouygues Télécom, 3:16:06; **118.** Giovanni Lombardi (I), CSC, 3:18:21; **119.** Laszlo Bodrogi (Hun), Crédit Agricole, 3:18:44; **120.** Matthieu Sprick (F), Bouygues Télécom, 3:20:47

121. Stéphane Augé (F), Cofidis, 3:21:30; **122.** Inaki Isasi (Sp), Euskaltel-Euskadi, 3:21:50; **123.** Matthew White (Aus), Cofidis, 3:23:41; **124.** Thomas Voeckler (F), Bouygues Télécom, 3:25:32; **125.** Marcus Ljungqvist (Swe), Liquigas-Bianchi, 3:25:36; **126.** Simons Gerrans (Aus), ag2r Prévoyance, 3:27:03; **127.** Thierry Marichal (B), Cofidis, 3:30:59; **128.** Fabian Cancellara (Swi), Fassa Bortolo, 3:32:40; **129.** Frédéric Bessy (F), Cofidis, 3:34:59; **130.** Michael Rich (G), Gerolsteiner, 3:37:13

131. Manuel Quinziato (I), Saunier Duval, 3:37:31; **132. Fred Rodriguez (USA), Davitamon-Lotto, 3:37:58; 133.** Alessandro Vanotti (I), Domina Vacanze, 3:38:43; **134.** Robbie McEwen (Aus), Davitamon-Lotto, 3:41:52; **135.** Karsten Kroon (Nl), Rabobank, 3:42:03; **136.** Johan Van Summeren (B), Davitamon-Lotto, 3:43:05; **137.** Mauro Gerosa (I), Liquigas-Bianchi, 3:44:22; **138.** Nicolas Jalabert (F), Phonak, 3:44:26; **139. Guido Trenti (USA), Quick Step, 3:46:24; 140.** Marc Wauters (B), Rabobank, 3:46:54

141. Kjell Carlström (F), Liquigas-Bianchi, 3:47:02; **142.** Baden Cooke (Aus), Française des Jeux, 3:47:17; **143.** Bernhard Eisel (A), Française des Jeux, 3:47:35; **144.** Mauro Facci (I), Fassa Bortolo, 3:49:30; **145.** Michael Albasini (Swi), Liquigas-Bianchi, 3:51:03; **146.** Peter Wrolich (A), Gerolsteiner, 3:51:50; **147.** Rafael Nuritdinov (Uzb), Domina Vacanze, 3:54:14; **148.** José Vicente Garcia Acosta (Sp), Illes Balears, 3:56:34; **149.** Servais Knaven (Nl), Quick Step, 3:59:07; **150.** David Etxebarria (Vz), Euskaltel-Euskadi, 4:00:24

151. Robert Förster (G), Gerolsteiner, 4:01:40; **152.** Daniel Becke (G), Illes Balears, 4:02:16; **153.** Janek Tombak (Est), Cofidis, 4:03:09; **154.** Wim Vansevenant (B), Davitamon-Lotto, 4:09:25; **155.** Iker Flores (Sp), Euskaltel-Euskadi, 4:20:24

POINTS CLASSIFICATION

1. Thor Hushovd (N), Crédit Agricole, 194 points; **2.** Stuart O'Grady (Aus), Cofidis, 182; **3.** Robbie McEwen (Aus), Davitamon-Lotto, 178; **4.** Alexander Vinokourov (Kaz), T-Mobile, 158; **5.** Allan Davis (Aus), Liberty Seguros, 130; **6.** Oscar Pereiro (Sp), Phonak, 118; **7.** Robert Förster (G), Gerolsteiner, 101; **8. Lance Armstrong (USA), Discovery Channel, 93; 9.** Baden Cooke (Aus), Française des Jeux, 91; **10.** Bernhard Eisel (A), Française des Jeux, 88

MOUNTAINS CLASSIFICATION

1. Michael Rasmussen (Dk), Rabobank, 185 points; **2.** Oscar Pereiro (Sp), Phonak, 155; **3. Lance Armstrong (USA), Discovery Channel, 99; 4.** Christophe Moreau (F), Crédit Agricole, 93; **5.** Michael Boogerd (Nl), Rabobank, 90; **6.** Santiago Botero (Col), Phonak, 88; **7.** Alexander Vinokourov (Kaz), T-Mobile, 75; **8.** Laurent Brochard (F), Bouygues Télécom, 75; **9. George Hincapie (USA), Discovery Channel, 74; 10.** Pietro Caucchioli (I), Crédit Agricole, 73

YOUNG RIDERS CLASSIFICATION

1. Yaroslav Popovych (Ukr), Discovery Channel, 86:34:04; **2.** Andrey Kashechkin (Kaz), Crédit Agricole, 09:02; **3.** Alberto Contador (Sp), Liberty Seguros, 44:23; **4.** Maxim Iglinskiy (Kaz), Domina Vacanze, 59:42; **5.** Jérôme Pineau (F), Bouygues Télécom, 1:12:36; **6.** Vladimir Karpets (Rus), Illes Balears, 1:24:43; **7.** David Arroyo (Sp), Illes Balears, 1:35:10; **8.** Patrik Sinkewitz (G), Quick Step, 1:48:46; **9.** Thomas Lövkvist (Swe), Française des Jeux, 1:48:46; **10.** Philippe Gilbert (B), Française des Jeux, 2:04:58

TEAM CLASSIFICATION

1. T-Mobile Team, 256:10:29; **2.** Discovery Channel Team, 14:57; **3.** Team CSC, 25:15; **4.** Crédit Agricole, 55:24; **5.** Illes Balears, 1:06:09; **6.** Phonak Hearing Systems, 1:09:20; **7.** Liberty Seguros–Würth Team, 1:47:56; **8.** Rabobank, 2:26:30; **9.** Saunier Duval–Prodir, 2:48:58; **10.** ag2r Prévoyance, 2:52:04; **11.** Gerolsteiner, 3:05:20; **12.** Bouygues Télécom, 3:13:31; **13.** Française des Jeux, 3:32:15; **14.** Davitamon-Lotto, 3:37:45; **15.** Euskaltel-Euskadi, 3:41:05; **16.** Domina Vacanze, 4:20:38; **17.** Lampre-Caffita, 4:33:06; **18.** Liquigas-Bianchi, 4:50:57; **19.** Cofidis Credit Par Telephone, 5:03:04; **20.** Fassa Bortolo, 6:13:26; **21.** Quick Step–Innergetic, 6:36:48

TOUR DE FRANCE
Winners

1903	Maurice Garin (F)	1925	Ottavio Bottechia (I)
1904	Henri Cornet (F)	1926	Lucien Buysse (B)
1905	Louis Trousselier (F)	1927	Nicolas Frantz (Lux)
1906	René Pottier (F)	1928	Nicolas Frantz (Lux)
1907	Lucien Petit-Breton (F)	1929	Maurice De Waele (B)
1908	Lucien Petit-Breton (F)	1930	André Leducq (F)
1909	François Faber (Lux)	1931	Antonin Magne (F)
1910	Octave Lapize (F)	1932	André Leducq (F)
1911	Gustave Garrigou (F)	1933	Georges Speicher (F)
1912	Odile Defraye (B)	1934	Antonin Magne (F)
1913	Philippe Thys (B)	1935	Romain Maes (B)
1914	Philippe Thys (B)	1936	Sylvére Maes (B)
		1937	Roger Lapébie (F)

STOPPED BECAUSE OF WWI

		1938	Gino Bartali (I)
		1939	Sylvére Maes (B)
1919	Firmin Lambot (B)		
1920	Philippe Thys (B)		
1921	Léon Scieur (B)		

STOPPED BECAUSE OF WWII

1922	Firmin Lambot (B)		
1923	Henri Pelissier (F)	1947	Jean Robic (F)
1924	Ottavio Bottechia (I)	1948	Gino Bartali (I)
		1949	Fausto Coppi (I)

1950	Ferdi Kubler (Swi)	1978	Bernard Hinault (F)
1951	Hugo Koblet (Swi)	1979	Bernard Hinault (F)
1952	Fausto Coppi (I)	1980	Joop Zoetemelk (Nl)
1953	Louison Bobet (F)	1981	Bernard Hinault (F)
1954	Louison Bobet (F)	1982	Bernard Hinault (F)
1955	Louison Bobet (F)	1983	Laurent Fignon (F)
1956	Roger Walkowiak (F)	1984	Laurent Fignon (F)
1957	Jacques Anquetil (F)	1985	Bernard Hinault (F)
1958	Charly Gaul (Lux)	**1986**	**Greg LeMond (USA)**
1959	Federico Bahamontes (Sp)	1987	Stephen Roche (Ire)
1960	Gastone Nencini (I)	1988	Pedro Delgado (Sp)
1961	Jacques Anquetil (F)	**1989**	**Greg LeMond (USA)**
1962	Jacques Anquetil (F)	**1990**	**Greg LeMond (USA)**
1963	Jacques Anquetil (F)	1991	Miguel Induráin (Sp)
1964	Jacques Anquetil (F)	1992	Miguel Induráin (Sp)
1965	Felice Gimondi (I)	1993	Miguel Induráin (Sp)
1966	Lucien Aimar (F)	1994	Miguel Induráin (Sp)
1967	Roger Pingeon (F)	1995	Miguel Induráin (Sp)
1968	Jan Janssen (Nl)	1996	Bjarne Riis (Dk)
1969	Eddy Merckx (B)	1997	Jan Ullrich (G)
1970	Eddy Merckx (B)	1998	Marco Pantani (I)
1971	Eddy Merckx (B)	**1999**	**Lance Armstrong (USA)**
1972	Eddy Merckx (B)	**2000**	**Lance Armstrong (USA)**
1973	Luis Ocaña (Sp)	**2001**	**Lance Armstrong (USA)**
1974	Eddy Merckx (B)	**2002**	**Lance Armstrong (USA)**
1975	Bernard Thévenet (F)	**2003**	**Lance Armstrong (USA)**
1976	Lucien Van Impe (B)	**2004**	**Lance Armstrong (USA)**
1977	Bernard Thévenet (F)	**2005**	**Lance Armstrong (USA)**

About the Authors

John Wilcockson is editorial director of *VeloNews* and author of ten books, including *23 Days in July* and *John Wilcockson's World of Cycling*. He has served as editor of five cycling magazines—*International Cycle Sport, Cyclist Monthly, Winning: Bicycling Racing Illustrated, Inside Cycling,* and *VeloNews*. He lives in Boulder, Colorado.

Andrew Hood is a European correspondent for *VeloNews* and has covered the Tour de France since 1996. He is author of *The 2004 Tour de France: Armstrong Rewrites History*. He has worked for the *Dallas Morning News, Denver Post, USA Today,* ESPN.com, and the Associated Press, as well as for cycling publications in the United States, Europe, and Australia. He has also appeared on ESPN radio, BBC, TXCN, and NPR. He lives in Spain.

Photo Credits

Page 105: Armstrong and Ullrich in time trial, Getty Images

Page 106: Levi Leipheimer, AFP/Getty Images; David Zabriskie, Graham Watson

Page 107: Tom Boonen, stage 2, Graham Watson; Floyd Landis, Getty Images

Page 108: Discovery team time trial, stage 20, Graham Watson

Page 109: Robbie McEwen, stage 7; Georg Totschnig, stage 10, Graham Watson

Page 110: Joseba Beloki, stage 10, Cor Vos; Allejandro Valverde, stage 10, Graham Watson

Page 111: Tom Boonen with trainer, stage 11; Chris Horner and Sylvain Chavanel, stage 13, AFP/Getty Images

Page 112–13: Peloton riding Col de Mente, stage 15, Graham Watson

Page 114: Ivan Basso with Lance Armstrong, stage 15, AFP/Getty Images; Michael Rassussen, stage 15, Cor Vos

Page 115: George Hincapie and Oscar Pereiro, stage 15; Yaroslav Popovych, AFP/Getty Images

Page 116: Cadel Evans climbing up Col de Marie-Blanque, stage 16; Paolo Savoldelli wins, stage 17, Graham Watson

Page 117: Ivan Basso and Lance Armstrong, stage 18, Getty Images; Viaduc de Millau, stage 18, Graham Watson

Page 118: Jan Ullrich, stage 20, Graham Watson

Page 119: Oscar Pereiro escape, stage 19, Graham Watson; Alexander Vinokourov, stage 21, AFP/Getty Images

Page 120: Discovery Channel team on podium, stage 21, Lance Armstrong, Graham Watson

Page 177: Lance Armstrong, 2005; Armstrong with Greg LeMond, 1996, Getty Images

Page 178: Armstrong back at the tour, 1999; Armstrong's parade in Austin, 1999, Getty Images

Page 179: Armstrong with Marco Pantani, 2000; Armstrong passes Ullrich, 2001, AFP/Getty Images

Page 180: Armstrong wins the stage, 2001, Graham Watson

Page 181: Armstrong and Beloki, 2002; Mont Ventoux and Armstrong, 2002, AFP/Getty Images

Page 182: Ullrich attacks to Ax-3 Domaines, 2003, Getty Images

Page 183: Armstrong on the podium, 2003; Armstrong, Ullrich, and Vinokourov, 2003, AFP/Getty Images

Page 184–85: Armstrong and Mayo crash, 2003, AFP/Getty Images

Page 186: Five-time Tour winners, 2003; Jean-Marie Leblanc with Armstrong, 2004, AFP/Getty Images

Page 187: Armstrong and Fillippo Simeoni, 2004, AFP/Getty Images

Page 188: The press, 2004, Getty Images; Armstrong with Johan Bruyneel, 2005, AFP/Getty Images

Page 189: Armstrong signing his autograph, 2005, Graham Watson; Armstrong and Hincapie, 2005, Getty Images

Page 190: Discovery team time trial, 2005, Getty Images

Page 191: Armstrong's time trial, 2005, Getty Images

Page 192: Armstrong on the scale, 2005, Graham Watson